The
Supreme
Court

The Supreme Court

Tenth Edition

Lawrence Baum
Ohio State University

CQ PRESS

A Division of SAGE
Washington, D.C.

CQ Press
2300 N Street, NW, Suite 800
Washington, DC 20037

Phone: 202-729-1900; toll-free, 1-866-4CQ-PRESS (1-866-427-7737)

Web: www.cqpress.com

Cover design: Auburn Associates, Inc.
Cover photos: Corbis (left): © Jose Fuste Raga and Getty Images (right):
Charles Ommanney
Composition: C&M Digitals (P) Ltd.

AP Images: 18 (The Oklahoman, Nate Billings), 34 (Jim Bourg), 61 (Nate
Billings), 73 (Mike Groll), 108 (Dana Verkouteren), 181 (AP Photo), 203
(Charlie Neibergall), 221 (Lawrence Jackson).
Corbis: 115 (Paul Buck).
Getty Images: 15 (David Hume Kennerly), 45 (Alex Wong, left, Chip Somod-
evilla, right), 84 (Chip Somodevilla), 99 (David Hume Kennerly), 143 (David
Paul Morris), 158 (Mike Simons), 171 (Museum of the City of New York), 195
(MPI).
Reuters: 137 (Jason Reed).

♾ The paper used in this publication exceeds the requirements of the
American National Standard for Information Sciences—Permanence of
Paper for Printed Library Materials, ANSI Z39.48-1992.

Printed and bound in the United States of America

13   12   11   10   09   1   2   3   4   5

Library of Congress Cataloging-in-Publication Data

Baum, Lawrence.
  The Supreme Court / Lawrence Baum. — 10th ed.
      p. cm.
  Includes bibliographical references and index.
  ISBN 978-1-60426-462-3 (pbk. : alk. paper) 1. United States. Supreme
Court. 2. Constitutional law—United States. 3. Courts of last resort—United
States. 4. Judicial review—United States. I. Title.

  KF8742.B35 2010
  347.73'26—dc22

                                                        2009032495

To my students

Contents

Tables, Figures, and Boxes

Tables

Figures

Boxes

Preface

In May 2009 Justice David Souter announced that he would retire from the Supreme Court at the end of the Court's term in June. His announcement triggered a wave of speculation about who his successor might be. A few weeks later President Barack Obama nominated Judge Sonia Sotomayor to succeed Souter. The nomination became a subject of intense scrutiny and debate that lasted until the Senate confirmed the nomination in midsummer.

While all this was going on, the Court completed its annual term in June. As it does every year, the Court issued many of its most important decisions in the last few weeks of the term. These decisions attracted considerable interest, and the Court's work over the term raised speculation about whether it was moving in a strongly conservative direction on such issues as racial discrimination and environmental protection.

The attention that the Supreme Court received in the spring and summer of 2009 underlines the importance of the Court for many people. But those who care a great deal about the Court do not always understand it well. The Supreme Court is a complicated institution, and on the whole it is more difficult to comprehend than the other branches of government. As a result, even some experts in American politics have substantial gaps in their knowledge of the Court.

I have written this book to provide a better understanding of the Supreme Court. The book is intended to serve as a short but comprehensive guide, both for readers who already know much about the Court and for those who have a more limited sense of it. I discuss how the Court functions, the work that it carries out, and the effects that its decisions have on the lives of people in the United States. And I provide some explanation of the decisions that the Court and its justices make, of actions by other people and groups that participate in cases, and of the Court's impact on government and society.

The book puts the Court in its historical context, but it focuses primarily on the current era. This edition incorporates recent developments in and around the Court. Most evident are President Obama's 2009 appointment of Justice Sotomayor and the effects of President George W. Bush's two appointments to the Court in 2005 and 2006. I discuss decisions made in the past few years that illuminate what the Court does and why, such as its rulings on gun control and the rights of suspected terrorists. And I take advantage of recent work by scholars that provides new information and insights about the Court.

The first chapter introduces the Supreme Court. In it I discuss the Court's role in general terms, examine the Court's place in the judicial system, analyze the Court as an institution, and present a brief summary of its history.

Each of the other chapters deals with an important aspect of the Court. Chapter 2 focuses on the justices: their selection, their backgrounds and careers, and the circumstances under which they leave the Court. Chapter 3 contains a discussion of how cases reach the Court and how the Court selects the small portion of those cases that it will hear.

In Chapter 4 I look at decision making in the cases that the Court accepts for full consideration. After outlining the Court's decision-making procedures, I turn to the chapter's primary concern: the factors that influence the Court's choices among alternative decisions and policies. Chapter 5 deals with the kinds of issues on which the Court concentrates, the policies it supports, and the extent of its activism in the making of public policy. I give special attention to changes in the Court's role as a policymaker and the sources of those changes. The final chapter examines the ways in which other government policymakers respond to the Court's decisions as well as the Court's impact on American society as a whole. The chapter concludes with an assessment of the Court's significance as a force in American life.

This new edition of the book reflects the very considerable help that many people gave me with earlier editions. In writing this edition I benefited from the information provided by Melanie Oberlin, Thomas Walker, Alan Wiseman, Lawrence Wrightsman, the Office of the Solicitor General, and the Public Information Office of the Supreme Court. The book was strengthened by suggestions for revision from Chris Bonneau, University of Pittsburgh; Saul Brenner, University of North Carolina–Charlotte; Sheldon Goldman, University of Massachusetts; Mark Petracca, University of California–Irvine; and Kim Seckler, New Mexico State University.

As always, the professionals at CQ Press did a great deal to make my life easier and, more important, to make the book better. I appreciate the assistance of Joanne S. Ainsworth, Belinda Josey, and Allison McKay in the editing process; I benefited from their careful work and good judgment. I am grateful for everything that Charisse Kiino and Brenda Carter do to ensure that CQ Press books, including this one, are of the highest possible quality.

My faculty colleagues at Ohio State University are an abundant source of ideas, and the same is true of the students in my classes. This book reflects all the things I have learned from them.

Chapter 1

The Court

Among the general public, Supreme Court justice Anthony Kennedy hardly qualifies as famous. But among people who follow government, Kennedy is widely regarded as very important. In 2007 a magazine ranked him as the fourth most powerful person in Washington. Four years earlier an interest group leader went further, calling him "the most dangerous man in America."[1]

What accounts for those characterizations of Kennedy? President Bush's selection of two new justices in 2005 put Kennedy at the ideological center of the nine-member Court, a position he has maintained since then. As a result, he has cast the decisive fifth vote in major decisions on issues such as gun control and the death penalty. Most people who follow politics and government believe that Supreme Court decisions have considerable impact on life in the United States. From that perspective, it is easy to see why Justice Kennedy is considered powerful.

In reality the effect of the Supreme Court is probably more limited than most people think it is. But it is still quite substantial. For this reason, its members—and not only Justice Kennedy—*are* powerful. And for the same reason, it is impossible to understand American government and society without understanding the Supreme Court.

This book is an effort to provide that understanding. Who serves on the Court, and how do they get there? What determines which cases and issues the Court decides? In resolving the cases before it, how does the Court choose between alternative decisions? In what policy areas is it active, and what kinds of policies does it make? Finally, what happens to the Court's decisions after they are handed down, and what impact do they actually have?

Each of these questions is the subject of a chapter in the book. As I focus on each question, I try to show not only what happens in and around the Court but also why things work the way they do. This first chapter is an introduction to the Court, providing background for the chapters that follow.

A Perspective on the Court

The Supreme Court's position in government is more ambiguous than the positions of the other branches, so a good place to begin is with the Court's attributes as an institution and its work as a policymaker.

The Court in Law and Politics

The Supreme Court is, first of all, a court—the highest court in the federal judicial system. Like other courts, it has jurisdiction to hear and decide certain kinds of cases. Like other courts, it can decide legal issues only in cases that are brought to it. And as a court, it makes decisions within a legal framework. Congress writes new law, but the Court interprets existing law. In this respect, the Court operates within a constraint from which legislators are free.

In another respect, however, the Supreme Court's identity as a court reduces the constraints on it. The widespread belief that courts should be insulated from the political process gives the Court a degree of actual insulation. The justices' lifetime appointments allow them some freedom from concerns about whether political leaders and voters approve of their decisions. Justices usually avoid open involvement in partisan activity, because such involvement is perceived as inappropriate. And because direct contact between lobbyists and justices is generally considered unacceptable, interest group activity in the Court is basically restricted to the formal channels of legal argument.

The Court's insulation from politics should not be exaggerated, however. People sometimes speak of courts as if they are, or at least ought to be, "nonpolitical." In a literal sense, this is impossible: as a part of government, courts are political institutions by definition. What people really mean when they refer to courts as nonpolitical is that courts are separate from the political process and that their decisions are affected only by legal considerations. This too is impossible for courts in general and certainly for the Supreme Court.

The Court is political chiefly because it makes important decisions on major issues. People care about those decisions and want to influence them. As a result, political battles regularly arise over appointments to the Court. Interest groups bring cases and present arguments to the Court in an effort to help shape its policies. Because members of Congress pay attention to the Court's decisions and hold powers over the Court, the justices may take Congress into account when they decide cases. Finally, the justices' political values affect the votes they cast and the opinions they write in the Court's decisions.

Thus, the Supreme Court should be viewed as both a legal institution and a political institution. The political process and the legal system each influence what the Court does. This ambiguous position adds to the complexity of the Court. It also makes the Court an interesting case study in political behavior.

The Court as a Policymaker

This book examines the Supreme Court broadly, but it emphasizes the Court's role in making public policy—the authoritative rules by which people in government institutions seek to influence government itself and to shape society as a whole. Legislation to provide subsidies for wheat farmers, a trial judge's ruling in an auto accident case, and a Supreme Court decision on rules of police procedure are all examples of public policy. The Court can be viewed as part of a policymaking system that includes lower courts and the other branches of government.

As I have noted, the Supreme Court makes public policy by interpreting provisions of law. Issues of public policy come to the Court in the form of legal questions. In this respect the Court's work as a policymaker differs fundamentally in form from that of Congress.

The Court does not face legal questions in the abstract. Rather, it addresses these questions in the process of settling specific controversies between parties (sometimes called litigants) that bring cases to it. In a sense, then, every decision by the Court has three aspects: it is a judgment about the specific dispute brought to it, an interpretation of the legal issues in that dispute, and a position on the policy questions that are raised by the legal issues.

These three aspects of the Court's rulings are illustrated by a 2008 decision, *Riegel v. Medtronic, Inc.* Donna Riegel carried forward a lawsuit against the Medtronic company after her husband's death. Her husband had been injured by the rupture of a Medtronic catheter during heart surgery. The lawsuit was based on New York law. Medtronic argued that a federal law disallowed such lawsuits under the circumstances of this case. The lower federal courts ruled in favor of Medtronic, and the Supreme Court agreed.

In the first aspect of its decision, the Supreme Court affirmed the court of appeals decision against Riegel. As a result, Riegel lost her case and received nothing from Medtronic. If the Court had reversed the court of appeals decision and remanded the case to that court for further action, Riegel would have gained the chance to go to trial with her case.

The Court's decision was also a judgment about the meaning of the federal statute in question, the Medical Device Amendments of 1976 (MDA). The MDA has a clause that preempts certain state regulations of medical devices. Accepting Medtronic's argument, the Court ruled that this clause prohibits state "common law" suits relating to the safety or effectiveness of a medical device, if the marketing of that device was in a form that the federal Food and

Drug Administration had already approved. In any future case, lower courts would be obliged to follow that interpretation of the MDA.

Finally, the Supreme Court's decision cut off one use of state law to challenge practices that are also regulated by federal law. In recent years the Court has decided a series of cases involving federal preemption of state laws that provide protections for consumers, employees, and people who have been injured. The decision in *Riegel* is consistent with the dominant theme of those decisions, a theme that limits the power of states to regulate business practices on issues that federal laws address. In adopting that theme, the Court has helped to shape government policy on business regulation.

The Supreme Court's role in business regulation policy is not unusual. Through its individual decisions and lines of decisions, the Court contributes to the content of government policy on a variety of issues. The Court's assumption of this role reflects several circumstances. For one thing, as the French observer Alexis de Tocqueville noted more than a century ago, "Scarcely any political question arises in the United States that is not resolved, sooner or later, into a judicial question."[2] In part, this is because the United States has a written Constitution that can be used to challenge the legality of government actions. Because so many policy questions come to the courts and ultimately to the Supreme Court, the Court has the opportunity to shape a wide range of policies. And the justices often accept and even welcome that opportunity, ruling on major issues and shaping public policy on those issues.

At the same time, the Court's role in policymaking is limited by several conditions, of which two are especially important. First, the Court can do only so much with the relatively few decisions it makes in a year. The Court currently issues decisions with full opinions in an average of about eighty cases each year. In deciding such a small number of cases, the Court addresses only a select group of policy issues. Inevitably, there are whole fields of policy that it barely touches. Even in the areas in which the Court does act, it deals with only a limited number of the issues that exist at a given time.

Second, the actions of other policymakers narrow the impact of the Court's decisions. The Court is seldom the final government institution to deal with the policy issues it addresses. Its decisions are implemented by lower-court judges and administrators, who often have considerable discretion over how they put a ruling into effect. The impact of a decision concerning police searches for evidence depends largely on how police officers react to it. Congress and the president influence how the Court's decisions are carried out, and they can overcome its interpretations of federal statutes simply by amending those statutes. As a result, there may be a great deal of difference between what the Court rules on an issue and the public policy that ultimately results from government actions on that issue.

For these reasons, those who see the Supreme Court as the dominant force in the U.S. government almost surely are wrong. But the Court does contribute a good deal to the making of public policy.

The Court in the Judicial System

The Supreme Court is part of a court system, and its place in that system structures its role by determining what cases it can hear and the routes those cases take.

State and Federal Court Systems

The United States has a federal court system and a separate court system for each state. Federal courts can hear only those cases that Congress has put under their jurisdiction. Nearly all of this jurisdiction falls into three categories.

First are the criminal and civil cases that arise under federal laws, including the Constitution. A prosecution for bank robbery, which violates federal law, is brought to federal court. So are civil cases based on federal patent and copyright laws.

Second are cases to which the U.S. government is a party. When the federal government sues an individual to recover what it claims to be owed from a student loan, or when an individual sues the federal government over disputed Social Security benefits, the case almost always goes to federal court.

Third are civil cases involving citizens of different states in which the amount in question is more than $75,000. If this condition is met, either party may bring the case to federal court. If a citizen of New Jersey sues a citizen of Texas for $100,000 as compensation for injuries from an auto accident, the plaintiff (the New Jersey resident) might bring the case to federal court, or the defendant (the Texan) might have the case "removed" from state court to federal court. If neither does so, the case will be heard in state court—generally, in the state where the accident occurred or the defendant lives.

These categories encompass only a small proportion of all court cases. The most common kinds of cases—criminal prosecutions, personal injury suits, divorces, actions to collect debts—typically are heard in state court. The trial courts of a single populous state such as Illinois or Florida hear far more cases than do the federal trial courts. However, federal cases are more likely than state cases to raise major issues of public policy.

State court systems vary considerably in their structure, but some general patterns exist (see Figure 1-1). Each state system has courts that are primarily

FIGURE 1-1
Most Common State Court Structures

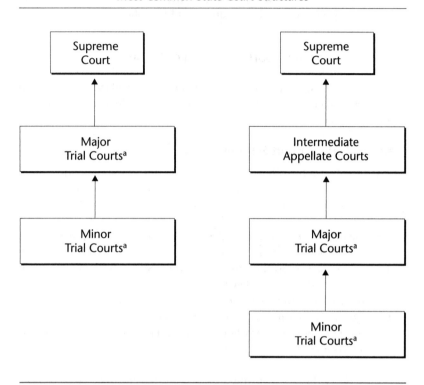

Note: Arrows indicate most common routes of appeals.

a. In many states, major trial courts or minor trial courts (or both) are composed of two or more different sets of courts. For instance, New York has several types of minor trial courts.

trial courts, which hear cases initially as they enter the court system, and courts that are primarily appellate courts, which review lower-court decisions that are appealed to them. Most states have two sets of trial courts, one to handle major cases and the other to deal with minor cases. Major criminal cases usually concern what the law defines as felonies. Major civil cases are those involving large sums of money. Most often, appeals from decisions of minor trial courts are heard by major trial courts.

Appellate courts are structured in two ways. Eleven states, generally those with small populations, have a single appellate court—usually called the state supreme court. All appeals from major trial courts go to this supreme court. The other thirty-nine states have a set of intermediate appellate courts below the supreme court. These intermediate courts initially hear most appeals from major trial courts. In those states supreme courts have discretionary jurisdiction over most challenges to the decisions of intermediate courts. Discretionary jurisdiction means simply that a court can choose which cases to hear; cases that a court is required to hear fall under its mandatory jurisdiction.

The structure of federal courts is shown in Figure 1-2. At the base of the federal court system are the federal district courts. The United States has ninety-four district courts. Each state has between one and four district courts, and there is a district court in the District of Columbia and in some of the territories, such as Guam. District courts hear all federal cases at the trial level, with the exception of a few types of cases that are heard in specialized courts.

Above the district courts are the twelve courts of appeals, each of which hears appeals in one of the federal judicial circuits. The District of Columbia constitutes one circuit; each of the other eleven circuits covers three or more states. The Second Circuit, for example, includes Connecticut, New York, and Vermont. Appeals from the district courts in one circuit generally go to the court of appeals for that circuit, along with appeals from the Tax Court and from some administrative agencies. Patent cases and some claims against the federal government go from the district courts to the specialized Court of Appeals for the Federal Circuit, as do appeals from three specialized trial courts. The Court of Appeals for the Armed Forces hears cases from lower courts in the military system.

The Supreme Court's Jurisdiction

The Supreme Court stands at the top of the federal judicial system. Its jurisdiction, summarized in Table 1-1, is of two types. First is the Court's original jurisdiction: the Constitution gives the Court jurisdiction over a few categories of cases as a trial court, so these cases may be brought directly to the Court without going through lower courts. The Court's original jurisdiction includes some cases to which a state is a party and cases involving foreign diplomatic personnel.

Most cases within the Court's original jurisdiction can be heard alternatively by a district court. Lawsuits between two states can be heard only by the Supreme Court, and these lawsuits account for most of the decisions based on the Court's original jurisdiction. These cases often involve disputed state borders, but increasingly they are battles over water rights.[3] The Court frequently refuses to hear cases under its original jurisdiction, even some lawsuits by one state against another. In part for this reason, full decisions in these cases are not plentiful—fewer than two hundred in the Court's history.[4] When the Court does accept a case under its original jurisdiction, it ordinarily appoints a "special master" to gather facts and

FIGURE 1-2
Basic Structure of the Federal Court System

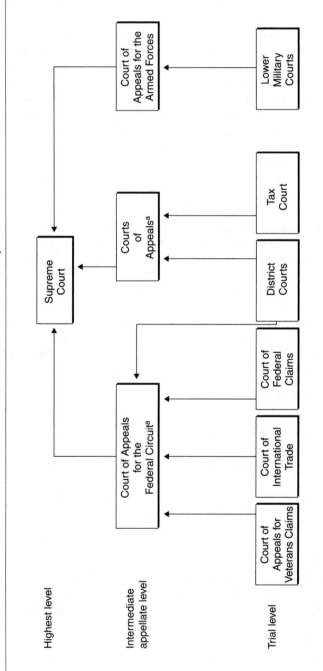

Note: Arrows indicate most common routes of appeals. Some specialized courts of minor importance are excluded.

a. These courts also hear appeals from administrative agencies.

TABLE 1-1
Summary of Supreme Court Jurisdiction

Types of jurisdiction	Categories of cases
Original	Disputes between states[a]
	Some types of cases brought by a state
	Disputes between a state and the federal government
	Cases involving foreign diplomatic personnel
Appellate[b]	All decisions of federal courts of appeals and specialized federal appellate courts
	All decisions of the highest state court with jurisdiction over a case, concerning issues of federal law
	Decisions of special three-judge federal district courts (mandatory)

a. It is unclear whether these cases are mandatory, and the Court treats them as discretionary.
b. Some minor categories are not listed.

propose a decision, which the Court tends to ratify.[5] Most of the original cases that the Court hears are more technical than interesting, but the justices take them seriously. In *New Jersey v. Delaware* (2008), to take one example, three justices dissented from all or part of the Court's decision.

The second type of jurisdiction, appellate jurisdiction, accounts for the overwhelming majority of cases that the Court hears. Under its appellate jurisdiction the Court hears cases brought by parties that are dissatisfied with the lower-court decisions in their cases. Within the federal court system, such cases can come from the federal courts of appeals and from the two specialized appellate courts. Cases may also come directly from special three-judge district courts; most of these cases involve voting and election issues.

State cases can come to the Supreme Court after decisions by the state supreme courts if they involve claims arising under federal law, including the Constitution. If a state supreme court chooses not to hear a case, the losing party can then go to the Supreme Court. As a result of this rule, in 2003 the Court decided a case that had been heard only by a West Virginia trial court.[6] Table 1-2 shows that a substantial majority of the cases that come to the Court, and an even larger majority of the cases that it hears, originated in federal court rather than in state court.

The rule under which state cases come to the Supreme Court may be confusing, because cases arising under federal law ordinarily start in federal court. But cases brought to state courts on the basis of state law sometimes contain issues of federal law as well. This situation is common in criminal cases. A person accused of burglary under state law will be tried in a state

TABLE 1-2
Sources of Supreme Court Cases in Recent Periods (percent)

	Federal courts			
	Courts of appeals	District courts	Specialized courts	State courts
Cases brought to the Court[a]	74	0	2	24
Cases heard by the Court[b]	82	2	4	12

Source: Data on cases heard by the Court are from the U.S. Supreme Court Database, compiled by Harold Spaeth, Michigan State University, at http://www.cas.sc.edu/poli/juri/sctdata.htm.

Note: Original jurisdiction cases are not included. Nonfederal courts of the District of Columbia and of U.S. territories are treated as state courts. For cases heard by the Court, each oral argument is counted once unless it involves consolidated cases from two different categories of courts.

a. Cases in which the Court ruled on petitions for hearings, October 6, 2008.
b. Cases in which the Court heard oral argument, 2006 and 2007 terms.

court. During the state court proceedings, the defendant may argue that the police violated rights protected by the U.S. Constitution during a search. The case eventually can be brought to the Supreme Court on that issue. If it is, the Court will have the power to rule only on the federal issue, not on the issues of state law involved in the case. Thus the Court cannot rule on whether the defendant actually committed the burglary.

Nearly all cases brought to the Court are under its discretionary jurisdiction, so it can choose whether or not to hear them. Nearly all discretionary cases come to the Court in the form of petitions for a writ of certiorari, a writ through which the Court calls up a case for decision from a lower court. The Court must hear certain cases, called appeals. In a series of steps culminating in 1988, Congress converted the Court's jurisdiction from mostly mandatory to almost entirely discretionary. Today, appeals can be brought in only the few small classes of cases that come directly from three-judge district courts. The Bipartisan Campaign Reform Act of 2002 provided this procedure for constitutional challenges to the law, so the cases that the Court heard on these challenges between 2003 and 2008 came to it as appeals from decisions of three-judge district courts.[7]

The Supreme Court hears only a fraction of 1 percent of the cases brought to federal and state courts. As this figure suggests, courts other than the Supreme Court have ample opportunity to make policy on their own. Moreover, their decisions help to determine the ultimate impact of the Court's policies. Important though it is, the Supreme Court certainly is not the only court that matters.

An Overview of the Court

Some attributes of the Supreme Court itself should be examined to provide background for the chapters that follow. This section considers several aspects of the Court, with emphasis on the justices and the people who help them do their work.

The Court's Building

The Supreme Court did not move into its own building until 1935. In its first decade, the Court met first in New York and then in Philadelphia. The Court moved to Washington, D.C., with the rest of the federal government at the beginning of the nineteenth century. For the next 130 years, it sat in the Capitol, a "tenant" of Congress.

The Court's accommodations in the Capitol were not entirely adequate. Among other things, the lack of office space meant that justices did most of their work at home. After an intensive lobbying effort by Chief Justice William Howard Taft, Congress appropriated money for the Supreme Court building in 1929. The five-story structure occupies a full square block across the street from the Capitol. Because the primary material in the impressive building is marble, it has been called a "marble palace." The aging of the Court's building and the need to house a staff that had grown considerably led to a major renovation project that began in 2003. After some delay, it is now scheduled for completion in 2010.

The building houses all the Court's facilities. Formal sessions are held in the courtroom on the first floor. Behind the courtroom is the conference room, where the justices meet to decide cases. Also near the courtroom are the chambers that contain offices for the associate justices and their staffs. Reflecting the chief justice's special status, the chief's chambers are attached to the conference room.

Personnel: The Justices

Under the Constitution, Supreme Court justices must be nominated by the president and confirmed by the Senate. By long-established Senate practice, a simple majority is required for confirmation. The Constitution says that justices will hold office "during good behavior"—that is, for life unless they relinquish their posts voluntarily or are removed through impeachment proceedings. Beyond these basic rules, questions such as the number of justices, their qualifications, and their duties have been settled by federal statutes and by tradition.

The Constitution says nothing about the number of justices, and that number was changed several times during the Court's first century. The Judiciary Act of 1789 provided for six justices. Subsequent statutes changed the number successively to five, six, seven, nine, ten, seven, and nine.

The changes were made in part to accommodate the justices' duties in the lower federal courts, in part to serve partisan and policy goals of the president and Congress. The most recent change to nine members was made in 1869, and any further changes in size appear quite unlikely.

In 2009 each associate justice received a salary of $213,900, and the chief justice received $223,500. Substantial as these salaries are, they are considerably lower than leading lawyers receive at large private law firms. Justices are limited to about $26,000 in outside income from activities such as teaching, but there are no limits on income from books. Clarence Thomas received an advance payment of more than $1 million for his memoir, *My Grandfather's Son*. Based on the information in their financial disclosure reports, it appears that about half of the current justices are wealthy by most standards.[8]

The primary duty of the justices is to participate in the collective decisions of the Court: determining which cases to hear, deciding cases, and writing and contributing to opinions. Ordinarily, the Court's decisions are made by all nine members, but exceptions occur. At times the Court has only eight members because a justice has left the Court and a replacement has not been appointed. A justice's illness may leave the Court temporarily shorthanded, or a justice may decide not to participate in a case because of a perceived conflict of interest. Under federal law, judges should withdraw from cases—"recuse" themselves—when a decision would affect their self-interest substantially or their impartiality "might reasonably be questioned."[9] The Court leaves this decision entirely to the individual justice.

Justices do not explain the reasons for their recusals, but those reasons often can be discerned. The most common reason is a financial interest in a case, usually a result of a justice's stock holdings. In a 2008 case Chief Justice John Roberts recused himself but then "un-recused" and participated in the case. As it turned out, after the original recusal he sold the stock that created a conflict of interest.[10] In the same year Stephen Breyer began to sell some of his stocks, and the Court's public information officer explained that he wanted to "minimize the number of instances in which financial conflicts require recusal."[11]

Other recusals result from personal ties between justices and the litigants or lawyers in a case. Antonin Scalia received some criticism because he chose not to recuse himself from a 2004 case in which Vice President Richard Cheney was a litigant in his official capacity. Scalia and Cheney were friends, and after the Court accepted this case the two were among the participants in a duck-hunting trip to Louisiana. One of Cheney's opponents in the case asked that Scalia recuse himself, but he declined to do so and issued a detailed memorandum explaining why he thought recusal was unnecessary.[12]

When only eight justices participate in a decision, the Court may divide 4–4. This was the result in two cases during the Court's 2007 term.[13] A tie vote affirms the lower-court decision, the votes of individual justices are not announced, and no opinions are written. Similarly, the lower-court decision in a case is affirmed if the Court cannot reach a quorum of six members. That situation is rare, but it occurred twice in the 2007 term. One case involved more than fifty companies, and four justices owned stock in at least one of the companies. In the other case a litigant had sued every Supreme Court justice on the basis of their handling of his prior lawsuits. Seven of the defendant justices remained on the Court in 2007, and they all recused themselves.[14]

In addition to their participation in collective decisions, the justices make some decisions individually as circuit justices. The United States has always been divided into federal judicial circuits. Originally, most appeals within a circuit were heard by ad hoc courts composed of a federal trial judge and two members of the Supreme Court who were assigned to that area as circuit justices. The circuit duties were arduous, especially when long-distance travel was difficult. Some justices even suffered ill health from "circuit riding."[15] Actions by Congress and by the justices themselves gradually reduced the extent of their circuit riding, and this duty ended altogether when Congress created the courts of appeals in 1891.

The justices today retain some duties as circuit justices, with each justice assigned to one or more circuits. As circuit justices they deal with applications for special action, such as a request to stay a lower-court decision (prevent it from taking effect) until the Court decides whether to hear the case. Such an application generally must go first to the circuit justice. That justice may rule on the application as an individual or refer the case to the whole Court. If the circuit justice rejects an application, it can then be made to a second justice. That justice ordinarily refers it to the whole Court.

One common subject of stay requests is the death penalty. The Court is confronted with numerous requests to stay executions or vacate (remove) stays of execution, many of which come near the scheduled execution time. The Court grants only a small proportion of requests for stays of execution. But it did grant several in the 2007 term while a case involving a challenge to state methods of lethal injunction was pending.[16] Requests for stays of execution sometimes produce disagreement among the justices, and the Court's decision to deny a stay of execution in a complicated 2008 case, *Medellin v. Texas,* drew four dissenting opinions.

For the most part, the nine justices are equal in formal power. The exception is the chief justice, who is the formal leader of the Court. The chief justice presides over the Court's public sessions and conferences and assigns the Court's opinion whenever the chief voted with the majority.

The chief also supervises administration of the Court, with the assistance of committees of justices. Justice Stephen Breyer disclosed in 2007 that he had "risen to the highest administrative level I'm likely ever to rise to, which is being ... the judges' representative on the court's cafeteria committee."[17]

The chief justice is the formal leader of the federal judicial system as well.[18] That role is symbolized by the official title, "Chief Justice of the United States." In this role the chief chairs the federal Judicial Conference and conveys to Congress the views of the conference on legislative issues. The chief justice appoints judges to administrative committees and some specialized courts. The chief also delivers an annual "state of the judiciary" message, directed primarily at Congress. In his messages Chief Justice Roberts has emphasized what he sees as inadequate salaries for federal judges. Roberts received some criticism for the strong tone of the concerns he expressed about judicial salaries in his message at the end of 2006.[19] His tone was not as strong in 2007 and 2008, although he continued to argue for at least modest increases in judicial salaries.

The chief justice traditionally swears in the president on Inauguration Day. When John Roberts performed this duty for President Barack Obama in 2009, it was the first time that a chief justice had sworn in a president who had voted in the Senate against the chief's confirmation to the Supreme Court.[20] After Roberts and Obama stumbled over the words of the oath specified by the Constitution, Roberts came to the White House the next day to administer the oath once again and thus eliminate any doubt that the constitutional requirement had been met.

Personnel: Law Clerks and Other Support Staff

A staff of about 450 people supports the justices. Most of the staff members carry out custodial and police functions under the supervision of the marshal of the Court. The police force has grown with concerns about security for the Court. These concerns were heightened by an incident in 2001: after anthrax bacteria were discovered in the Court's mailroom, the Court building was closed for a week, and oral arguments were held at a nearby federal court building.

Several other offices help carry out the Court's work. The clerk of the Court is responsible for the clerical processing of all the cases that come to the Court. The reporter of decisions supervises preparation of the official record of the Court's decisions, the *United States Reports*. The librarian is in charge of the libraries in the Supreme Court building.

Of all the members of the support staff, the law clerks have the most direct effect on the Court's decisions.[21] Associate justices may employ four clerks each, the chief justice five. Clerks usually work with a justice for only one year. The typical clerk is a recent, high-ranked graduate of a

Justice Clarence Thomas with three of his law clerks in 2002. The clerks play important roles in assisting the justices, but the extent of their influence is debated.

prestigious law school. In the 2004–2008 terms, 49 percent came from Harvard and Yale.[22] The great majority clerked in a federal court of appeals before coming to the Supreme Court, and some spent a short time in legal practice after their stints in a court of appeals. There has been a growing tendency for the justices, especially the most conservative, to draw clerks from court of appeals judges who share the justices' ideological positions.[23]

Clerks typically spend much of their time on the petitions for hearings by the Court, reading the petitions and the lower-court records and summarizing them for the justices. Clerks also work on cases that have been accepted for decision. This work includes analysis of case materials and issues, discussions of issues with their justices, and drafting opinions. According to a 2004 report, John Paul Stevens was the only justice who wrote the first drafts of opinions rather than delegating them to law clerks.[24]

The extent of law clerks' influence over the Court's decisions is a matter of considerable interest and wide disagreement.[25] Observers who depict the clerks as quite powerful probably underestimate the justices' ability to maintain control over their decisions. Still, the jobs that justices give to their clerks ensure significant influence, influence that has grown over time. Writing drafts of opinions, for instance, allows clerks to shape the content of those opinions, whether or not they seek to do so. The same is true of the other work that clerks do. Whatever their influence may be, law clerks certainly make the justices' jobs easier. Indeed, one legal scholar argued that the justices "don't have to do too much work; they have clerks who can write their opinions for them. It's no sweat."[26]

After leaving the Court, most law clerks initially go into the private practice of law. With "signing bonuses" that can run as high as $200,000, these clerks often earn far more than the justices in their first year after Court service.[27] Many former clerks go on to distinguished careers. Indeed, Stephen Breyer, William Rehnquist, Byron White, John Roberts, and John Paul Stevens were once law clerks in the Court. Roberts is a "second-generation" clerk-turned-justice, having clerked for Rehnquist in the Court's 1980 term and then succeeding him as chief justice.

The Court and the Outside World

In May 2008 a contestant on the television show "Who Wants to Be a Millionaire" faced a challenge: in order to move on to the next round, she needed to identify the Chief Justice of the United States. Provided with the names of four Supreme Court justices, she used the show's "fifty-fifty lifeline" to eliminate two of the four and reduce her options to John Roberts and John Paul Stevens. She then chose Stevens, and her quest for a million dollars reached an unhappy end.[28]

That contestant was hardly alone in her limited knowledge of the justices. Surveys find that most Americans can recall few if any of the justices' names. A typical survey found that 77 percent of the public remembered two of the Seven Dwarfs, but only 24 percent could identify two justices. (Far more people named Clarence Thomas than any other justice.)[29] Nor are the justices' faces widely recognized. Even among people who thought they knew the justices, Stephen Breyer and David Souter were regularly confused with each other. Souter once met two people who thought he was Breyer and politely chose not to correct them. One of the two asked what he liked most about the Court, and he responded, "Working with Justice Souter."[30]

To a degree, the anonymity of the justices results from their own choices. One key choice is a refusal to allow the Court's public sessions to be televised, despite considerable pressure from Congress to change that policy. Anthony Kennedy even appeared before the Senate Judiciary Committee in 2007 to ask that the committee not approve legislation to require televising of sessions.[31] (However, the Court now posts transcripts of oral arguments within a few hours, and it has allowed immediate release of argument audiotapes in a few cases that attracted great interest.)

The Court's position on televising its sessions is part of a broader practice of limiting disclosure of information about the Court's decision-making processes. The primary goal behind this practice may be to maintain an impression that the Court is above ordinary politics. Barbara Perry has argued that the justices and the Court's staff engage in a careful strategy to give the Court an exalted image with the general public.[32] If there is such a strategy, it has achieved some success. The Court receives more deferential news coverage than the other branches of government.[33] It enjoys a certain aura in popular culture, and its public approval ratings are usually more positive than those of the president and Congress.[34] That high level of approval may provide the Court with some protection from criticism and attacks by other policymakers.

Yet the Court and its members are not entirely isolated from the outside world. For instance, justices often appear before legal groups and visit law schools. The willingness of some justices to participate in summer law-school programs may have something to do with the location of the programs: in 2007, justices crossed the Atlantic to carry out this duty in London, Vienna, Salzburg, Innsbruck, and Sorrento.[35] Some justices have published writings about legal and nonlegal subjects. None of the current justices seems to have the direct relationships with presidents and members of Congress that were common in earlier eras, but some interact with political interest groups. In 2007, for instance, four justices appeared at the twenty-fifth anniversary celebration of the Federalist Society, a conservative legal group.[36]

Over the past several years, the justices have become more willing to interact with groups outside the Court. They give more interviews to the news media, some of them on television. The current justices who have written books—Stephen Breyer, Antonin Scalia, and Clarence Thomas—each has made appearances to publicize the books and the ideas in them. (In a 2009 appearance by Justice Scalia at which his book was displayed, a college student asked him whether there was any inconsistency between Scalia's opposition to televising of oral arguments and the fact that justices go "out on book tours." "That's a nasty, impolite question," Scalia said.)[37]

Several current justices have offered their views about public issues in speeches and interviews. Justice Scalia is especially active in this regard, speaking about issues such as interrogation of suspected terrorists and the relationship between government and religion. In 2003 he agreed to a litigant's request that he recuse himself from a case because he had criticized the lower court's decision in a speech.[38]

Among the justices who have served in recent years David Souter was probably the one who made the fewest public appearances. "In a perfect world," he told a colleague in 1990, "I would never give another speech, address, talk, lecture or whatever as long as I live."[39] After one Court

Justice Stephen Breyer at American University, in a discussion with Justice Antonin Scalia. Breyer and Scalia are two of the justices who make frequent appearances at public events.

session, according to a reporter, Souter walked out the Court's front door. Even among the people who had just attended the Court's session, nobody recognized him except for one of the lawyers who had argued a case at the session.[40] Undoubtedly, Souter was very pleased to go unnoticed.

The Court's Schedule

The Court keeps to a constant annual schedule. It holds one term each year, lasting from the first Monday in October until the beginning of the succeeding term a year later.[41] The term is designated by the year in which it begins: the 2009 term began in October 2009. (However, the clerk's office treats a term as ending when the Court finishes its work in June.) Ordinarily, the Court does its collective work from late September to late June. This work begins when the justices meet to act on the petitions for hearings that have accumulated during the summer and ends when the Court has issued decisions in all the cases it heard during the term.

Most of the term is divided into sittings of about two weeks, when the Court holds sessions to hear oral arguments in cases and to announce decisions in cases that were argued earlier in the term, and recesses of two weeks or longer. In May and June the Court hears no more cases and holds one or more sessions each week to announce decisions. It issues few decisions early in the term because of the time required after oral arguments to write opinions and reach final positions. Typically, about one-third of the decisions are announced in June, as the justices scramble to finish their work by the end of the term. According to Justice Scalia, "Toward the end of the term when there are a lot of opinions outstanding that haven't come in yet," former Chief Justice Rehnquist was "wont to say, 'Ladies and gentlemen, time to stop thinking and start writing.' "[42] As an associate justice, Rehnquist once wrote to Justice Marshall that "if this were November rather than June, I would prepare a masterfully crafted dissenting opinion exposing the fallacies" of Marshall's majority opinion in a case. "Since it is June, however, I join" Marshall's opinion.[43]

When the Court has reached and announced decisions in all the cases it heard during the term, the summer recess begins. Cases that the Court accepted for hearing but that were not argued during the term are carried over to the next term. In summer the justices generally spend time away from Washington but continue their work on the petitions for hearings that arrive at the Court. During that time the Court and individual circuit justices respond to applications for special action. When the justices meet at the end of summer to dispose of the accumulated petitions, the annual cycle begins again.

The schedule of weekly activities, like the annual schedule, is fairly regular. During sittings, the Court generally holds sessions on Monday through Wednesday for two weeks and on Monday of the next week. The sessions begin at ten o'clock in the morning. Oral arguments usually are held during each session except on the last Monday of the sitting. They may be preceded by several types of business. On Mondays the Court announces the filing of its order list, which is a report of the Court's decisions on petitions for hearing and other actions taken at its conference on the preceding Friday. On Tuesdays and Wednesdays, as well as the last Monday of the sitting, justices announce their opinions in any cases the Court has resolved. In May and June, however, opinions may be announced on any day of the week.

The oral arguments consume most of the time during sessions. The usual practice is to allot one hour, equally divided between the two sides, for arguments in a case. On most argument days the Court hears two cases. But the Court scheduled three arguments for most of its sessions in the first sitting of 2008, in an effort to reach decisions in more cases early in the term and thus relieve the pressure on the justices in June.[44]

During sittings, the Court holds two conferences each week. The Wednesday afternoon conference is devoted to discussion of the cases that were argued on Monday. In a longer conference on Friday, the justices discuss the cases argued on Tuesday and Wednesday, as well as petitions for certiorari and other matters the Court must decide. In May and June, after oral arguments have ended for the year, the Court has weekly conferences on Thursdays.

The Court also holds a conference on the last Friday of each recess to deal with the continuing flow of business. The remainder of the justices' time during recess periods is devoted to their individual work: study of petitions for hearing and cases scheduled for argument, writing of opinions, and reaction to other justices' opinions. That work continues during the sittings.

The Court's History

This book is concerned primarily with the Supreme Court at present and in the recent past, but I frequently refer to the Court's history to provide perspective on the current Court. For this reason, an overview of that history will provide background for later chapters. Even a brief overview makes clear the links between the Court's own history and that of the nation as a whole. The Court has played a role in American political development, and it has been shaped by the development of other political institutions.

The Court from 1790 to 1865

The framers of the Constitution explicitly created the Supreme Court, but the Constitution says much less about the Court than about Congress and the president. In the Judiciary Act of 1789, which set up the federal court system, the Court's jurisdiction under the Constitution was used as the basis for granting the Court broad powers. Still, what it would do with its powers was uncertain, in part because their scope was ambiguous.

The Court started slowly, deciding only about fifty cases and making few significant decisions between 1790 and 1799.[45] Several people rejected offers to serve on the Court, and two justices—including Chief Justice John Jay—resigned to take more attractive positions in state government. The Court's fortunes improved considerably under John Marshall, chief justice from 1801 to 1835. Marshall, appointed by President John Adams, dominated the Court to a degree that no other justice has matched. He used his dominance to strengthen the Court's position and advance the policies he favored.

The Court's most important assertion of power under Marshall was probably its decision in *Marbury v. Madison* (1803), in which the Court struck down a federal statute for the first time. In his opinion for the Court, Marshall argued that when a federal law is inconsistent with the Constitution, the Court must declare the law unconstitutional and refuse to enforce it. A few years later, the Court also claimed the right of judicial review over state acts.

The Court's aggressiveness brought denunciations and threats, including an effort by President Thomas Jefferson to have Congress remove at least one justice through impeachment. But Marshall's skill in minimizing confrontations helped to protect the Court from a successful attack. The other branches of government and the general public gradually accepted the powers that he claimed for the Court and the Court's role in policymaking.

This acceptance was tested by the Court's decision in *Scott v. Sandford* (1857), generally known as the *Dred Scott* case. Prior to that decision, the Court had overturned only one federal statute, the minor law involved in *Marbury v. Madison*. In *Dred Scott*, however, Marshall's successor Roger Taney (1836–1864) wrote the Court's opinion holding that Congress had exceeded its constitutional powers when it prohibited slavery in some territories. That decision was intended to resolve the legal controversy over slavery. Instead, the level of controversy increased, and the Court was vilified in the North. The Court's prestige suffered greatly, but its basic powers survived without serious challenge.[46]

During this period, the Court was concerned with more than its own position; it was addressing major issues of public policy. The primary area of its concern was federalism, the legal relationship between the national government and the states. Under Marshall, the Court gave strong support to national powers. Marshall wanted to restrict state policies where they interfered with activities of the national government, especially its power to regulate commerce. Under Taney, the Court was not as favorable to the national government, but Taney and his colleagues did not reverse the Marshall Court's general expansion of federal power. As a result, the constitutional power of the federal government remained strong; the Court had permanently altered the lines between the national government and the state governments.

The Court from 1865 to 1937

After the Civil War, the Court began to focus its attention on government regulation of the economy. By the late nineteenth century, all levels of government were adopting new laws to regulate business activities. Among them were the federal antitrust laws, state regulations of railroad practices, and federal and state laws regulating employment conditions. Inevitably, much of this legislation was challenged in the courts on constitutional grounds.

The Supreme Court upheld a great many government policies regulating business in this period, but it gradually became less friendly toward those policies. That position was reflected in the development of constitutional doctrines limiting government power to control business activities. Those doctrines were used with increasing frequency to attack regulatory legislation, and in the 1920s the Supreme Court struck down more than 130 regulatory laws as unconstitutional.[47]

In the 1930s the Supreme Court's attacks on economic regulation brought it into serious conflict with the other branches. President Franklin Roosevelt's New Deal program to combat the Great Depression included sweeping statutes to control the economy, measures that enjoyed widespread support. In a series of decisions in 1935 and 1936, the Court struck down several of these statutes, including laws broadly regulating industry and agriculture, generally by 6–3 and 5–4 margins.[48]

Roosevelt responded in 1937 by proposing legislation under which an extra justice could be added to the Court for every sitting justice over the age of seventy who had served at least ten years, up to a maximum of six extra justices. If the legislation were enacted, Roosevelt could appoint six new justices, thereby "packing" the Court with justices favorable to his programs. While this plan was being debated in Congress, however, the Court weakened the impetus behind it. In several decisions in 1937, the Court reversed direction and upheld New Deal legislation and similar state laws by narrow margins.[49] Many observers, although not all, have concluded that this shift was a deliberate effort by one or two moderate justices to mend the Court's contentious relationship with the other branches.[50] In any event, the Court-packing plan died.

The Court from 1937 to 1969

During the congressional debate in 1937, one of the justices who had voted to strike down New Deal laws retired. Several other justices left the Court in the next few years, giving Roosevelt the ideological control of the Court that he had sought through the Court-packing legislation. The new Court created by his appointments fully accepted New Deal regulation of the economy, giving very broad interpretations to the constitutional powers to tax and to regulate interstate commerce. And in the decades that followed, the Court continued to uphold major economic policies of the federal government.

Because of the Court's consistent position on issues of economic regulation, this field gradually became less central to its role. Instead, the Court increasingly focused on civil liberties. By the mid-1960s, the Court was giving the most attention to interpretation of legal protections for freedom of expression and freedom of religion, for the procedural rights of criminal defendants and others, and for equal treatment of disadvantaged groups.

During this period, the Court's overall support for civil liberties issues in conflict with other values varied considerably. That support peaked in the 1960s, the latter part of the period when Earl Warren was chief justice (1953–1969). The Court's policies during that period are often identified with Warren, but other liberal justices played roles of equal or greater importance: Roosevelt appointees Hugo Black and William Douglas, as well as Eisenhower appointee William Brennan.

The most prominent decision of the Warren era was *Brown v. Board of Education* (1954), in which the Court ordered desegregation of school systems that assigned students to separate schools by race. The Court supported the rights of African Americans in several other areas as well. During the 1960s the Court expanded the rights of criminal defendants in state cases. It issued landmark decisions on the right to counsel (*Gideon v. Wainwright,* 1963), police search and seizure practices (*Mapp v. Ohio,* 1961), and the questioning of suspects (*Miranda v. Arizona,* 1966). The Court supported freedom of expression by expanding First Amendment rights, especially on obscenity and libel. In a line of cases beginning with *Baker v. Carr* (1962), the Court required that legislative districts be equal in population.

The Court from 1969 to the Present

When Earl Warren retired in 1969, he was succeeded as chief justice by Warren Burger, President Nixon's first Court appointee. In 1970 and 1971 Nixon made three more appointments. The Court's membership changed much more slowly after that. But each new member until 1993 was appointed by a conservative Republican president—one by Gerald Ford, three by Ronald Reagan, and two by George H. W. Bush. In 1986 Reagan named Nixon appointee William Rehnquist, the Court's most conservative justice, to succeed Warren Burger as chief justice. The string of Republican appointments was broken with Bill Clinton's appointments of Ruth Bader Ginsburg in 1993 and Stephen Breyer in 1994. After eleven years without any change in the Court's membership, George W. Bush chose two justices—John Roberts and Samuel Alito—in 2005.

The Republican appointments from 1969 through 1991 gradually moved the Court's civil liberties policies in a conservative direction, to a greater degree on some issues than on others. Perhaps the most decisive shift came on issues of criminal procedure. The Court did not directly overturn any of the Warren Court's landmark decisions expanding defendants' rights, but it cut back on the reach of decisions such as *Mapp* and *Miranda.* The Rehnquist Court generally gave narrow interpretations to federal statutes prohibiting discrimination, and in 1991 Congress acted to overturn several of those interpretations. One noteworthy exception to the general trend in civil liberties was the Burger Court's series of decisions striking down state and federal laws on the basis of sex discrimination.

The Court also shifted direction in economic policy. Its interpretations of federal laws on environmental protection and labor-management relations became more conservative. Beginning in 1995 it narrowed congressional power to regulate the private sector and state governments in some respects, although it interpreted that power broadly in others.[51]

The absence of a more decisive shift in the Court's policies frustrated some conservative observers of the Court. President Bush's appointments to the Court were widely expected to produce such a shift, and in the first few years under Chief Justice Roberts the Court did seem to move to the right. In *District of Columbia v. Heller* (2008), for instance, the Court held for the first time that the Second Amendment protected the right to individual gun ownership, taking a position that conservatives had championed. But some important decisions were liberal. One example was the 2006 and 2008 rulings that provided legal protections for suspected terrorists who were detained at the Guantánamo Bay Naval Station.[52]

The Court's path during the period since 1969 underlines the reality that its direction is largely a reflection of its membership. For that reason, the selection of justices is a crucial process. I examine that process in the next chapter.

NOTES

1   Raha Naddaf and Greg Veis, "The 50 Most Powerful People in D.C.," *GQ,* September 2007, 298; "Focus on the Family's Dobson Decries 'Concerted Effort to Drive God Out of the Public Square,'", U.S. Newswire, September 17, 2003.

2. Alexis de Tocqueville, *Democracy in America,* 2 vols., trans. Henry Reeve, rev. Francis Bowen (New York: Knopf, 1945), 1:280.

3. Tresa Baldas, "A Deluge of Water Wars," *National Law Journal,* March 24, 2008, 1, 17.

4. This figure is updated from Henry J. Abraham, *The Judicial Process,* 7th ed. (New York: Oxford University Press, 1998), 188.

5. Anne-Marie Carstens, "Lurking in the Shadows of Judicial Process: Special Masters in the Supreme Court's Original Jurisdiction Cases," *Minnesota Law Review* 86 (February 2002): 625–715.

6. *Norfolk & Western Railway Co. v. Ayers* (2003).

7. *McConnell v. Federal Election Commission* (2003); *Federal Election Commission v. Wisconsin Right to Life, Inc.* (2007); *Davis v. Federal Election Commission* (2008).

8. The justices' annual financial disclosure reports list the (very) approximate values of their investments at the end of each calendar year. They also list the justices' outside income, including book royalties. The reports for the justices since 2002 are posted at http://moneyline.cq.com/pml/home.do.

9. 28 U.S.C., sec. 455.

10. The case was *Stoneridge Investment Partners v. Scientific-Atlanta* (2008). See "Supreme Court Records" (editorial), *Washington Post,* September 28, 2007, A18.

11. Adam Liptak, "Supreme Court Opens Term with a Tobacco Fraud Case," *New York Times,* October 7, 2008, A17.

12. Justice Scalia's memorandum is at *Cheney v. United States District Court* (2004).

13. The cases were *Board of Education v. Tom F.* (2007) and *Warner-Lambert Co. v. Kent* (2008). As I discuss later in the chapter, the Court's terms span two calendar years; the 2007 term began in October 2007 and ended a year later.

14. The cases were, respectively, *American Isuzu Motors, Inc. v. Ntsebeza* (2008) and *Sibley v. Breyer* (2007).

15. David N. Atkinson, *Leaving the Bench: Supreme Court Justices at the End* (Lawrence: University Press of Kansas, 1999), chap. 2.

16. See Linda Greenhouse, "Justices Stay Execution, A Signal to Lower Courts," *New York Times,* October 31, 2007, A1, A18.

17. "Wait Wait ... Don't Tell Me!" National Public Radio, March 24, 2007 (www.npr.org/programs/waitwait/archives.html).

18. See Russell R. Wheeler, "Chief Justice Rehnquist as Third Branch Leader," *Judicature* 89 (November–December 2005): 116–120.

19. Robert Barnes, "Outside Court, Roberts Hears Dissent," *Washington Post,* January 8, 2007, A13.

20. Lawrence Hurley, "Will Obama Have an Awkward Inaugural Moment?" *Daily Journal,* November 20, 2008.

21. The law clerks are discussed in Todd C. Peppers, *Courtiers of the Marble Palace: The Rise and Influence of the Supreme Court Law Clerk* (Stanford: Stanford University Press, 2006); and Artemus Ward and David L. Weiden, *Sorcerers' Apprentices: 100 Years of Law Clerks at the United States Supreme Court* (New York: New York University Press, 2006).

22. This figure was calculated from information sheets provided by the Supreme Court.

23. Corey Ditslear and Lawrence Baum, "Selection of Law Clerks and Polarization in the U.S. Supreme Court," *Journal of Politics* 63 (August 2001): 869–885.

24. David G. Savage, "Anthony M. Kennedy and the Road Not Taken," in *A Year at the Supreme Court,* ed. Neal Devins (Durham, N.C.: Duke University Press, 2004), 41.

25. See Peppers, *Courtiers of the Marble Palace,* chap. 6; Ward and Weiden, *Sorcerers' Apprentices,* chap. 6; Todd C. Peppers and Christopher Zorn, "Law Clerk Influence on Supreme Court Decision Making: An Empirical Assessment," *DePaul Law Review* 58 (2008): 410–427.

26. Richard Brust, "Supreme Court 2.0," *ABA Journal* 94 (October 2008): 39.

27. Charles Lane, "Former Clerks' Signing Bonuses Rival Salaries on the High Court," *Washington Post,* May 15, 2006, A15.

28. This incident was reported in the blog "How Appealing" (http://howap pealing.law.com/), May 23, 2008.

29. Jennifer Harper, "Superman Tops Supremes," *Washington Times,* August 15, 2006. Citing other survey results, two scholars argue that Americans know the justices better than their recall of justices' names suggests. James L. Gibson and Gregory A. Caldeira, "Knowing the Supreme Court? A Reconsideration of Public Ignorance of the High Court," *Journal of Politics,* forthcoming.

30. Greg Stohr, "Souter Fiercely Protects His Own Right to Privacy about His Anonymity," *Pittsburgh Post-Gazette,* May 18, 2008, A-7.

31. Joan Biskupic, "Justice Pleads with Senate: No Cameras in High Court," *USA Today,* February 15, 2007, 8A.

32. Barbara A. Perry, *The Priestly Tribe: The Supreme Court's Image in the American Mind* (Westport, Conn.: Praeger, 1999).

33. On coverage of the Court, see Elliot E. Slotnick and Jennifer A. Segal, *Television News and the Supreme Court: All the News That's Fit to Air?* (New York: Cambridge University Press, 1998); and Rorie L. Spill and Zoe M. Oxley, "Philosopher Kings or Political Actors? How the Media Portray the Supreme Court," *Judicature* 87 (July–August 2003): 23–29.

34. Norman L. Rosenberg, "The Supreme Court and Popular Culture: Image and Projection," in *The United States Supreme Court: The Pursuit of Justice*, ed. Christopher Tomlins (Boston: Houghton Mifflin, 2005), 421.

35. This information is taken from the justices' financial disclosure reports, discussed in note 8.

36. Robert Barnes, "Federalists Relish Well-Placed Friends," *Washington Post*, November 16, 2007, A3.

37. Frank Cerabino, "Student Fails to Persuade Justice Scalia," *Palm Beach Post*, February 7, 2009.

38. Charles Lane, "High Court to Consider Pledge in Schools," *Washington Post*, October 15, 2003, A1, A9. The case was *Elk Grove v. Newdow* (2004).

39. Elizabeth Walters, "Breaking Ground with the Justices," *Concord (N.H.) Monitor*, April 9, 2006.

40. Stohr, "Souter Protects Anonymity."

41. The Court's schedule is described in Eugene Gressman, Kenneth S. Geller, Stephen M. Shapiro, Timothy S. Bishop, and Edward A. Hartnett, *Supreme Court Practice*, 9th ed. (Arlington, Va.: BNA Books, 2007), 11–16.

42. Joan Biskupic, "It's Crunch Time for Some of High Court's Biggest Decisions," *USA Today*, June 6, 2005, 7A.

43. Joan Biskupic, *Sandra Day O'Connor* (New York: HarperCollins, 2005), 125.

44. Tony Mauro, "Next Term: A Fatter, Faster Calendar for Supreme Court," Law.Com, July 3, 2008 (www.law.com/jsp/law/LawArticleFriendly.jsp?id=1202422731447).

45. See William R. Casto, *The Supreme Court in the Early Republic: The Chief Justiceships of John Jay and Oliver Ellsworth* (Columbia: University of South Carolina Press, 1995). For another perspective, see Scott Douglas Gerber, ed., *Seriatim: The Supreme Court before John Marshall* (New York: New York University Press, 1998).

46. Robert G. McCloskey, *The American Supreme Court*, 4th ed., rev. by Sanford Levinson (Chicago: University of Chicago Press, 2005), 64–66.

47. This figure was calculated from data in Congressional Research Service, *The Constitution of the United States of America: Analysis and Interpretation* (Washington, D.C.: Government Printing Office, 1987), 1885–2113.

48. The cases included *Carter v. Carter Coal Co.* (1936); *United States v. Butler* (1936); and *Schechter Poultry Corp. v. United States* (1935).

49. The cases included *National Labor Relations Board v. Jones & Laughlin Steel Corp.* (1937); *Steward Machine Co. v. Davis* (1937); and *West Coast Hotel Co. v. Parrish* (1937).

50. William G. Ross, *The Chief Justiceship of Charles Evans Hughes, 1930–1941* (Columbia: University of South Carolina Press, 2007), ix–xi and chap. 4.

51. See *United States v. Morrison* (2000) and *Gonzales v. Raich* (2005).

52. The decisions were *Hamdan v. Rumsfeld* (2006) and *Boumediene v. Bush* (2008).

Chapter 2

The Justices

The most direct influence on the Supreme Court's decisions, and probably the strongest, is the Court's membership. In turn, the ability to determine who sits on the Court is a power of considerable importance. Although other issues dominated the 2008 elections, one major consequence of those elections was that any nominations to the Court for the next two years would be made by Barack Obama and reviewed by a Senate with a Democratic majority. That consequence was underlined when Justice David Souter announced his retirement three months after Obama became president.

With Obama's appointment of Sonia Sotomayor in 2009, presidents have made 152 nominations to the Supreme Court, and 111 justices have served. Four candidates were nominated and confirmed twice, and eight declined appointments or died before beginning service on the Court. Twenty-nine did not secure Senate confirmation; a few of these nominees dropped out before the Senate could consider them.[1]

Table 2-1 lists the thirty-two nominations to the Court since 1953 and the twenty-five justices chosen since that time. This chapter focuses on that period and primarily on the past few decades. In the chapter's three sections I discuss the selection of justices, the characteristics of the people who are selected, and how and why they leave the Court.

The Selection of Justices

The formal process for selection of Supreme Court justices is simple. When a vacancy occurs, the president makes a nomination. The nomination must then be confirmed by the Senate, with a simple majority of participating senators required for confirmation. When the chief justice's position is vacant, the president has two options: to nominate a sitting justice to that position and also nominate a new associate justice, or to nominate a person as chief justice from outside the Court.

TABLE 2-1

Nominations to the Supreme Court since 1953

Name	Nominating president	Justice replaced	Years served
Earl Warren (CJ)	Eisenhower	Vinson	1953–1969
John Harlan	Eisenhower	Jackson	1955–1971
William Brennan	Eisenhower	Minton	1956–1990
Charles Whittaker	Eisenhower	Reed	1957–1962
Potter Stewart	Eisenhower	Burton	1958–1981
Byron White	Kennedy	Whittaker	1962–1993
Arthur Goldberg	Kennedy	Frankfurter	1962–1965
Abe Fortas	Johnson	Goldberg	1965–1969
Thurgood Marshall	Johnson	Clark	1967–1991
Abe Fortas (CJ)	Johnson	(Warren)	Withdrew, 1968
Homer Thornberry	Johnson	(Fortas)	Moot, 1968
Warren Burger (CJ)	Nixon	Warren	1969–1986
Clement Haynsworth	Nixon	(Fortas)	Defeated, 1969
G. Harrold Carswell	Nixon	(Fortas)	Defeated, 1970
Harry Blackmun	Nixon	Fortas	1970–1994
Lewis Powell	Nixon	Black	1971–1987
William Rehnquist	Nixon	Harlan	1971–2005
John Paul Stevens	Ford	Douglas	1975–
Sandra Day O'Connor	Reagan	Stewart	1981–2006
William Rehnquist (CJ)	Reagan	Burger	1986–2005
Antonin Scalia	Reagan	Rehnquist	1986–
Robert Bork	Reagan	(Powell)	Defeated, 1987
Douglas Ginsburg	Reagan	(Powell)	Withdrew, 1987
Anthony Kennedy	Reagan	Powell	1988–
David Souter	G. H. W. Bush	Brennan	1990–2009
Clarence Thomas	G. H. W. Bush	Marshall	1991–
Ruth Bader Ginsburg	Clinton	White	1993–
Stephen Breyer	Clinton	Blackmun	1994–
John Roberts (CJ)	G. W. Bush	Rehnquist	2005–
Harriet Miers	G. W. Bush	(O'Connor)	Withdrew, 2005
Samuel Alito	G. W. Bush	O'Connor	2006–
Sonia Sotomayor	Obama	Souter	2009–

Note: CJ = chief justice. Fortas and Rehnquist were associate justices when nominated as chief justice. Roberts was originally nominated to replace O'Connor, then was nominated for chief justice after Rehnquist's death.

Defeated = Senate voted against confirmation.

Withdrew = Nomination or planned nomination was withdrawn. The Fortas nomination was withdrawn after a vote to end a filibuster failed. Douglas Ginsburg withdrew before he was formally nominated.

Moot = When Fortas withdrew as nominee for chief justice, the Thornberry nomination to take Fortas's position as associate justice became moot.

Presidents usually take the latter course, as President Bush did when he selected John Roberts to succeed William Rehnquist in 2005. But President Ronald Reagan elevated Rehnquist from associate justice to chief justice after Warren Burger retired in 1986.

The actual process of selection is more complicated than the simple formal process suggests. The president and the Senate make their decisions surrounded by individuals and groups with a strong interest in these decisions, and the process of nomination and confirmation can be complex. It will be useful to discuss the roles of unofficial participants in the process and then consider how the president and Senate reach their decisions.

Unofficial Participants

Because Supreme Court appointments are so important, many people seek to influence the president and Senate. When a vacancy occurs, presidents and other administration officials may hear from a wide array of individuals and groups. The same is true of senators who are deciding whether to support a nominee's confirmation. The most important of these individuals and groups fall into three categories: the legal community, other interest groups, and people who seek nominations for themselves.

The Legal Community. Lawyers have a particular interest in the Court's membership, and their views about potential justices may carry special weight. As the largest and most prominent organization of lawyers, the American Bar Association (ABA) occupies an important position. An ABA committee investigates presidential nominees who await confirmation and evaluates them as "well qualified," "qualified," or "not qualified."

Because they believe that the ABA committee is biased against conservative nominees, some Republican senators give little weight to its judgment. Still, the committee's level of enthusiasm for a nominee can affect the confirmation process. (It has never rated a Supreme Court nominee as "not qualified.") A unanimous rating of "well qualified," which most nominees receive, assists a nominee in winning Senate approval. By the same token, when four committee members rated Robert Bork as "not qualified" in 1987 and two gave that rating to Clarence Thomas in 1991, the nominees' prospects for confirmation were weakened. Those negative ratings of two conservative Republicans, one of them (Bork) a prestigious legal scholar, fostered the perception of bias in the ABA committee's decisions.

Other legal groups and individual lawyers also participate in the selection process. Law professors and other prominent attorneys often announce their evaluations of nominees the Senate is considering. For Republican presidents, the conservative Federalist Society of lawyers serves as one source of advice. Seven of Samuel Alito's current and past colleagues on the federal court of appeals for the Third Circuit testified on his behalf in the Judiciary Committee.

Supreme Court justices sometimes participate in the selection process, most often by recommending a potential nominee. Chief Justice Warren Burger went further. Appointed by Richard Nixon in 1969, he was active in suggesting names to fill other vacancies during the Nixon administration. He played an important role in G. Harrold Carswell's nomination and a crucial role in the nomination of his longtime friend Harry Blackmun. Some years later, Burger lobbied the Reagan administration on behalf of Sandra Day O'Connor.[2]

Other Interest Groups. Many interest groups have a stake in Supreme Court decisions, so groups often seek to influence the selection of justices. The level of group activity has grown substantially in the past half century, and it now pervades both the nomination and confirmation stages of the selection process.

At the nomination stage, interest groups would like to influence the president's choice from the large number of potential nominees. The groups that actually exert influence are typically those that are politically important to the president. Democratic presidents usually give some weight to the views of labor and civil rights groups. Republican presidents usually pay attention to groups that take conservative positions on social issues such as abortion and school religious observances.

The influence of these core groups was underlined in 2005. After Sandra Day O'Connor announced her retirement, the Bush administration consulted with leaders of conservative groups about potential nominees. At the same time, conservative groups lobbied publicly in favor of a strong conservative. They even attacked Attorney General Alberto Gonzales, thought to be a candidate for nomination, for his perceived moderation. Conservatives welcomed President Bush's nominee John Roberts, in part because the administration had worked for a year to win their support for Roberts.[3] After Chief Justice William Rehnquist died and Bush nominated Roberts to succeed Rehnquist, he chose his White House counsel Harriet Miers for O'Connor's position. Many conservatives were uncertain that Miers held views similar to their own, and conservative groups and individuals mounted a strong campaign against her. After their campaign secured Miers's withdrawal, President Bush chose Samuel Alito, a judge who was popular with conservative groups.

Once a nomination has been announced, groups often work for or against Senate confirmation. Significant interest group activity at the confirmation stage can be traced back as far as 1881, but it was fairly limited and sporadic until the late 1960s.[4] Its growth since then reflects growth in the number of interest groups and in the intensity of group activity, greater awareness that nominations to the Court are important, and group leaders' increased understanding of how to influence the confirmation process. Ideological groups have also found that opposition to controversial nominees is a good way to generate interest in their causes and monetary contributions from their supporters.

Groups that opposed specific nominees achieved noteworthy successes between 1968 and 1970. Conservative groups helped to defeat Abe Fortas, nominated for elevation to chief justice by President Lyndon Johnson in 1968, and labor and civil rights groups helped to secure the defeats of Nixon nominees Clement Haynsworth and G. Harrold Carswell. Liberal groups opposed some later nominees between 1971 and 1986 but achieved no more successes.

President Reagan's nomination of Robert Bork in 1987 gave rise to an unprecedented level of group activity.[5] Liberal groups feared that the strongly conservative Bork would move an ideologically divided Court to the right. Accordingly, they devoted considerable effort, and an estimated $12 million to $15 million, to achieving his defeat.[6] Their activities ranged from newspaper advertisements to direct lobbying of senators. Groups that favored Bork's nomination took action as well. The pro-Bork groups did not mobilize as quickly or as fully as the opposition groups, and the higher level of activity against Bork helped to bring about his defeat.[7]

That episode led to an escalation of interest group conflict over confirmations. When it seems possible that a nominee might lose in the Senate, groups on both sides work actively to influence the outcome. A heated battle broke out over Clarence Thomas in 1991, and groups were highly active when the Senate considered Samuel Alito in 2006. Those two Republican nominees were confirmed with more than forty negative votes, opposition that resulted in part from the direct and indirect lobbying of Democratic senators by liberal groups.

Interest group activity for and against Alito was intense, with groups on both sides using advertisements and other means of communication to make their cases to the public. There was a good deal of group activity on Sonia Sotomayor's nomination as well. Indeed, when David Souter announced his retirement in 2009, conservative groups mobilized even before a nominee was chosen to succeed Souter.[8] A Web site set up by the conservative Judicial Confirmation Network posted ads criticizing three prospective nominees, including Sotomayor. After Sotomayor was nominated, conservative groups mounted strong attacks on her despite the expectation that she would be difficult to defeat. On the other side, liberal groups worked on behalf of Sotomayor in cooperation with the Obama administration. But interest group activity was not as extensive as it had been on some earlier nominations.

Candidates for the Court. When presidents make nominations to the Supreme Court, they sometimes choose people who never thought of themselves as potential justices. Some prospective nominees withdraw from consideration, some turn down nominations, and others accept them reluctantly. Among the reluctant justices were Byron White in 1962, Abe Fortas in 1965, and Lewis Powell in 1971. But for many lawyers, the Supreme Court is a long-standing dream. A decade before his appointment to the Court, Clarence Thomas told a reporter, "I want to be on the Supreme Court."[9] For Samuel Alito, that goal may have come much earlier. According to the 1972 Princeton yearbook, Alito's intent was to "warm a seat on the Supreme Court."[10] Not surprisingly, most people who are offered nominations accept them readily.

Some lawyers with ambition for the Supreme Court conduct concerted private campaigns for nominations. William Howard Taft became chief justice in 1921 after years of efforts that began even when he was president. As an ex-president he had a great deal of influence, and one commentator described Taft as "virtually appointing himself" chief justice.[11] While serving on a federal court of appeals, Warren Burger exerted considerable effort to make himself a candidate for the Supreme Court. When his effort succeeded, President Nixon's attorney general—overlooking Taft's example—said that "Burger's the first guy to run for the job of Chief Justice—and get it."[12] Burger and Taft are unusual cases, both in the extent of their efforts and in their success. More often, prospective nominees engage in quieter campaigns to enhance their chances through means such as writing opinions that garner attention. Because there are only a limited number of nominations to the Court, however, most of these campaigns fail.

Sitting justices might welcome a promotion to chief justice. During the last few years of the Rehnquist Court, some observers perceived that Anthony Kennedy was trying to improve his chances of promotion through his off-the-Court activities, which included collaboration with First Lady Laura Bush on a "Dialogue on Freedom" program for students. But Kennedy never had a real chance for promotion because conservatives strongly disagreed with the positions he had taken in some cases.[13]

In past eras, nominees typically played little part in the confirmation process. Today, they participate actively in that process. Nominees visit with senators, provide voluminous written materials to the Senate Judiciary Committee, and testify before the Committee at its hearings on confirmation. The visits have become a major activity. Sonia Sotomayor met with 89 senators before her confirmation hearings.[14]

Because so much attention is focused on nominees' testimony, it has become a key to confirmation. When Harriet Miers was pushed to withdraw after her 2005 nomination, one reason was that Bush administration officials concluded she would not do well at the committee hearings.[15] Nominees work hard to prepare for the hearings. In their testimony they seek to present an attractive image and to avoid taking positions on judicial issues that could arouse opposition.

For their part, senators who seek to defeat a nominee look for ways to elicit acknowledgments of unpopular positions from nominees. But well-prepared nominees can usually overcome those efforts. They can turn back questions about matters such as abortion or the death penalty on the ground—largely legitimate—that they do not want to "prejudge" issues that might come before the Court. According to one count, John Roberts refused to answer questions on that ground sixty-seven times.[16] Nominees can limit criticism for being unresponsive by addressing questions about issues on which they know their answers will be popular or uncontroversial.

In 1987 Robert Bork's testimony weakened his prospects for confirmation because it left the impression that he was strongly conservative and because it exposed his rough edges. Clarence Thomas's testimony four years later increased opposition to him because what he said about his views on issues raised doubts about his candor. Nominees since then have done better, in part because they have learned from the Bork and Thomas experiences. John Roberts in 2005 impressed senators with his expertise and with his personality, and he adroitly avoided the traps that some Democratic committee members sought to lay for him. Samuel Alito was not quite as effective in putting forth a positive image, but he too avoided traps. One commentator said, "John Roberts charmed his way through the proceedings. Sam Alito has chosen to simply bore his way through"— and he too did well as a result.[17] In particular, he succeeded in turning back questions based on controversial positions he had taken in the past.

Frustrated by the performances of Roberts and Alito, then-senator Joseph Biden suggested that the Senate should eliminate nominees' testimony and assess the nominees solely on the basis of their prior records.[18] In 2007 several senators complained that the records of both justices on the Court, especially their treatment of the Court's precedents, diverged from what they had said during their confirmation hearings.[19] But it is not surprising that some nominees tailor their testimony to make themselves appear more moderate than they are and thereby improve their chances for confirmation.

Democratic senator Patrick Leahy of Vermont, chair of the Judiciary Committee, swearing in Supreme Court nominee Sonia Sotomayor at her confirmation hearing in 2009. A nominee's appearance before the Judiciary Committee has become a key event in the confirmation process.

At Sonia Sotomayor's appearance before the Judiciary Committee, Republican senators questioned her closely about some of her decisions and statements outside of court. Sotomayor was cautious in her testimony while seeking to address the concerns that Republicans raised. Her testimony did not satisfy her critics, but she did not say anything that aroused broader opposition. As a result, her confirmation was assured.

The President's Decision

For the president, a Supreme Court vacancy provides a valuable opportunity to influence the Court's direction, and presidents seek to make the most of these opportunities. But the individuals and groups for whom nominations are important can subject the president to heavy and conflicting pressures, and the pressures have grown stronger in recent years.[20]

Presidents do not make their decisions alone, although they differ in how much they participate in the selection process. Bill Clinton and George W. Bush played a more active role in the process than did Ronald Reagan and George H. W. Bush. Barack Obama, a former constitutional law professor with a strong interest in the Court, was even more involved in the process that led to the nomination of Sonia Sotomayor.[21] Before his inauguration, according to news reports, he suggested several potential nominees for a future vacancy on the Court (including Sotomayor) to his staff. After David Souter announced his retirement, Obama read memoranda of sixty to seventy pages on each of the leading candidates for a nomination and gathered information from other sources. He chose the four finalists and interviewed each for an hour before reaching his decision.

Still, all presidents delegate most of the search process to other officials in the executive branch, increasingly to White House officials rather than the Justice Department.[22] In 2005 Vice President Richard Cheney led a committee that chose five prospective nominees for an expected vacancy on the Court, and the committee held long interviews with the candidates.[23] President Obama's search for a nominee in 2009 involved intensive activity within his administration. Staff in the White House counsel's office and Vice President Biden's office, among others, worked to identify and gather information on prospective nominees (including having candidates fill out highly detailed questionnaires), and they enlisted people within and outside the administration to do intensive research on the candidates. Staff members and Biden himself interviewed candidates.

As the examples of George W. Bush and Obama indicate, administrations in the current era typically do a good deal of preparatory work even before a vacancy on the Court actually arises. Once a vacancy occurs, occasionally a president fixes on a single candidate for nomination. When Chief Justice Rehnquist died, President Bush quickly chose John Roberts for that position; he had already nominated Roberts to succeed Justice O'Connor. More often, administrations create a short list and then work to identify the best candidate from that list.[24] This process allows presidents and other officials to work systematically through the advantages and disadvantages of choosing different names from the list. But uncertainties about potential nominees and shifting conditions often introduce an element of chaos to the process. That was certainly true of President Clinton's nominations. And there was a degree of chaos even in the George W. Bush nominations, despite the administration's careful preparations.

Administrations differ in the mix of criteria that presidents and their advisers use in choosing nominees. The possible criteria fall into several categories: the "objective" qualifications of potential nominees, their policy preferences, rewards to political and personal associates, and building political support. Cutting across these criteria and helping to determine their use is the reality that the Senate must confirm a nominee.

"Objective" Qualifications. Presidents have strong incentives to select Supreme Court nominees who have demonstrated high levels of legal competence and adherence to ethical standards. One reason is most presidents' respect for the Court. Another is that highly competent justices are in the best position to influence their colleagues. Finally, serious questions about a candidate's competence or ethical behavior can make confirmation considerably more difficult.

In general, presidents' choices reflect a concern for competence. This does not mean that all nominees are highly skilled in the law, but only in a few cases has a nominee's capacity to serve on the Court been seriously questioned. One of those was Nixon nominee G. Harrold Carswell, who was denied confirmation. Perceptions that Harriet Miers had only limited knowledge of constitutional law, perceptions shared by some senators who talked with her, were one source of the opposition that ultimately led her to withdraw as a nominee.

The ethical behavior of several nominees has been questioned. Abe Fortas (when nominated to be chief justice), Clement Haynsworth, Stephen Breyer, and Samuel Alito were attacked for alleged financial conflicts of interest; Fortas was also criticized for continuing to consult with President Johnson while serving as an associate justice. The charges against Fortas and Haynsworth helped bring about their defeats in the Senate. After Douglas Ginsburg was announced as a Reagan nominee, disclosures were made about a possible financial conflict of interest when he was in the Justice Department and about his past use of marijuana. The latter disclosure was especially damaging, and Ginsburg withdrew his name from consideration. An allegation that Clarence Thomas had sexually harassed an assistant while he was a federal administrator resulted in a special set of Senate hearings on the charge and put his confirmation in jeopardy.

To minimize the possibility of such embarrassments, administrations today give close scrutiny to potential nominees, using competence and ethics as screening criteria. Although these criteria eliminate some people from consideration, enough candidates survive the screening process to give presidents a wide range of choices for a nomination.

Policy Preferences. By policy preferences I mean an individual's attitudes toward policy issues. These criteria have always been a consideration in the selection of Supreme Court justices, because presidents recognize that their appointees' impact on the Court's policies is among a president's major legacies.

In the current era every president gives considerable weight to the policy preferences of prospective nominees, because of the Court's prominence as a policymaker and because interest groups associated with both parties care so much about the Court's direction. But presidents continue to differ in the weight they give to this consideration. Understandably, presidents who want to change the Supreme Court's direction give particular emphasis to policy considerations. This was true of both Richard Nixon and Ronald Reagan. Speaking of potential nominees, Nixon told his chief of staff that he did not care "if the guy can read or write, just so he votes right."[25] Policy considerations were also important to George W. Bush, in part because he and other conservatives were unhappy that a string of appointments by his Republican predecessors had changed the Court less than they had hoped. In contrast, Bill Clinton was less concerned with the policy views of his prospective nominees.

It is in relation to this criterion that the Senate's role creates the greatest complications. Most Democratic presidents are distinctly liberal, most Republicans distinctly conservative. If a Democratic president chose a nominee whose preferences were also strongly liberal, that nominee's views would be somewhat distant from the views of Senate moderates and quite distant from the views of most Republican senators. A strongly conservative president is in a similar situation with Democratic senators. Thus, presidents often perceive that they must choose between two imperfect options. One is to select a nominee whose views seem to mirror their own views, as well as those of interest groups associated with their party, and risk difficulty with confirmation. The other is to choose a more moderate nominee and reduce their impact on the Court's direction. Presidents have responded to this dilemma in different ways, depending in part on their willingness to get into conflicts over nominees. President Obama's choice of Sonia Sotomayor probably reflected a desire to minimize conflict, in that Sotomayor seemed less likely to attract strong opposition than did candidates with more distinctly liberal records.

Presidents who want to put like-minded people on the Supreme Court need to ascertain that their nominees really *are* like-minded. This is one reason that every nominee since 1986 except for Harriet Miers has come from a federal court of appeals. If a judge has a long record of judicial votes and opinions on issues of federal law, as Samuel Alito and Sonia Sotomayor did, presidents and their advisers can be fairly confident about the kinds of positions the judge would take on many issues as a justice. In the George W. Bush administration, one prospective nominee with a strong conservative reputation was nonetheless eliminated from consideration because of a single opinion in which he had taken a liberal position.[26]

Some nominees do not have these long records. Sandra Day O'Connor had served only on state courts, and nearly all of David Souter's judicial service was at the state level. Most kinds of issues that come to the Supreme Court are uncommon in state courts. Clarence Thomas had served only one year on a federal court of appeals, John Roberts only two. For candidates such as these, other sources of information can be consulted, such as records in nonjudicial positions and people who know a prospective nominee well. In Harriet Miers's case, George W. Bush had a good sense of her views from their long association, including her work in the White House. Sometimes presidents or their representatives ask prospective nominees directly about their views. According to one report, presidential advisers questioned John Roberts closely in order to ascertain the strength of his conservatism.[27]

Presidents concerned with confirmation of their nominees might prefer a situation in which the president has a clear sense of a nominee's views but there is little public evidence of those views for opponents to attack. As George W. Bush said about Harriet Miers, who had not served as a judge, "there's not a lot of opinions for people to look at."[28] But the lack of hard evidence that Miers was strongly conservative on judicial issues aroused concern from members of the president's own party. In the case of David Souter, President George H. W. Bush had what he thought was good evidence of Souter's conservatism from people who knew him, but Senate Democrats had little evidence of their own with which to raise questions about Souter. Souter was confirmed with little difficulty, but his record as a justice indicates that he was not nearly as conservative as Bush thought. That record has served as a cautionary tale for conservatives, and fear of another Souter helps to explain the strong opposition to Miers.

Exceptions such as Souter get considerable attention, but most justices turn out to be ideologically compatible with the presidents who appoint them. Those who deviate from the appointing president generally fall into two categories. First, some were chosen by presidents who were not especially interested in choosing compatible justices or who were not careful about doing so. Gerald Ford selected John Paul Stevens without regard for his nominee's policy preferences, so the gap between Ford's conservatism and Stevens's liberalism is not surprising. According to a story that is widely circulated but of uncertain accuracy, Dwight Eisenhower cited his appointees Earl Warren and William Brennan as the two mistakes he had made as president.[29] But as a California governor Warren had shown signs of the liberalism he later manifested as chief justice, and Brennan's own liberalism was apparent from his record as a state judge.

Second, some justices shift their ideological positions after reaching the Court. Richard Nixon's one "failure" was Harry Blackmun, who had a distinctly conservative record in his early years on the Court but gradually adopted more liberal positions. Anthony Kennedy also may have shifted in a liberal direction after reaching the Court, albeit to a lesser degree. A conservative publication later referred to Kennedy as "surely Reagan's biggest disappointment."[30]

Presidents cannot be assured of their appointees' support even on cases that affect the president directly. Three of President Nixon's appointees joined in the unanimous decision in *United States v. Nixon* (1974) that required Nixon to hand over tape recordings of his conversations as president. (The fourth, William Rehnquist, did not participate, because he had worked in the Justice Department during the Nixon administration.) After learning of the Court's decision, Nixon reportedly "exploded, cursing the man he had named chief justice, reserving a few choice expletives for Blackmun and Powell, his other appointees."[31]

Political and Personal Reward. When George W. Bush nominated Harriet Miers to the Supreme Court in 2005, he had known Miers for a dozen years. In Texas she was general counsel for Bush's transition team after he was elected governor, and she was also his personal lawyer. She joined his presidential administration in 2001, serving in the White House as staff secretary, deputy chief of staff, and counsel to the president.

In choosing Miers, Bush took what had been a common approach for most of the Supreme Court's history. As of the late 1960s, about 60 percent of the nominees to the Court had known the nominating president personally.[32] With the exception of Dwight Eisenhower, all the presidents from Franklin Roosevelt through Lyndon Johnson selected primarily personal acquaintances. Reward for political associates seemed to be the main criterion for Harry Truman in selecting justices.

Some appointments to the Court were direct rewards for political help. Eisenhower selected Earl Warren to serve as chief justice largely because of Warren's crucial support of Eisenhower at the 1952 Republican convention. As governor of California and leader of that state's delegation, Warren had provided needed votes on a preliminary issue, and Eisenhower's success on that issue helped to secure his nomination.

But since 1968 Miers is the only close associate or political ally that a president has nominated to the Court. Indeed, few nominees have had any contact with the president before being considered for the Court. President Obama first met Sonia Sotomayor a few days before choosing her as his nominee in 2009.[33] Perhaps the main reason for the decline in the selection of personal acquaintances is that such nominees are vulnerable to charges of "cronyism." That charge was made in 1968 when President Johnson nominated Justice Abe Fortas for elevation to chief justice and nominated Judge Homer Thornberry to succeed Fortas as associate justice; both Fortas and Thornberry were close to Johnson. The charge played a small role in building opposition to Fortas and Thornberry in the Senate. Ultimately, Fortas's confirmation was blocked by a filibuster, and Thornberry's nomination thus became moot. Miers's nomination was also attacked as a case of cronyism, and that charge was one factor in the pressures that led to her withdrawal.

One element of political reward has remained strong, however: about 90 percent of all nominees to the Court—and all those chosen since 1975—have been members of the president's party. One reason is that lawyers who share the president's policy views are more likely to come from the same party, but there is also a widespread feeling that such an attractive prize should go to one of the party faithful.

Building Political Support. Nominations can reward people who helped the president in the past, but they can also be used to seek political benefits in the future. Most often, presidents select justices with certain characteristics in order to appeal to leaders and voters who share those characteristics.

Geography and religion were important criteria for selecting justices in some past eras, but their role in nominations has nearly disappeared. In contrast, representation by race, gender, and ethnicity has become quite important. President George H. W. Bush's nomination of Clarence Thomas to succeed Thurgood Marshall reflected the pressure he felt to maintain black representation on the Court. And according to one scholar, "gender was the primary and decisive factor" in President Reagan's nomination of Sandra Day O'Connor at a time when there was a widespread feeling that a woman should be appointed.[34] When O'Connor announced her retirement in 2005, President George W. Bush felt some pressure to replace her with a woman, and he chose Harriet Miers after restricting consideration to women.[35] But before and after Miers, Bush nominated men to succeed O'Connor. (As noted earlier, before William Rehnquist died, John Roberts was nominated to O'Connor's position.) In searching for a successor to David Souter four years later, President Obama focused primarily on female candidates, and all four finalists were women. His choice of Sonia Sotomayor over the other finalists was heavily influenced by the desire to select the first Hispanic justice, largely as a means to please an important group in the electorate.

Demographic characteristics aside, presidents may seek nominees whose positions on judicial issues appeal to political activists and voters. This consideration does not lead in a single direction. Nominees who appear to be moderates might strengthen a president's support among undecided voters. But nominees who seem strongly liberal or conservative are more likely to garner approval from people who are active in the president's party, including financial contributors and leaders of allied interest groups. These activists typically give greater weight to Supreme Court nominations than do ordinary voters, for whom such nominations are generally not a key consideration.

Summary. Presidents use several criteria to choose Supreme Court nominees. The importance of these considerations changes over time and varies from one nomination to another.

The Court's importance has at least two effects on the criteria for selection of justices. First, it makes presidents and their representatives weigh all the criteria more carefully than they generally do in nominating judges to lower courts. Second, it leads to an emphasis on competence and policy preferences rather than the "political" considerations of reward and support building. If Supreme Court justices are better jurists than the judges on lower federal courts, and if their policy preferences are more accurate reflections of their nominators' views, it is chiefly because presidents have a strong incentive to achieve those results.

Senate Confirmation

A president's nomination to the Court goes to the Senate for confirmation. The nomination is referred to the Judiciary Committee, which gathers extensive information on the nominee, holds hearings at which the nominee and other witnesses testify, and then votes its recommendation for Senate action. After this vote, the nomination is referred to the floor, where it is debated and a confirmation vote taken.

A simple majority is needed for confirmation, although a large minority of senators (under the current rules, forty-one) could block confirmation through a filibuster that uses extended debate to prevent a confirmation vote. That was the fate of Abe Fortas's nomination for chief justice in 1968. In 2006 some Democrats called for a filibuster against confirmation of Samuel Alito, but the Senate voted 75–25 to end debate and proceed to a vote.

The length of this process varies, in part with the degree of controversy over a nominee. By historical standards, the period from nomination to confirmation vote has been extraordinarily long in the past two decades, typically running between two and three months.[36]

The Senate's Role and Record. When the president nominates someone to any position, the presumption typically is in favor of confirmation. That presumption applies to the Supreme Court. But the Senate gives Supreme Court nominations close scrutiny, and confirmation is far from automatic.

Indeed, defeats of nominees are hardly rare. Through mid-2009 the Senate has refused to confirm twenty-six nominations to the Supreme Court, either through an adverse vote or nonaction. These twenty-six cases constitute about one-sixth of the nominations that the Senate considered. This proportion of defeats is the highest of any position to which the president makes appointments. For example, presidents have made far more nominations of cabinet members, but only nine have been defeated.

Presidents have been more successful with Supreme Court nominations in the twentieth century and the early twenty-first century than

TABLE 2-2
Senate Votes on Supreme Court Nominations since 1949

Nominee	Year	Vote
Tom Clark	1949	73–8
Sherman Minton	1949	48–16
Earl Warren	1954	NRV
John Harlan	1955	71–11
William Brennan	1957	NRV
Charles Whittaker	1957	NRV
Potter Stewart	1959	70–17
Byron White	1962	NRV
Arthur Goldberg	1962	NRV
Abe Fortas	1965	NRV
Thurgood Marshall	1967	69–11
Abe Fortas[a]	1968	Withdrawn
Homer Thornberry	(1968)	No action
Warren Burger	1969	74–3
Clement Haynsworth	1969	45–55
G. Harrold Carswell	1970	45–51
Harry Blackmun	1970	94–0
Lewis Powell	1971	89–1
William Rehnquist	1971	68–26
John Paul Stevens	1975	98–0
Sandra Day O'Connor	1981	99–0
William Rehnquist[b]	1986	65–33
Antonin Scalia	1986	98–0
Robert Bork	1987	42–58
Douglas Ginsburg	(1987)	No action
Anthony Kennedy	1988	97–0
David Souter	1990	90–9
Clarence Thomas	1991	52–48
Ruth Bader Ginsburg	1993	96–3
Stephen Breyer	1994	87–9
John Roberts	2005	78–22
Harriet Miers	(2005)	No action
Samuel Alito	2006	58–42
Sonia Sotomayor	2009	68–31

Source: Joan Biskupic and Elder Witt, *Guide to the U.S. Supreme Court,* 3d ed. (Washington, D.C.: Congressional Quarterly, 1997), 1099; table updated by the author.

Note: NRV = no recorded vote.

a. Elevation to chief justice; nomination withdrawn after the Senate vote of 45–43 failed to end a filibuster against the nomination (two-thirds majority was required).
b. Elevation to chief justice.

in the nineteenth. Since 1900 only five of the sixty-two nominations considered by the Senate have failed: Herbert Hoover's nomination of John Parker in 1930, Johnson's elevation of Abe Fortas to chief justice in 1968 (withdrawn after Fortas's supporters failed to end the filibuster against him), Nixon's nominations of Clement Haynsworth in 1969 and G. Harrold Carswell in 1970 (both for the same vacancy), and Reagan's nomination of Robert Bork in 1987. Only four successful nominees were confirmed by less than a two-thirds margin in the Senate.

This record of success is a bit misleading, however, because the Senate has continued to scrutinize nominations carefully. This has been especially true since the late 1940s. Of the thirty-one nominees the Senate considered from 1949 through mid-2009, four were defeated, ten others received more than ten negative votes, and others faced serious opposition. And the withdrawals of Douglas Ginsburg in 1987 and Harriet Miers in 2005 came primarily because of concerns about their prospects for confirmation. The Senate votes in this period are shown in Table 2-2. As suggested by these votes, nominees have faced especially close scrutiny since 1968.

Nominees vary a great deal in the degree of difficulty they face in the Senate, from those who face no opposition to those who fail to win the needed majority. This variation reflects the characteristics of nominees and of the situations in which the Senate considers them.[37]

Nominees and Situations. The attributes of nominees that affect confirmation the most are their perceived ideological positions and qualifications. Nominees who are thought to be highly liberal or highly conservative have greater difficulty than those who seem to be moderate, simply because extremists are more distant ideologically from the average senator. Nominees who seem less qualified than they should be also may arouse opposition. Senators who are ideologically distant from a nominee often use questions about a nominee's legal skills or ethical standards as a seemingly objective justification for opposing the nominee. And senators who are not distant from a nominee may oppose confirmation because they conclude that the nominee's qualifications are deficient.

Several aspects of the situation at the time of nomination also affect the Senate's action. One is the president's political strength in the Senate. According to one count, presidents whose party holds a Senate majority have had 90 percent of their nominees confirmed, as against 61 percent for presidents who faced an opposition majority.[38] One reason for this difference is that senators of the majority party chair the Judiciary Committee and schedule votes on the floor. Another reason is that a Senate controlled by the opposition has more senators who are politically opposed to the president and who are ideologically distant from a nominee. For both reasons, President Obama began with a significant advantage when he had the chance to nominate a successor to Justice Souter.

Other factors affect the president's strength. Presidents with high public approval ratings have an advantage, because strong public support deters opposition to their nominees. And nominations made late in a president's term are more vulnerable for several reasons: the president's popularity tends to decline, second-term presidents are "lame ducks" who will leave office shortly, and partisanship often increases. Nearly half of the nominees selected in the last year of a presidential term were defeated in the Senate.[39]

A second aspect of the situation is the mobilization of support and opposition to the nominee. A strong interest group campaign against a nomination can overcome the assumption that the nominee will be confirmed and thus cause senators to consider voting against confirmation. It is also important whether some senators decide to play an active role in mustering votes against a nominee and whether the administration mounts a strong effort to secure confirmation.[40]

Finally, the perceived impact of a nomination helps to determine whether senators believe that efforts to defeat the nominee are worthwhile. In part, the intense scrutiny given to recent nominations reflects the increased prominence of the Supreme Court as policymaker on controversial issues. If a nominee has the potential to change the Court's policies substantially, senators will attach particular importance to that nomination.

Among nominees in the past three decades, David Souter and Clarence Thomas illustrate the importance of personal characteristics. The two were chosen by President George H.W. Bush a year apart, with the Democrats holding majorities in the Senate. Each would replace a strongly liberal justice, so they seemed likely to change the Court's ideological balance considerably. Souter won confirmation with only moderate difficulty, but Thomas's margin was only four votes. The difference can be explained primarily by two widespread perceptions: that Souter was a moderate conservative and Thomas a strong conservative and that Souter was well qualified but Thomas's qualifications might be questioned.

Another pair of nominees illustrates the importance of the situation. President Reagan selected Antonin Scalia in 1986 and Robert Bork in 1987. Both were viewed as highly conservative, and both were considered well qualified for service on the Court. Scalia was confirmed unanimously, and Bork was defeated. One difference was that the Senate had a Republican majority in 1986 but a Democratic majority the next year. Another was that Scalia would replace another strong conservative, but Bork would replace a moderate conservative on a Court with a close

Robert Bork (left) and Antonin Scalia. The Senate confirmed Scalia's nomination to the Supreme Court unanimously in 1986; a year later, Judge Bork—also nominated by President Reagan—failed to win confirmation to the Court. Scalia benefited from the more favorable situation in which his nomination was made.

ideological balance. Finally, in 1986, liberal senators and interest groups focused their efforts on defeating William Rehnquist's nomination for chief justice and largely ignored Scalia. In 1987, in contrast, liberals in and out of the Senate gave intense attention to Bork.

These generalizations can be illustrated further by looking at two sets of nominations. The first set includes the four defeats of nominees in the past half century. The second includes the five nominees considered by the Senate since 1993, all of whom won confirmation.

The Defeats. From 1930 to 1967, a long series of Supreme Court nominees won confirmation. Then, in the period from 1968 to 1970, three nominees lost in the Senate. The first was Abe Fortas, a sitting justice whom President Johnson nominated to be chief justice in 1968. The Senate had a Democratic majority, but many of the Democrats were conservative, and Fortas's strong liberalism on the liberal Warren Court aroused conservative opposition. Further, some Republicans wanted to prevent Fortas's confirmation in order to reserve the vacancy for a new president—expected to be Republican—in 1969. These opponents pointed to two activities that raised doubts about Fortas's ethical fitness: his continued consultation with the president about policy matters while serving on the Court and an arrangement by which he gave nine lectures at American University, in Washington, D.C., for a fee of $15,000 raised from businesses. The Judiciary Committee approved the nomination by a divided vote, but it ran into a filibuster on the Senate floor. A vote to end the filibuster fell fourteen votes short of the two-thirds majority then required; the opposition came almost entirely from Republicans and southern Democrats. President Johnson then withdrew the nomination at Fortas's request.

In 1969 Fortas resigned from the Court. President Nixon selected Clement Haynsworth, chief judge of a federal court of appeals, to replace him. Haynsworth was opposed by labor groups and the National Association for the Advancement of Colored People (NAACP), both of which disliked his judicial record. Liberal senators, concerned about that record, sought revenge for Fortas's defeat as well. Haynsworth was also charged with unethical conduct: he had sat on two cases involving subsidiaries of companies in which he owned stock, and in another case he had bought the stock of a corporation in the interval between his court's decision in its favor and the announcement of the decision. These charges led to additional opposition from Senate moderates. Haynsworth ultimately was defeated by a 45–55 vote, with a large minority of Republicans voting against confirmation.

President Nixon then nominated another court of appeals judge, G. Harrold Carswell. After the fight over Haynsworth, most senators were inclined to support the next nominee. One senator predicted that any new Nixon nominee "will have no trouble getting confirmed unless he has committed murder—recently."[41] But Carswell drew opposition from civil rights groups for what they perceived as his hostility to their interests, and their cause gained strength from a series of revelations about the nominee that suggested an active opposition to racial equality. Carswell was also criticized for an alleged lack of judicial competence. After escorting Carswell to talk with senators, one of Nixon's staffers reported to the president that "they think Carswell's a boob, a dummy. And what counter is there to that? He is."[42] The nomination was defeated by a 45–51 vote, with a lineup similar to the vote on Haynsworth.

Robert Bork's 1987 defeat differed from the three that preceded it in that no serious charges were made about Bork's competence or his ethical standards. But liberals were concerned about his strong conservatism on civil liberties issues and his potential to shift the Court's ideological balance. Senator Ted Kennedy and liberal interest groups worked hard to secure votes against Bork. Concern about Bork's views was intensified by his testimony before the Senate Judiciary Committee, in which he discussed in detail his positions on issues such as the right to privacy.

This growing concern, combined with the unprecedented level of interest group activity against Bork, made his defeat possible. Also important was President Reagan's political weakness: not only did the Democrats control the Senate, but Reagan's popularity both inside and outside Congress had declined. Even so, a more effective campaign for Bork by the administration might have secured his confirmation. In any event, confirmation was denied by a 42–58 vote. All but eight senators voted along party lines; the overwhelming and unexpected opposition of southern Democrats made the difference in the outcome.

These four defeats, different though they were, have some things in common. In each instance, many senators were inclined to oppose the nominee on ideological grounds. All but Fortas faced a Senate controlled by the opposite party, and Fortas was confronted by a conservative majority. And each nominee was weakened by a "smoking gun" that could rally opposition: the ethical questions about Fortas and Haynsworth, the allegations of racism and incompetence against Carswell, and the charge that Bork was outside the mainstream in his views about judicial issues. The combination of these problems created a basis for enough opposition to prevent confirmation in each instance.

The Recent Confirmations. Between 1993 and 2009, the Senate voted on five nominations. All five nominees won confirmation, although their paths to victory differed considerably.

When President Clinton nominated Ruth Bader Ginsburg in 1993 and Stephen Breyer in 1994, there remained a good deal of resentment among Republicans over the defeat of Robert Bork. As the fates of Haynsworth and Carswell indicate, such resentment can lead to retaliation. However, the Democrats held a majority in the Senate.

Just as important, Clinton made a greater effort than most other presidents to avoid confirmation battles.[43] Because of this goal, his two nominees were both relatively moderate liberals. Ginsburg had helped lead the litigation campaign on behalf of equal rights for women, but her record as a court of appeals judge was fairly centrist. And neither nominee would change the Court's ideological balance very much.

Ginsburg won confirmation with no serious obstacles and only three negative votes. Breyer had a slightly more difficult time. Some Republican senators argued that he had shown a lack of prudence in investing in an insurance syndicate and that the investment had created conflicts of interest in some cases. Ultimately, nine Republicans cast votes against him, but his nomination was never in real jeopardy.

George W. Bush's nominations of John Roberts and Samuel Alito in 2005 came at a time of increased polarization between the parties and concern over the Supreme Court's future direction. As a result, it was likely that

Senate Democrats would oppose a nominee who seemed to be a strong conservative. Yet interest groups allied with the Republican Party were adamant that the president should choose strong conservatives, and the president's own inclination seemed to be the same. Bush had the advantage of a moderately large Republican majority in the Senate, increasing the chances of a favorable outcome for any nominee. Under the circumstances, he chose two nominees whose records suggested that they were quite conservative. (Harriet Miers, who withdrew before Senate consideration of her nomination, also appeared to Bush to be strongly conservative.)

Nothing like a smoking gun emerged for Roberts. Indeed, his testimony in the Judiciary Committee left most observers with a highly positive image of him. Ultimately, he was confirmed by a 78–22 vote, with all the negative votes coming from Democrats.

Like Roberts, Alito had demonstrated a high level of legal skills. But he was more vulnerable than Roberts because he had a more extensive record of strongly conservative positions. Some opponents thought they had a smoking gun in two statements he had made in 1985. In those statements Alito said that he was proud of his contributions to the Reagan administration's arguments that the "Constitution does not protect the right to an abortion" and implied that his goal was "the eventual overruling of *Roe v. Wade.*"[44] Alito was also criticized for participating as a judge in one case involving a mutual fund firm that held a substantial investment of his, despite a pledge to recuse himself from such cases when he was nominated to the court of appeals.

Most senators seemed to regard that participation as inadvertent and inconsequential. In contrast, Alito's efforts to reassure senators that he was not an extreme conservative and that he would not necessarily vote to overturn *Roe* had limited success with Democrats. But it was clear early in the process that nearly all Republican senators would vote for him. As the minority party in the Senate the Democrats could block Alito only with a successful filibuster, and many Democratic senators saw a filibuster as inappropriate or at least bad political strategy. After the vote to end debate, Alito won confirmation by a 58–42 margin. One Republican and all but four Democrats voted against him.

Sonia Sotomayor entered the confirmation process with the great advantage of a large Democratic majority in the Senate and the additional advantage that her replacement of David Souter was unlikely to change the Court's overall ideological balance very much. Still, some Senate Republicans joined conservative interest groups in expressing strong opposition to Sotomayor. She had said in one talk, "I would hope that a wise Latina woman with the richness of her experiences would more often than not reach a better conclusion than a white male who hasn't lived that life."[45] Opponents argued that this passage and other statements and actions indicated a lack of impartiality on her part.

They also charged that some of her positions in court of appeals decisions were unduly liberal and departed from good interpretations of the law.

None of these criticisms constituted the kind of smoking gun that might have attracted Democratic opposition to the nomination. Indeed, no Democratic senator voted against Sotomayor. But the great majority of Republicans—31 of 40—voted against Sotomayor. Although senators who cast negative votes cited specific concerns about Sotomayor, their votes were primarily a product of ideological considerations: conservative senators and interest groups that were important to those senators saw the nominee as unduly liberal. Thus the sources of Republican opposition to Sotomayor were similar to the sources of widespread Democratic opposition to Samuel Alito three years earlier. Perhaps most fundamentally, the large numbers of votes against both Sotomayor and Alito reflect the strong polarization between the congressional parties in the current era.

Summary. The Senate's use of its power over confirmation of Supreme Court nominees has varied a good deal over time. Since 1968 the Senate has taken an assertive role in scrutinizing nominees. One reason for this change is the growth in efforts by interest groups to defeat nominees whose views run counter to group positions. Another spur has been the growing awareness that a single Court appointment can affect national policy in important ways. In both respects one issue—abortion—has been especially important.

Even so, the great majority of nominees since 1968 have been confirmed. There is still a presumption in favor of confirming nominees, and those who vote against a nominee have the burden of justifying their negative votes. Presidents have further improved the chances of confirmation by selecting nominees carefully, sometimes choosing moderates to avoid conflicts and usually looking closely for attributes of prospective nominees that might provide senators with a basis for opposition.

We are now in an era of strong party polarization in national politics. The confirmation of Samuel Alito illustrates the effects of that polarization. Except for Clarence Thomas, no successful nominee in more than a century has won by a closer margin than Alito. Yet there was never much uncertainty about the outcome. Because of the ideological gap and the bitterness between the parties, a nominee with a strong ideological position is certain to garner negative reactions from the opposition party. For the same reasons, senators from the president's party are strongly inclined to support a nominee.

Thus, if the nominee's objective qualifications are at least reasonably strong and the president's party controls the Senate, confirmation is nearly guaranteed. But if the opposing party has a Senate majority, a nominee similar to Alito runs a serious risk of defeat, and a president who seeks to avoid that risk will be inclined to choose a nominee with a record of ideological moderation. In the current period, even more than in some past periods, the kinds of people who reach the Supreme Court depend on Senate elections as well as presidential elections.

Who Is Selected

In some respects, the people who have become Supreme Court justices are a diverse group. But because of the workings of the selection process, certain kinds of people are far more likely to reach the Court than others.

Career Paths

The kinds of people who become justices can be understood from the paths they take to the Court. These paths have changed over time. In order to highlight that change, in this section I examine the set of thirty-six justices appointed since 1937. Recent justices are of particular interest, and the box on pages 52–53 summarizes the careers of the justices who sat on the Court in 2009.

The Legal Profession. The Constitution specifies no requirements for Supreme Court justices, so they need not be attorneys. In practice, however, this restriction has been absolute. Nearly everyone involved in the selection process assumes that only a person with legal training can serve effectively on the Court. If a president nominated a nonlawyer to the Court, this assumption—and the large number of lawyers in the Senate—almost surely would prevent confirmation.

Thus, holding a law degree constitutes the first and least flexible requirement for recruitment to the Court. Most of the justices who served during the first century of the Court's history followed what was then the standard practice, apprenticing under a practicing attorney. In several instances, the practicing attorney was a leading member of the bar.[46] James Byrnes (chosen in 1941) was the last justice to study law through apprenticeship; all his successors have taken what is now the nearly universal route of law school training. A high proportion of justices have graduated from prestigious schools. Of the nine justices sitting in 2009, seven received their law degrees from Harvard or Yale.

High Positions. If legal education is a necessary first step in the paths to the Court, almost equally important as a last step is attaining a high position in government or the legal profession. Obscure private practitioners or state trial judges might be superbly qualified for the Court, but their qualifications would be questioned because of their lowly positions. A high position in government or the legal profession also makes a person more visible to the president and to the officials who identify potential nominees.

At the time they were selected, the thirty-six justices appointed since 1937 held positions of four types. They were judges, executive branch officials, elected officials, or well-respected leaders in the legal profession.

Nineteen of the justices appointed in this period were appellate judges at the time of selection. Seventeen sat on the federal courts of appeals; the other two (William Brennan and Sandra Day O'Connor) served on state courts. Six of the seventeen federal judges came from the District of Columbia circuit, which is especially visible to the president and other federal officials.

Ten justices served in the federal executive branch, seven of them in the Justice Department. The other three justices served as chair of the Securities and Exchange Commission (William Douglas), secretary of the Treasury (Fred Vinson), and secretary of labor (Arthur Goldberg).

Of the other seven justices appointed since 1937, four held high elective office; three were senators (Hugo Black, James Byrnes, and Harold Burton) and the fourth was the governor of California (Earl Warren). The other three held positions outside government. Each had attained extraordinary success and respect—as a legal scholar (Felix Frankfurter), a Washington lawyer (Abe Fortas), and a leader of the legal profession (Lewis Powell). Frankfurter and Fortas had also been informal presidential advisers.

The Steps Between. The people who have become Supreme Court justices took several routes from their legal education to the high positions that made them credible candidates for the Court. Frankfurter, Fortas, and Powell illustrate one simple route: entry into legal practice or academia, followed by a gradual rise to high standing in the legal profession. Some justices took a similar route through public office. Earl Warren held a series of appointive and elective offices, leading to his California governorship. Clarence Thomas and Samuel Alito each served in several nonelected government positions and then as a judge on a federal court of appeals.

Since 1975 the most common route to the Court has been through private practice or law teaching, often combined with some time in government, before appointment to a federal court of appeals. Antonin Scalia, Ruth Bader Ginsburg, and Stephen Breyer were law professors. John Paul Stevens, Anthony Kennedy, and John Roberts went directly from private practice to a court of appeals. During their careers, all six had held government positions or participated informally in the governmental process.

Careers of the Supreme Court...

John G. Roberts Jr. (born 1955)
Law degree, Harvard University, 1979
Law clerk, U.S. Court of Appeals, 1979–1980
Supreme Court law clerk, 1980–1981
U.S. Justice Department, 1981–1982
White House Counsel's Office, 1982–1986
U.S. Solicitor General's Office, 1989–1993
Private law practice, 1986–1989, 1993–2003
Judge, U.S. Court of Appeals, 2003–2005
Appointed chief justice, 2005

John Paul Stevens (born 1920)
Law degree, Northwestern University, 1947
Supreme Court law clerk, 1947–1948
Private law practice, 1949–1970
Judge, U.S. Court of Appeals, 1970–1975
Appointed to Supreme Court, 1975

Antonin Scalia (born 1936)
Law degree, Harvard University, 1960
Private law practice, 1960–1967
Law school teaching, 1967–1971
Legal positions in federal government, 1971–1977
Law school teaching, 1977–1982
Judge, U.S. Court of Appeals, 1982–1986
Appointed to Supreme Court, 1986

Anthony M. Kennedy (born 1936)
Law degree, Harvard University, 1961
Private law practice, 1961–1975
Judge, U.S. Court of Appeals, 1975–1988
Appointed to Supreme Court, 1988

Clarence Thomas (born 1948)
Law degree, Yale University, 1974
Missouri attorney general's office, 1974–1977
Attorney for Monsanto Company, 1977–1979
Legislative assistant to a U.S. senator, 1979–1981
Assistant U.S. secretary of education, 1981–1982
Chair, U.S. Equal Employment Opportunity Commission, 1982–1990
Judge, U.S. Court of Appeals, 1990–1991
Appointed to Supreme Court, 1991

...Justices (2009)

Ruth Bader Ginsburg (born 1933)
Law degree, Columbia University, 1959
Federal district court law clerk, 1959–1961
Law school research position, 1961–1963
Law school teaching, 1963–1980
Judge, U.S. Court of Appeals, 1980–1993
Appointed to Supreme Court, 1993

Stephen G. Breyer (born 1938)
Law degree, Harvard University, 1964
Supreme Court law clerk, 1964–1965
U.S. Justice Department, 1965–1967
Law school teaching, 1967–1980
Staff, U.S. Senate Judiciary Committee, 1974–1975,
  1979–1980
Judge, U.S. Court of Appeals, 1980–1994
Appointed to Supreme Court, 1994

Samuel A. Alito Jr. (born 1950)
Law degree, Yale University, 1975
Law clerk, U.S. Court of Appeals, 1976–1977
Assistant U.S. Attorney, 1977–1981
U.S. Solicitor General's Office, 1981–1985
U.S. Justice Department, 1985–1987
U.S. Attorney, 1987–1990
Judge, U.S. Court of Appeals, 1990–2006
Appointed to Supreme Court, 2006

Sonia Sotomayor (born 1954)
Law degree, Yale University, 1979
Assistant district attorney, 1979–1984
Private law practice, 1984–1992
Judge, U.S. District Court, 1992–1998
Judge, U.S. Court of Appeals, 1998–2009
Appointed to Supreme Court, 2009

Sources: Based chiefly on information in Kenneth Jost, *The Supreme Court Yearbook, 1998–1999* (Washington, D.C.: CQ Press, 2000), 321–339; for Roberts, Alito, and Sotomayor, based on information in *Biographical Directory of Federal Judges,* Federal Judicial Center (www.fjc.gov/public/home.nsf/hisj).

Note: With the exception of Justice Breyer's Senate staff service, only the primary position held by a future justice during each career stage is listed.

Justice O'Connor took a unique path to the Court. She spent time in private practice and government legal positions, with some career interruptions for family reasons, before becoming an Arizona state senator and majority leader of the senate. O'Connor left the legislature for a trial judgeship. Her promotion to the state court of appeals through a gubernatorial appointment put her in a position to be considered for the Supreme Court.

Implications of the Career Paths

The paths to the Supreme Court help to explain some significant characteristics of the justices. They also underline the role of chance in determining who becomes a justice.

Age. Since 1937, most Supreme Court justices have been in their fifties at the time of their appointments and the rest in their forties or early sixties. William Douglas was the youngest appointee, at age forty; at the other end of the spectrum, Lewis Powell was sixty-four.

The ages of Court appointees reflect a balance between two considerations. On the one hand, lawyers need time to develop the record of achievement that makes them credible candidates for the Court. On the other hand, presidents would like their appointees to serve for many years in order to achieve the maximum impact on the Court. Thus, a candidate such as Clarence Thomas, forty-three when George H. W. Bush appointed him, can be especially attractive. Of course, people of the same age can vary considerably in their prospects for future good health. Perhaps this was the reason that George W. Bush asked at least one prospective nominee about how much he exercised. That candidate, Judge J. Harvie Wilkinson, reported that the president admonished him for limiting himself to running despite his doctor's advice to engage in cross-training. "He thought I was well on my way to busting my knees," Judge Wilkinson reported. "He warned me of impending doom." [47]

Class, Race, and Sex. The Supreme Court's membership has diverged from the general population in regard to social class; most justices grew up in families that were relatively well off. One study found that one-third of the justices were from the upper class and one-quarter were from the upper middle class. Less than one-quarter were from the lower middle class or below. [48]

Since the 1930s an unusually high percentage of appointees to the Court have had lower-status backgrounds. Of the justices on the 2009 Court, Clarence Thomas's family was impoverished, and Sonia Sotomayor's family can be characterized as lower middle class. Still, the recent justices as a group grew up in better than average circumstances. Among the other seven justices on the 2009 Court, the family of John Paul Stevens came from an upper-class family, and the other six justices' families were divided evenly between the middle class and upper middle class.

The predominance of higher-status backgrounds can be explained by the career paths that most justices take. First and most important, a justice must obtain a legal education. To do so is easiest for individuals of high status, because of the cost of law school and the college education that precedes it. Second, individuals of high status have a variety of advantages in their careers. Those who can afford to attend elite law schools, for instance, have the easiest time obtaining Supreme Court clerkships and positions in successful law firms.

The partial deviation from this pattern since the 1930s reflects the increased availability of legal education. In addition, the larger size of the legal profession, the judiciary, and the federal government has made high positions in these sectors more accessible to individuals with lower-status backgrounds. If these explanations have some validity, the proportion of justices with lower-status backgrounds may increase further in the future.

Until 1967 all the justices were white men. This pattern is not difficult to understand. Because of various restrictions, women and members of racial minority groups long had extreme difficulty pursuing an education in the law. As a result, few members of these groups passed the first barrier to selection. In addition, prejudice limited their ability to advance in the legal profession and in politics. Thus, very few individuals who were not white men could achieve the high positions that people generally must obtain to be considered for nomination to the Court.

Since 1967 three women (Sandra Day O'Connor, Ruth Bader Ginsburg, and Sonia Sotomayor), two African Americans (Thurgood Marshall and Clarence Thomas), and an Hispanic American (Sotomayor) have won appointments to the Court. These appointments reflect changes in a society that made it somewhat less difficult for people other than white men to achieve high positions. They also reflect the growing willingness of presidents to consider women and members of racial minority groups as prospective nominees. Still, because of the various advantages they enjoy, white men are likely to enjoy disproportionate representation on the Court for some time.

If the Court has been composed primarily of white men with higher-status backgrounds, what has been the effect on its policies? One possible effect concerns the legal claims of racial minority groups and of women. It seems likely that those claims would have been taken seriously at an earlier time if members of these groups had sat on the Court, because these justices would have influenced their colleagues' perceptions of discrimination. As Justice O'Connor pointed out, Thurgood Marshall had that kind of influence once he joined the Court.[49] The same may have been true of O'Connor and Ginsburg, who both faced serious discrimination early in their legal careers.

Political and social attitudes differ somewhat between people of higher and lower socioeconomic status, so justices' class origins might affect the Court's decisions. But the justices typically are people who have achieved high status themselves even if their origins were humble. The sympathies of people who have "climbed" upward from a low socioeconomic level may differ little from those of people who started out with social and economic advantages. Notably, the justices with humble backgrounds have included solid conservatives such as Warren Burger and Clarence Thomas as well as liberals such as Earl Warren and Thurgood Marshall. Some commentators argue that the Court's decisions generally reflect the values and interests of people who are well off. If so, this may reflect the status that the justices achieve in their own lives as much as their origins.

Partisan Political Activity. One characteristic shared by most current justices, like their predecessors, is a degree of involvement in partisan politics. Antonin Scalia, John Roberts, and Samuel Alito each held multiple positions in Republican administrations. Anthony Kennedy drafted a state ballot proposition for California governor Ronald Reagan. Clarence Thomas worked with John Danforth when Danforth was the Missouri attorney general and a U.S. senator, and Thomas later served in the Reagan and George H.W. Bush administrations. Stephen Breyer interrupted his law school teaching twice to work with Democrats on the Senate Judiciary Committee.

This pattern reflects the criteria for selecting judges. Even when nominations to the Court are not used as political rewards, presidents look more favorably on people who have contributed to their party's success. Partisan activity also brings people to the attention of presidents, their staff members, and others who influence nomination decisions. Perhaps more important, it enables people to win the high government positions that make them credible candidates for the Court. For instance, lawyers who avoid any involvement in politics are unlikely to become federal judges.

The Role of Chance. No one becomes a Supreme Court justice through an inevitable process. Rather, advancement from membership in the bar to a seat on the Court results from luck as much as anything else. This luck comes in two stages. First, good fortune is often necessary to achieve the high positions in government or law that make individuals possible candidates for the Court. Second, even after they achieve such positions, whether candidates are seriously considered for the Court and actually win an appointment depends largely on several circumstances.

For one thing, a potential justice gains enormously by belonging to a particular political party at the appropriate time. Every appointment to the Court between 1969 and 1992 was made by a Republican president. As a result, a whole generation of potential justices who were liberal Democrats had no chance to win appointments. Further, someone whose friend or associate achieves a powerful position becomes a far stronger candidate for a seat on the Court. David Souter was fortunate that some-one who described Souter as "my closest friend" (Warren Rudman) became a U.S. senator and that a person who knew and admired him (John Sununu) became the president's chief of staff.[50]

More generally, everyone appointed to the Court has benefited from a favorable series of circumstances. Eisenhower's attorney general became aware of William Brennan because Brennan gave a conference address in place of a colleague on the New Jersey Supreme Court who was ill. John Paul Stevens has reported that his pro bono volunteer services for a client led to favorable publicity that later helped him win a judicial appoint-ment.[51] If William Rehnquist had retired during George W. Bush's first term rather than remaining on the Court, almost surely someone other than John Roberts would have succeeded him as chief justice, because Roberts did not become a lower-court judge until 2003.[52]

This does not mean that the effects of presidential appointments to the Court are random. No matter which individuals they choose, Democratic presidents generally nominate people with liberal views and Republicans tend to select conservatives, and presidents and their aides increasingly make systematic efforts to identify the best nominees from their perspective. But it does mean that specific individuals achieve membership on the Court in large part through good fortune. "You have to be lucky," said Sandra Day O'Connor about her appointment, a statement that reflects realism as well as modesty.[53]

Changes in Paths to the Court

The most noteworthy characteristic of the justices' backgrounds in the period since 1937 is the extent to which they have changed. As noted earlier, the numerical dominance of people from privileged backgrounds has declined somewhat. But more striking is the change in justices' pre-Court careers. Put simply, those careers have come to involve less politics and more law. As shown in Table 2-3, there is a substantial differ-ence in those respects between the justices who were appointed between 1937 and 1968 and the justices chosen since then.

The twenty-one justices appointed to the Court between 1937 and 1968 were reasonably typical of those selected in earlier periods. About half had judicial experience, nearly as many had held elective office, and more than a quarter had headed a federal administrative agency.

TABLE 2-3
Selected Career Experiences of Justices Appointed since 1937 (in percentages)

Years appointed	Elective office	Head of federal agency	Judgeship
	Experience during career		
1937–1968	43	29	48
1969–2009	7	0	87
	Position at appointment		
1937–1968	19	29	29
1969–2009	0	0	87

Source: Biographical Directory of Federal Judges, compiled by the Federal Judicial Center, at www. fjc.gov/public/home.nsf/hisj.

Note: Federal agencies include cabinet departments and independent agencies.

The fifteen justices who have arrived at the Court since then are a different kind of group. All but two have come directly from lower courts. Only one, Sandra Day O'Connor, ever held elective office. None headed a federal agency, and several spent little or no time in government before winning judgeships. Among these justices, the median proportion of their careers spent in what might be called the legal system—private practice, law school teaching, and the judiciary—was 87 percent. For the justices appointed between 1937 and 1968, the median was 67 percent.[54] The extent of this change was underlined when Samuel Alito joined the Court in 2006: all nine justices had come to the Court from a federal court of appeals.

One reason for this change, perhaps the primary one, is that a prior judicial record helps presidents and their advisers to predict the positions that prospective nominees might take as justices. In an era in which most presidents care a great deal about the Court's direction, any help in making these predictions is valued. There may also be a growing feeling that service on a lower court helps to prepare a judge for the Supreme Court. Harriet Miers, the first nominee since 1971 without judicial experience, was criticized for this lack.

Whether or not lower-court experience is needed as preparation for the Supreme Court, the change in paths to the Court since 1968 may affect the justices' perspectives and their thinking about legal issues. Some commentators argue that justices do not understand government and politics as much as their counterparts in earlier periods and that this lack of understanding reduces their ability to recognize the likely consequences of some decisions.[55] There may be some truth to this argument, and the shift from politics to law in the backgrounds of justices may have other effects on the Court's decisions.[56] But today, as in the past, people who had no contact with the political world would have little chance to reach the Court. None of the current justices fits that description.

Leaving the Court

In the Supreme Court's first century, Congress sometimes increased the Court's size to allow new appointments of justices. Such legislation has become very unlikely, almost unthinkable. Today new members come to the Court only when a sitting justice leaves.

Justices can leave the Court in three ways: through death, a voluntary decision, or external pressure.[57] In contrast with the nineteenth century, justices today seldom stay on the Court until they die. Before William Rehnquist's death in 2005, the last justice to die in office had been Robert Jackson in 1954. Thus, departures from the Court result primarily from voluntary choices and external pressure. Table 2-4 summarizes the reasons for departures since 1965.

Voluntary Departures

After its somewhat rocky start, the Supreme Court became a prestigious body with considerable influence on American life. As a result, justices typically are reluctant to leave the Court.

This reluctance is reflected in the infrequency with which justices leave to take other positions or opportunities. In the past century, only a handful of justices have done so. The most recent was Arthur Goldberg, who resigned in 1965 to become U.S. ambassador to the United Nations.

Still, justices must decide whether and when to retire from the Court. Financial considerations once played an important part in those choices: several justices stayed on the Court, sometimes with serious infirmities, to keep receiving their salaries. Congress established a judicial pension in 1869, and it is now quite generous. Justices who have served as federal judges for at least ten years and who are at least sixty-five years old can retire and continue to receive the salary earned at the time of retirement if their age and years of service add up to eighty or more. Justices can also receive any salary increases granted sitting justices if they are disabled or if they perform a certain amount of service for the federal courts—generally equal to one-quarter of full-time work. For some retired justices, among them Sandra Day O'Connor, that service has included sitting on lower federal courts.

TABLE 2-4
Reasons for Leaving the Court since 1965

Year	Justice	Age	Primary reasons for leaving	Length of time from leaving until death
1965	Goldberg	56	Appointment as ambassador to United Nations	24 years
1967	Clark	67	Son's appointment as attorney general	10 years
1969	Fortas	58	Pressures based on possible ethical violations	13 years
1969[a]	Warren	78[b]	Age	5 years
1971	Black	85	Age and ill health	1 month
1971	Harlan	72	Age and ill health	3 months
1975	Douglas	77	Age and ill health	4 years
1981	Stewart	66	Age	4 years
1986	Burger	78	Uncertain: age, demands of service on a federal commission may have been factors	9 years
1987	Powell	79	Age and health concerns	11 years
1990	Brennan	84	Age and ill health	7 years
1991	Marshall	83[b]	Age and ill health	2 years
1993	White	76[b]	Desire to allow another person to serve, possibly age	9 years
1994	Blackmun	85	Age	5 years
2005	Rehnquist	80	Death	Same time
2006[a]	O'Connor	75	Spouse's ill health	NA
2009	Souter	69	Desire to return to New Hampshire	NA

Sources: Joan Biskupic and Elder Witt, *Guide to the U.S. Supreme Court,* 3d ed. (Washington, D.C.: Congressional Quarterly, 1997), 931–954; other biographical sources, newspaper stories.

Note: NA = not applicable.

a. Warren originally announced the intent to leave the Court in 1968, O'Connor in 2005.
b. When they announced their intent to leave the Court, Warren was 77, Marshall 82, White 75.

Free from financial concerns, then, older justices weigh the satisfactions of remaining on the Court against the somewhat different satisfactions of retirement and against concern about their capacity to handle their work. David Souter left the Court at the age of sixty-nine, when he was in good health. By all accounts, he did so because he found it attractive to return to his native New Hampshire, which he much preferred to Washington, D.C.[58]

Retired Justice Sandra Day O'Connor, with Justice Stephen Breyer (left) and University of Oklahoma president David Boren, at the Oklahoma Museum of Natural History. O'Connor has engaged in a wide range of work and public activities since her retirement in 2006.

But the satisfactions of Court service are so great that most justices stay well past the usual retirement age, and most are reluctant to leave. Early in his time on the Court, William Rehnquist would tell his law clerks that he "never can understand why justices stay so long." Toward the end of his career, some of his former clerks reminded him of that view. Rehnquist's response was that "it turns out you look at it differently" at that later point in one's career.[59]

Rehnquist did remain on the Court until his death, even after his thyroid cancer weakened him considerably and he was unable to fully participate in the Court's work. Writing in 2000, one scholar argued that since World War II, seven justices had stayed on the Court "years or months" too long after their mental capacities should have led to their departures.[60] But most justices do leave the Court when they can no longer ignore their infirmities. It is noteworthy that Rehnquist was the only justice in the past half century to die in office. John Paul Stevens has disclosed that he designated a colleague whom he trusts to tell him when he reaches the point that he should retire. Stevens speculated that "he's apt to do it when I'm dissenting on one of his decisions."[61]

There has been limited turnover on the Court since the mid-1990s. Indeed, no justices left the Court between 1994 and 2005. For some observers this lack of turnover raised the question of whether justices were staying on the Court too long, whether or not they were capable of doing their work. Some legal scholars have even suggested a form of term limits for the justices.[62] But justices in the current era do not stand out from their predecessors for the length of their tenure on the Court or for their ages, and the lack of turnover in one recent period may be an anomaly.[63] The biggest change, one that reflects improvements in health care and the Court's increased attractiveness, is the nearly complete disappearance of justices who serve for only short periods.[64]

Other factors affect decisions whether to leave the Court. Some justices (although not as many as some observers think) time their retirements so that a president whose views are compatible with theirs will choose their successor. It appears that the election of President Obama made retirement more attractive to David Souter, a relatively liberal Republican; Souter reportedly said that he "probably" would have retired if John McCain had won the 2008 election.[65] Family considerations sometimes come into play. According to his administrative assistant at the time, William Rehnquist would have retired in 1991, but his wife's death made retirement less attractive and he changed his mind.[66] Sandra Day O'Connor retired when she was still in good health in order to care for her ailing husband. Referring to other justices, she later said that "most of them get ill and are really in bad shape, which I would've done at the end of the day myself, I suppose, except my husband was ill and I needed to take action there."[67]

One current justice gave very early notice of his retirement. In 1992, a year after he joined the Court, Clarence Thomas told two of his clerks that he would remain on the Court until 2034. He explained, "The liberals made my life miserable for 43 years, and I'm going to make their lives miserable for 43 years."[68]

External Pressure

Although justices make their own decisions whether to resign or retire, Congress and the president can try to influence those decisions. For example, the legislation creating attractive pension rights has had considerable effect. The other branches can also try to persuade specific justices to leave the Court. Presidents have good reason to do so—to create vacancies they can fill. John Kennedy reportedly persuaded Felix Frankfurter to retire after ill health had decreased his effectiveness, but Thurgood Marshall bitterly resisted efforts by the Carter administration to persuade him to retire.[69]

Presidents can also try to lure justices away from the Court by offering them other positions. Lyndon Johnson offered Arthur Goldberg the position of ambassador to the United Nations and then exerted intense personal pressure on him to accept that position. Byron White, however, rejected the idea of becoming FBI director when the Reagan administration sounded him out about it.

In contrast with those kinds of pressures, impeachment is beyond the justices' control. Under the Constitution, justices, like other federal officials, can be removed through impeachment proceedings for "treason, bribery, or other high crimes and misdemeanors."[70] President Thomas Jefferson actually sought to gain control of the largely Federalist (and anti–Jefferson) judiciary through the use of impeachment, and Congress did impeach and convict a federal district judge in 1803. Justice Samuel Chase made himself vulnerable to impeachment by participating in President John Adams's campaign for reelection in 1800 and by making some injudicious and partisan remarks to a Maryland grand jury in 1803. Chase was impeached, an action justified chiefly by his handling of political trials, but the Senate acquitted him in 1805. His acquittal effectively ended Jefferson's plans to seek the impeachment of other justices.

No justice has been impeached since then, but the possible impeachment of two justices has been the subject of serious discussion. Several efforts were made to remove William Douglas (most seriously in 1969 and 1970), motivated by opposition to his strong liberalism. The reasons stated publicly by opponents were his financial connections with a foundation and his outside writings.[71] A special House committee failed to approve a resolution to impeach Douglas, however, and the resolution died in 1970.

Had Abe Fortas not resigned from the Court in 1969, he actually might have been removed by Congress.[72] Fortas had been criticized for his financial dealings at the time of his unsuccessful nomination as chief justice in 1968. A year later, it was disclosed that he had a lifetime contract as a consultant to a foundation and had received money from the foundation at a time when the person who directed it was being prosecuted by the federal government. Under considerable pressure, Fortas resigned. The resignation came too quickly to determine how successful an impeachment effort would have been, but it almost certainly would have been serious.

The campaigns against Douglas and Fortas came primarily from the Nixon administration, which sought to replace the two liberals with more conservative justices. John Dean, a lawyer on Nixon's staff, later reported that Fortas's resignation led to "a small celebration in the attorney general's office" that "was capped with a call from the president, congratulating" Justice Department officials "on a job well done."[73] In contrast, according to Dean, the unsuccessful campaign against Douglas "created an intractable resolve by Douglas never to resign while Nixon was president."[74]

The Fortas episode seems unlikely to be repeated, in part because it reminded justices of the need to avoid questionable financial conduct. The removal of three federal judges through impeachment proceedings between 1987 and 1989 makes it clear that impeachment is a real option. But it is used only in cases with strong evidence of serious misdeeds, often involving allegations of corrupt behavior.

Thus, the timing of a justice's leaving the Court reflects primarily the justice's own inclinations, health, and longevity. Those who want to affect the Court's membership may have their say when a vacancy occurs, but they have little control over the creation of vacancies.

Conclusion

The recruitment of Supreme Court justices is a complex process. People do not "rise" to the Court in an orderly fashion. Rather, whether they become credible candidates for the Court and whether they actually win appointments depend on a wide range of circumstances. Indeed, something close to pure luck plays a powerful role in determining who becomes a justice.

The recruitment process has evolved over the Court's history. To take one example, the balance of power between president and Senate in selecting justices has shifted back and forth. Further, justices today are drawn from a broader subset of society than they were during most of the Court's history, and their backgrounds are more "legal" and less "political" than they once were.

The Court's power and prestige have fundamental effects on its membership. For one thing, presidents take nominations to the Court very seriously, and they have a wide range of prospective nominees to choose from. For another, justices are usually reluctant to give up their positions.

Also consequential is the perception of a strong link between the Court's membership and its decisions. Because of this perception, presidents accord heavy weight to the policy preferences of candidates when they choose a nominee. For the same reason, the Senate gives Court nominees greater scrutiny than it does nominees to any other positions. Interest groups regularly seek to influence president and Senate, and they sometimes engage in massive campaigns over nominees.

This perception is well founded. In later chapters I will discuss how the identities of the justices shape the Court's positions on legal and policy issues.

NOTES

1. The four who were nominated and confirmed twice include three individuals elevated from associate justice to chief justice (Edward White, Harlan Stone, and William Rehnquist) and one (Charles Evans Hughes) who resigned from the Court and was later appointed chief justice. Douglas Ginsburg is counted as a nominee even though he withdrew from

consideration in 1987, before he was officially nominated. Harriet Miers was nominated in 2005 but withdrew before the Senate could consider her nomination.

2. Joan Biskupic, *Sandra Day O'Connor* (New York: HarperCollins, 2005), 72–73. Burger's role in the Nixon nominations is discussed in John W. Dean, *The Rehnquist Choice* (New York: Free Press, 2001), 19, 52, 179–185.
3. David D. Kirkpatrick, "A Year of Work to Sell Roberts to Conservatives," *New York Times*, July 22, 2005, A14.
4. This discussion is based in part on John Anthony Maltese, *The Selling of Supreme Court Nominees* (Baltimore: Johns Hopkins University Press, 1995); and Gregory A. Caldeira and John R. Wright, "Lobbying for Justice: The Rise of Organized Conflict in the Politics of Federal Judgeships," in *Contemplating Courts*, ed. Lee Epstein (Washington, D.C.: CQ Press, 1995), 44–71.
5. Michael Pertschuk and Wendy Schaetzel, *The People Rising: The Campaign against the Bork Nomination* (New York: Thunder's Mouth Press, 1989); Patrick B. McGuigan and Dawn M. Weyrich, *Ninth Justice: The Fight for Bork* (Washington, D.C.: Free Congress Research and Education Foundation, 1990); Mark Gitenstein, *Matters of Principle: An Insider's Account of America's Rejection of Robert Bork's Nomination to the Supreme Court* (New York: Simon and Schuster, 1992).
6. Richard Hodder-Williams, "The Strange Story of Judge Robert Bork and a Vacancy on the United States Supreme Court," *Political Studies* 36 (December 1988): 628.
7. Gregory A. Caldeira and John R. Wright, "Lobbying for Justice: Organized Interests and the Bork Nomination in the United States Senate" (paper presented at the annual meeting of the American Political Science Association, Chicago, September 1992).
8. Stephen Clark, "Political Battle Over Obama's Supreme Court Pick Hits the Web," FOXNews.com, May 19, 2009, at www.foxnews.com/politics/2009/05/19/political-battle-obamas-supreme-court-pick-goes-viral-on-line/.
9. Andrew Peyton Thomas, *Clarence Thomas: A Biography* (San Francisco: Encounter Books, 2001), 179.
10. Laura Parker, "College Yearbook Described Goal of Becoming Justice," *USA Today*, November 1, 2005, 2A.
11. Henry J. Abraham, *Justices, Presidents, and Senators: A History of U.S. Supreme Court Appointments from Washington to Bush II*, 5th ed. (Lanham, Md.: Rowman and Littlefield, 2008), 146.
12. Dean, *The Rehnquist Choice*, 14.
13. Jan Crawford Greenburg, *Supreme Conflict: The Inside Story of the Struggle for Control of the United States Supreme Court* (New York: Penguin Press, 2007), 240–241.
14. Neil A. Lewis, "Nominee Wraps Up Rehearsale," *New York Times*, July 12, 2009, A16.
15. Greenburg, *Supreme Conflict*, 283.
16. Dahlia Lithwick, "More Fun than the Emmys," *Slate Magazine*, at www.slate.com, September 20, 2005.
17. Dahlia Lithwick, "Revenge of the Nerd," *Slate Magazine*, at www.slate.com, January 10, 2006.
18. Bob Dart, "Tears Trump Substance during Alito Hearings," *Atlanta Journal-Constitution*, January 13, 2006, 8A.

19. Carrie Budoff, "Specter to Probe Supreme Court Decisions," *Politico*, at www.politico.com/, July 25, 2007.
20. The discussion of nomination decisions that follows draws much from Christine L. Nemacheck, *Strategic Selection: President Nomination of Supreme Court Justices from Herbert Hoover through George W. Bush* (Charlottesville: University of Virginia Press, 2007), and from David Alistair Yalof, *Pursuit of Justices: Presidential Politics and the Selection of Supreme Court Justices* (Chicago: University of Chicago Press, 1999).
21. The discussion of the Sotomayor nomination in this paragraph and the one that follows is based primarily on Peter Baker and Jeff Zeleny, "Obama Nominates Hispanic Judge for Supreme Court," *New York Times*, May 27, 2009, A1, A17; Peter Baker and Adam Nagourney, "White House Set Strategy in Choosing New Justice," *New York Times*, May 28, 2009, A1, A17; and Jan Crawford Greenburg, "Becoming Nominee Sotomayor," Legalities Blog, May 26, 2009, at http://blogs.abcnews.com/legalities/2009/05/becoming-nomine.html.
22. Nemacheck, *Strategic Selection*, chap. 5.
23. Barton Gellman, *Angler: The Cheney Vice Presidency* (New York: Penguin Press, 2008), 359.
24. Nemacheck, *Strategic Selection*, chap. 3.
25. Dean, *The Rehnquist Choice*, 96.
26. Greenburg, *Supreme Conflict*, 199.
27. Steve Holland, "Bush Defends Pick for Supreme Court," *Toronto Star*, October 5, 2005, A11.
28. Fred Barnes, "Souter-Phobia," *Weekly Standard*, August 1, 2005, 11–12.
29. Alyssa Sepinwall, "The Making of a Presidential Myth," (letter), *Wall Street Journal*, September 4, 1990, A11; Tony Mauro, "Leak of Souter Keeps McGuigan in Plan," *Legal Times*, September 10, 1990, 11.
30. "Justice Anthony Kennedy: Surely Reagan's Biggest Disappointment," *Human Events*, May 31–June 7, 1996, 3.
31. J. Anthony Lukas, *Nightmare: The Underside of the Nixon Years* (New York: Viking Press, 1976), 569.
32. Robert Scigliano, *The Supreme Court and the Presidency* (New York: Free Press, 1971), 95.
33. Baker and Zeleny, "Obama Nominates Hispanic Judge," A17.
34. Barbara A. Perry, *A "Representative" Supreme Court? The Impact of Race, Religion, and Gender on Appointments* (New York: Greenwood Press, 1991), 122.
35. Greenburg, *Supreme Conflict*, 245.
36. Denis Steven Rutkus and Maureen Bearden, "Supreme Court Nominations, 1789–2005: Actions by the Senate, the Judiciary Committee, and the President," report of the Congressional Research Service, January 5, 2006.
37. See Lee Epstein, René Lindstädt, Jeffrey A. Segal, and Chad Westerland, "The Changing Dynamics of Senate Voting on Supreme Court Nominees," *Journal of Politics* 68 (May 2006): 296–307.
38. These percentages are based on figures in Jeffrey Segal, "Senate Confirmation of Supreme Court Justices: Partisan and Institutional Politics," *Journal of Politics* 49 (November 1987): 1008; percentages updated by the author. Percentages differ among sources, chiefly because of differences in assignment of partisan affiliation to some presidents.

39. Based on ibid., updated by the author. Nominations made during a president's fourth year but after the president's reelection are not included.
40. See Maltese, *Selling of Supreme Court Nominees.*
41. "Here Comes the Judge," *Newsweek,* February 2, 1970, 19. Quoted in John Massaro, *Supremely Political: The Role of Ideology and Presidential Management in Unsuccessful Supreme Court Nominations* (Albany: State University of New York Press, 1990), 105.
42. Richard Reeves, *President Nixon: Alone in the White House* (New York: Simon and Schuster, 2001), 161.
43. See George Stephanopoulos, *All Too Human: A Political Education* (Boston: Little, Brown, 1999), 168.
44. Ronald Brownstein, "Alito's Remarks on Roe May Not Be Fighting Words," *Los Angeles Times,* December 12, 2005, A11.
45. Sonia Sotomayor, "A Latina Judge's Voice," *Berkeley La Raza Law Journal* 13 (2002): 92.
46. This discussion is based in part on John R. Schmidhauser, *Judges and Justices: The Federal Appellate Judiciary* (Boston: Little, Brown, 1979), 41–100.
47. Elisabeth Bumiller, "An Interview by, Not with, the President," *New York Times,* July 21, 2005, A1.
48. Lee Epstein, Jeffrey A. Segal, Harold J. Spaeth, and Thomas G. Walker, *The Supreme Court Compendium,* 4th ed. (Washington, D.C.: CQ Press, 2007), 271–279. This source was also used in the next paragraph to classify the justices sitting in 2009.
49. Sandra Day O'Connor, *The Majesty of the Law: Reflections of a Supreme Court Justice* (New York: Random House, 2003), 132–138.
50. See Warren B. Rudman, *Combat: Twelve Years in the U.S. Senate* (New York: Random House, 1996), 152–194; quotation, 153.
51. Richard C. Reuben, "Justice Stevens: I Benefited from Pro Bono Work," *Los Angeles Daily Journal,* August 11, 1992, 11. See Kenneth A. Manaster, *Illinois Justice: The Scandal of 1969 and the Rise of John Paul Stevens* (Chicago: University of Chicago Press, 2001).
52. See Greenburg, *Supreme Conflict,* 242–243.
53. Laurence Bodine, "Sandra Day O'Connor," *American Bar Association Journal* 69 (October 1983): 1394.
54. These proportions are based on biographies in the *Biographical Directory of Federal Judges,* compiled by the Federal Judicial Center, at www.fjc.gov/public/home.nsf/hisj.
55. Terri L. Peretti, "Where Have All the Politicians Gone? Recruiting for the Modern Supreme Court," *Judicature* 91 (November–December 2007): 121–122.
56. See David J. Garrow, "The Once and Future Supreme Court," *American History,* 39 (February 2005): 28–36.
57. This discussion of resignation and retirement draws on David N. Atkinson, *Leaving the Bench: Supreme Court Justices at the End* (Lawrence: University Press of Kansas, 1999); and Artemus Ward, *Deciding to Leave: The Politics of Retirement from the United States Supreme Court* (Albany: State University of New York Press, 2003).
58. Philip Rucker, "Quiet N.H. Home Is Where Souter's Heart Has Always Been," *Washington Post,* May 3, 2009, A1.
59. Greenburg, *Supreme Conflict,* 194.

60. David J. Garrow, "Mental Decrepitude on the U.S. Supreme Court: The Historical Case for a 28th Amendment," *University of Chicago Law Review* 67 (fall 2000): 1085. See also Susan Okie, "Illness and Secrecy on the Supreme Court," *New England Journal of Medicine* 351 (December 23, 2004): 2675–2678.

61. Ken Kobayashi, "Justice Stevens Recalls War Years in Honolulu," *Honolulu Advertiser,* July 20, 2007.

62. Roger C. Cramton and Paul D. Carrington, eds., *Reforming the Court: Term Limits for Supreme Court Justices* (Durham, N.C.: Carolina Academic Press, 2006); Robert Barnes, "Legal Experts Propose Limiting Justices' Powers, Terms," *Washington Post,* February 23, 2009, A15.

63. Kevin T. McGuire, "An Assessment of Tenure on the U.S. Supreme Court," *Judicature* 89 (July–August 2005): 8–15.

64. Justin Crowe and Christopher F. Karpowitz, "Where Have You Gone, Sherman Minton? The Decline of the Short-Term Supreme Court Justice," *Perspectives on Politics* 5 (September 2007): 425–445.

65. Jeanette Lee, "Justice Souter's Dream," The Atlantic Politics Channel, May 4, 2009, at http://politics.theatlantic.com/2009/05/justice_souters_dream.php; see Peter Baker and Jeff Zeleny, "Souter Said to Have Plans to Leave Court in June," *New York Times,* May 1, 2009, A1.

66. Noel J. Augustyn, "The Chief I Knew," *Journal of Supreme Court History* 31 (March 2006): 14.

67. Debra Rosenberg, "Bench Player," *Newsweek,* February 12, 2007, 32.

68. Neil A. Lewis, "2 Years after His Bruising Hearing, Justice Thomas Still Shows the Hurt," *New York Times,* November 27, 1993, 6.

69. Juan Williams, "Marshall's Law," *Washington Post Magazine,* January 7, 1990, 29; from an interview with Marshall conducted by Carl Rowan, quoted in "The Justice and the President," *Washington Post,* September 11, 1987, A23.

70. U.S. Constitution, art. 2, sec. 4.

71. John Ehrlichman, *Witness to Power: The Nixon Years* (New York: Simon and Schuster, 1982), 122.

72. Laura Kalman, *Abe Fortas: A Biography* (New Haven: Yale University Press, 1990), 359–376; Bruce Allen Murphy, *Fortas: The Rise and Ruin of a Supreme Court Justice* (New York: Morrow, 1988).

73. Dean, *The Rehnquist Choice,* 11.

74. Ibid., 26.

Chapter 3

The Cases

The Supreme Court reaches full decisions in a limited number of cases, currently fewer than eighty a year. Those cases are a very small proportion of all the actions and events that create potential Supreme Court cases. This chapter examines the process of agenda setting that produces those rare events. In the first stage of that process, people make the series of decisions that bring their cases to the Supreme Court. In the second stage, the Court selects from those cases the few—currently about one in one hundred—that it will fully consider and decide.

Several sets of people and institutions help to set the Court's agenda. In the first stage, litigants file cases and bring them through the legal system to the Court. Most of these litigants are represented by lawyers through at least part of this process, and some receive direct or indirect assistance from interest groups. Although the Court plays no direct part at this stage, predictions of how the Court might respond to a case affect decisions about whether to bring it to the Court. In the second stage, the justices are the sole decision makers. But their choices may be influenced by the litigants, lawyers, and interest groups that participate in cases. And the other branches of government structure both stages by setting the Court's jurisdiction and writing the statutes on which most cases are based.

The first two sections of this chapter examine the two stages of agenda setting in the Court. In the first section, I consider how and why cases are brought to the Court. In the second I discuss how and why the justices choose certain cases to decide on the merits. In the final section, I take a different perspective on agenda setting by examining the size of the Court's agenda.

Reaching the Court: Litigants, Attorneys, and Interest Groups

Litigants, their attorneys, and interest groups are all important in determining which cases get to the Supreme Court, and I will examine the role of each in turn. The federal government is the most frequent and most distinctive participant in Supreme Court cases, and its role merits separate consideration.

Litigants

Every case that comes to the Supreme Court has at least one formal party, or litigant, on each side. For a case to reach the Court, one or more of the parties must have acted to initiate the litigation and move it upward through the court system.

Litigants in the Supreme Court are a diverse lot.[1] Of those who petition the Court to hear cases, the great majority are individuals. Most of these individuals are criminal defendants; the others occupy a variety of roles. Among respondents, the litigants who are brought to the Court by petitioners, the largest category consists of governments and government agencies, from the federal level to the local level. Individuals are also respondents in many cases. Businesses frequently appear as petitioners or respondents. Other kinds of organizations, such as nonprofit groups and labor unions, appear in some Court cases.

One key question about litigants is why they become involved in court cases and carry those cases to the Supreme Court. The motives of litigants can be thought of as taking two general forms. In the two ideal types of Supreme Court litigation, one motive or the other is dominant. Some litigants have mixed motives, so they fit neither ideal type.

The first ideal type of case can be called ordinary litigation because it is so common. Most of the time, parties bring cases to court or appeal unfavorable decisions because they seek to advance a direct personal or organizational interest. For instance, plaintiffs file personal injury suits because they hope to receive money through a court verdict or an out-of-court settlement.

One example of ordinary litigation is *Metropolitan Life Insurance Co. v. Glenn* (2008). Wanda Glenn, who worked for Sears, Roebuck in Ohio, was diagnosed with a serious heart condition. She took a medical leave from Sears and applied for long-term disability benefits to MetLife, which administered and insured the Sears employee disability plan. MetLife initially paid disability benefits to Glenn, but after two years the company ruled that she did not meet the stricter standard for continued benefits. After losing her appeal within the MetLife organization, Glenn sued the company in federal court. Her lawyer argued that the denial of benefits to her violated her rights under the federal ERISA law (Employee Retirement Income Security Act), which governed her disability plan. After Glenn lost in district court and won in the court of appeals, MetLife asked the Supreme Court to hear the case. The Court did so to resolve an issue in interpretation of ERISA, and it affirmed the court of appeals decision requiring MetLife to pay benefits to Glenn. She had said earlier that "never in a million years" had she expected her problem to go to the Supreme Court. Her goal was simply to obtain benefits that she needed.[2]

The second ideal type of case may be called political litigation. In political cases, litigants seek to advance policies they favor rather than their direct self-interest. Most often, political litigation is aimed at winning a judicial decision that supports the litigant's policy goals.

District of Columbia v. Heller (2008) exemplifies political litigation.[3] Three lawyers who were associated with conservative interest groups sought to establish that the Second Amendment applies to individual gun ownership. To do so they challenged the prohibition of handguns in the District of Columbia, in part because it was a highly restrictive gun law. They interviewed a large number of people before choosing the six plaintiffs in the case, selected because they were a diverse group who might be appealing to the courts. One of the three lawyers, who was wealthy, financed the litigation. After they won in a federal court of appeals, they joined the District of Columbia in asking the Supreme Court to hear the case, something that would never be done by an ordinary litigant who simply wanted to win the case. The Court did accept the case. When the Court then affirmed the court of appeals decision, it gave the original sponsors of the case just what they had sought.

Many cases have large elements of both ordinary and political litigation. Individuals or companies may bring lawsuits to gain something directly, but along the way they become concerned with the larger policy issues that arise from their cases. In cases brought by government agencies, ordinary and political elements may be difficult to separate: prosecutors file criminal cases to advance the specific mission of their agencies, but that mission is linked to the broader political goal of attacking crime.

The proportion of cases that can be classified as fully or partly political increases with each step upward in the judicial system, so political litigation is most common in the Supreme Court. This pattern is not accidental. Ordinary litigation usually ends at a relatively early stage because the parties find it more advantageous to settle their dispute or even to accept a defeat than to fight on. In contrast, political litigants often want to get a case to the highest court, where a victory may establish a national policy they favor. In addition, political litigation sometimes attracts the support of interest groups that help to shoulder the costs and other burdens of carrying a case through the judicial system.

Even so, the great majority of cases brought to the Supreme Court are best classified as ordinary litigation. Many are criminal cases in which a convicted defendant who wants to get out of prison, or to stay out, seeks a hearing. Other cases come from business corporations whose economic stake in the outcome justifies a petition to the Court. Still other cases concern a variety of individual grievances, big or small; in these cases, the aggrieved party cannot resist going to the Supreme Court in one final effort to obtain redress.

Political litigation is more common in the cases that the Court agrees to hear, because those cases are more likely to contain broad legal issues that interest the justices. Yet, as the *Glenn* case illustrates, ordinary litigation is by no means absent from the cases that the Court hears. Even in the biggest cases, the ones that attract the attention of large numbers of interest groups, the chief motivation of the litigants is often their own direct interests.

Organizations that are Supreme Court litigants often play active roles in their cases. Indeed, the lawyers that represent governments in the Court are usually employees of those governments. In contrast, most litigants who are individuals have limited involvement in their own cases. An extreme example is *Rasul v. Bush* (2004), which concerned the jurisdiction of federal courts to review the detention of suspected terrorists at the Guantánamo Bay Naval Station in Cuba. The cases were initiated by relatives of detainees on their behalf. Because detainees were kept isolated from the outside world at that time, those still in detention did not know that their cases existed.[4]

Attorneys

In January 2007 the Supreme Court heard oral arguments in *Safeco Insurance Company v. Burr,* a dispute between two insurance companies and their customers. The lawyer who argued for the insurance companies was Maureen Mahoney, an attorney in the Washington office of a large law firm. Mahoney had argued eighteen prior cases in the Supreme Court, and she had written briefs in many others. Arguing for the federal government as amicus curiae ("friend of the court") was Patricia Millett, who had even more experience in oral argument. The argument for the customers was made by Scott Shorr, a lawyer from a firm in Portland, Oregon. Shorr had never participated in a Supreme Court case before.

The lawyers who argued in the *Safeco* case illustrate some traditional and changing patterns in representation of clients before the Court. Scott Shorr was hardly unusual: every year, a high proportion of the lawyers who argue before the Court are doing so for the first time. A law professor who argued before the Court in 2006 was making only his second oral argument in *any* court.[5] Often these lawyers become involved in a case at its inception and continue to represent their clients when the case unexpectedly reaches the Supreme Court. One result is that many criminal defendants are represented by lawyers who have no Supreme Court experience.[6]

Patricia Millett served in the solicitor general's office within the Justice Department, which represents the federal government in the Supreme Court. The government participates in a high proportion of the cases that

Maureen Mahoney, one of the lawyers in private practice who regularly argue before the Supreme Court.

the Court hears, so the lawyers in the solicitor general's office regularly write briefs and argue cases in the Court. Millett had joined the office in 1996, and like other skilled long-term lawyers who have served in the office, she had the opportunity to present oral arguments in a large number of cases. One lawyer in the office, Edwin Kneedler, argued his one hundredth case before the Court in 2008.

In contrast with Shorr and Millett, Maureen Mahoney represents a relatively new phenomenon.[7] For many years not many attorneys outside the solicitor general's office argued more than a few cases in the Supreme Court. Most of the exceptions were lawyers for interest groups that had many cases in the Court, such as Thurgood Marshall of the NAACP Legal Defense Fund. But in the 1980s law firms began to seek out work in Supreme Court litigation, recruiting attorneys with experience as law clerks in the Court or in the solicitor general's office. Some, such as Mahoney, have both forms of experience. That trend has accelerated in the last decade. Business firms are involved in a substantial number of Supreme Court cases, and increasingly they go to the experienced lawyers in large firms. Those lawyers also represent some nonbusiness clients.

Because of this development, some big-firm lawyers are frequent participants in Supreme Court cases. Carter Phillips has argued fifty cases since leaving the solicitor general's office for private practice. Alongside these lawyers are some others who appear in the Court with some frequency. Ted Cruz, the former solicitor general of Texas, was a prominent part of a trend in which some lawyers for state governments regularly represent the state in the Supreme Court.[8] James Bopp, a lawyer in Terre Haute, Indiana, has argued against regulations of election campaign activity in five cases.[9] Most remarkable of all is Thomas Goldstein, who developed a thriving practice in Supreme Court litigation at a relatively young age while working out of his home in a very small law firm.[10] But Goldstein ultimately joined a large firm in 2006—the same firm that Patricia Millett joined a year later. Those two moves symbolize the increasing importance of large law firms in Supreme Court practice.

The effects of this change are reflected in Table 3-1. When lawyers for the federal government are excluded, about half of all oral arguments are still presented by lawyers who appear only once before the Court over a five-term period. But compared with fifteen years earlier, lawyers who argued cases in the 2007 term were much more likely to make multiple arguments over a five-term period, and a much higher proportion of arguments was presented by lawyers who appear in the Court with some regularity.

The larger number of lawyers and firms undertaking Supreme Court litigation has increased the competition for cases. In 2008 the Court granted certiorari in a case brought by a Texas prison inmate. Thomas Goldstein wrote to the inmate, offering his services for free. He then had two lawyers from his firm's Dallas office drive more than two hours to the prison in a successful effort to get the inmate's case.[11]

When the Court accepts a case in which one of the attorneys has no experience in the Court, the lawyer and the lawyer's client inevitably get entreaties to turn the case over to an experienced Court advocate. But the opportunity to go before the Court for the first time can be irresistible, and clients often feel more comfortable with a lawyer they know well. In an unusual conflict that arose in a 2008 case, Rhode Island and one of its towns disagreed about whether oral argument for their side should be presented by a town lawyer who had long been involved in the case or by an experienced Supreme Court advocate whom the state had hired. The dispute was not resolved until three days before oral argument, when the clerk of the Court reportedly told the town and state that if they did not settle on a lawyer in one hour, their side would lose its right to present oral argument. State officials told the town's lawyer that if he did not yield, the state would forgo oral argument. The town lawyer said, "I concluded they were not bluffing," and he gave up the case.[12]

After his first year on the Court, Justice Samuel Alito said in 2007, "I'm very impressed with the quality of the briefing and advocacy" before the Court. "I think it's considerably better than what I saw 20 years ago or so,"

TABLE 3-1
Numbers of Oral Arguments over a Five-Term Period by Lawyers Arguing Cases in the 1992 and 2007 Terms (Lawyers for Federal Government Excluded)

Number of arguments	1992 (%)	2007 (%)
1	81.4	53.0
2	6.6	7.0
3–5	8.2	19.1
6–10	3.8	9.6
11–15	0.0	2.6
16–25	0.0	8.7

Note: For lawyers who argued cases in 1992, the five-term period is 1988–1992; for lawyers who argued cases in 2007, the period is 2003–2007. Lawyers who argued multiple cases in 1992 or 2007 are counted each time they argued a case. Thus, the 8.7% in the lower-right cell of the table means that, leaving aside arguments by lawyers for the federal government, 8.7% of the oral arguments in the 2007 term were made by lawyers who had 16 to 25 arguments in the 2003–2007 terms.

when he was in the solicitor general's office.[13] Undoubtedly, this change reflects the growing participation of experienced Supreme Court advocates. It is true that some lawyers with little or no experience in the Court do very well. Justice Scalia has said that "I'm often amazed at how good some of these people from nowhere are—court appointed counsel from Podunk." But he also said that the "specialists" in Supreme Court litigation "generally are better."[14]

The quality of lawyers' representation affects the outcomes of Supreme Court cases. But it is only one factor that helps to shape the Court's decisions. As one lawyer put it, the justices "recognize they are deciding questions for the whole country, and they try to avoid having accidents of legal ability affect the outcome."[15] Thus it is not rare for a poor advocate to win a case.

In the legal system as a whole, a relationship exists between the wealth of an individual or institution and the quality of the legal services available to that party. To a considerable degree, this is true of the Supreme Court. The experienced Supreme Court advocates in private practice are most readily available to large corporations and other prosperous organizations that can afford their regular fees. In one case a leading Supreme Court advocate billed $43,500 (at $750 an hour) just for his effort to persuade the executive branch to support his side or at least to remain neutral.[16]

Parties without substantial resources are generally in a weaker position. This is especially true when they petition for hearings in the Court, because they may not have any legal assistance at all. However, prisoners may get informal help. One South Carolina inmate filed what he estimated to be seventy-five petitions on behalf of fellow prisoners. He finally succeeded with a petition in 2007, but his success resulted in a state investigation for practicing law without a license.[17]

If the Court accepts a case, the picture often changes. The Court appoints attorneys to represent indigent litigants, and some of those lawyers are highly skilled. Some experienced Supreme Court litigators occasionally take cases for low fees or for free, partly as a professional service and partly because they want to argue as many cases as possible in the Court.[18] In 2008, lawyers for Wilmer Cutler, a large law firm, won three Supreme Court cases in a two-week period—for a former criminal defendant, an immigrant, and a detainee at Guantánamo Bay Naval Station.[19] Several law schools have recently established Supreme Court clinics in which students work on cases for lower-income clients, often in conjunction with law firms that have Supreme Court specialists.[20] Still, as a group, those litigants that can afford to hire the most experienced advocates have a clear advantage over those that cannot.

Lawyers are eligible to participate in cases if they join the Supreme Court bar, for which the most important requirement is that they have been admitted to practice in a state for at least the last three years. Lawyers who cannot meet this requirement, however, usually are allowed to argue cases they have brought to the Court. Lawyers join the Supreme Court bar primarily for the prestige. More than 250,000 lawyers are members,[21] and the great majority will never participate in a Supreme Court case.

Interest Groups

Leaders of interest groups must decide how to allocate their limited resources. Many groups devote some of their resources to the Supreme Court, and some give a high priority to the Court. One reason is that the Court is highly visible, so groups can publicize themselves to members and others by giving attention to the Court. More important, the Court's decisions affect a wide range of interest groups, so groups want to influence those decisions. As a result, interest groups are regular participants in the Court.

Forms of Group Activity. Groups that seek to influence congressional decisions often communicate directly with individual members of Congress. In contrast, it is considered highly improper to lobby judges directly. Because of this norm, Supreme Court justices generally try to avoid contact with litigants and the groups that support them.

But interest groups can attempt to influence the Court in other ways. As described in Chapter 2, some groups participate in the nomination and confirmation of justices. Groups can also lobby the Court indirectly.

Groups on both sides of the abortion controversy conduct marches and demonstrations when the Court considers abortion cases. Some groups and litigants sponsor research that can be cited in support of their positions, although the Court said in a 2008 decision that it would not rely on research that was funded by a litigant.[22] Some interest groups hire public relations firms to try to obtain favorable coverage in the news media, and one group paid more than $200,000 to a firm for that purpose in a 2006 patent case.[23]

The primary route used to influence the Court is participation in the litigation process, participation that takes multiple forms.[24] First, groups can initiate litigation or help bring it to the Court. Organizations that exist primarily as interest groups generally lack standing, a legal stake in a case, to bring cases in their own names. But other organizations that may be considered interest groups, especially businesses and governments, are often parties in Supreme Court cases.

A group that is not a party can "sponsor" a case on an issue that concerns it, providing attorneys' services and bearing the costs from the start. Sponsorship is costly, and it can be difficult to carry out, so relatively few groups undertake full sponsorship of cases. But sometimes groups engage in limited sponsorship of cases that have already been initiated, helping to bear the financial costs and supplying legal services and advice. A substantial portion of the cases the Court agrees to hear involves full or limited sponsorship.

One example of sponsorship was *Kelo v. City of New London* (2005).[25] The Institute for Justice, a conservative public interest law firm, developed a litigation campaign in which it argued that governments were exceeding their eminent domain powers under the Constitution by taking property (with compensation) for private use rather than public use. New London, a Connecticut city, sought to buy property for a development project; when some homeowners and other property owners balked, the city condemned their property. The Institute for Justice sued the city on their behalf, and it carried the lawsuit forward through a mixed decision in the state trial court, a defeat in the state supreme court, and ultimately a 5–4 defeat in the Supreme Court.

Whether or not it sponsors cases, a group can try to influence the Court's decisions to accept or reject cases and how to decide those that it accepts. If a group effectively controls a case, its attorneys submit a brief that asks the Court to grant or deny a writ of certiorari. If the case is accepted for decision on the merits, the group's attorneys submit new briefs and participate in oral argument.

When a group does not control the case, it still may submit arguments to the Court in amicus curiae briefs.[26] With the consent of the parties to a case or by permission of the Court, any person or organization may submit an amicus brief to supplement the arguments of the parties. (Legal representatives of government do not need to obtain permission.) Most of the time, the parties give their consent for the submission of amicus briefs. When the Court's consent is needed, it seldom is denied. In the 2007 term, the Court granted consent to all seventy-five amici who sought it. Amicus briefs can be submitted on whether a case should be heard or, after a case is accepted for hearing, directly on the merits.

Amicus briefs are by far the most common means by which groups other than parties participate in litigation before the Court. As might be expected, amicus briefs are especially common in cases that the Court has accepted for consideration on the merits. In the 2007 term amicus briefs were submitted in almost 95 percent of the cases decided after oral argument; 60 percent of the cases had at least five briefs, and more than one-quarter had at least ten briefs.[27] And because groups or individuals can join in submitting a brief, the number of participants is considerably larger than the number of briefs. Amicus briefs are much less common at the certiorari stage, but they are not rare: in the Court's 2005 term, 270 amicus briefs were submitted on behalf of 144 paid petitions, about 10 percent of all the paid petitions.[28] (Paid petitions are those submitted by parties that are not indigent.)

The popularity of amicus briefs has several sources.[29] First, although the costs of preparing them are substantial, they are considerably cheaper than case sponsorship. Second, the logistics of submitting an amicus brief are relatively simple. Third, many lawyers and other people believe that amicus briefs influence the Court's decisions. For this reason, groups whose interests are implicated by a case may feel that they need to have their say, and parties to cases often encourage or even orchestrate supportive briefs. In *District of Columbia v. Heller* (2008), which attracted sixty-seven amicus briefs, lawyers for both sides coordinated the gathering of amicus briefs. The lawyers who were challenging the District of Columbia prohibition on handguns engaged in a careful effort to identify appropriate interest groups to raise particular issues.[30]

Group leaders can also use amicus briefs, like case sponsorship, as a means to attract support for the group. As one law professor pointed out, "they can recruit members and do direct fund raising, whether they win or lose. If they win, they say, 'We are only one justice away from losing,' and if they lose, they say, 'We are only one justice away from winning.' Both letters say, 'Send money.' "[31]

The Array of Groups in the Court. Interest group participation in Supreme Court litigation has increased dramatically in the past few decades. Groups are sponsoring more cases, and amicus briefs have proliferated. To take one indicator, in cases with oral arguments the Court received an average of

0.63 briefs per case in the 1956–1965 terms, 4.23 in the 1986–1995 period, and 8.09 in the 2007 term.[32] One reason for this growth is that the number of active interest groups and the level of their activity have increased considerably. Another is that the apparent success of some groups in shaping the Supreme Court's policies has encouraged other groups to seek similar success.

Hundreds of interest groups now participate in Supreme Court cases in some way. Among them are nearly all the groups that are most active in Congress and the executive branch. The box on page 80 provides a sampling of this participation by listing some of the groups that submitted amicus briefs in the 2008 term.

The groups that participate in Supreme Court cases can be placed in four broad categories. The first is economic: individual businesses, trade associations, professional groups, labor unions, and farm groups. Much of the Court's work affects the interests of these groups, on issues that range from employment discrimination to regulation of products. The business community is especially well represented in the Court. Individual businesses frequently are parties to cases, and businesses and business groups regularly submit amicus briefs. Over three recent terms of the Court, the National Chamber Litigation Center, the litigation arm of the U.S. Chamber of Commerce, submitted fifty-five amicus briefs in support of petitions for certiorari, far more than any other group.[33]

In the second category are groups that represent segments of the population defined by something other than economics. Most of these groups are based on personal characteristics such as race, gender, age, and sexual orientation. The prototype for these groups is the NAACP Legal Defense and Educational Fund (sometimes called the NAACP Legal Defense Fund or simply the Fund). The Fund initially focused its efforts on voting rights and school desegregation and later turned to other areas such as employment and criminal justice, giving special attention to the death penalty. The Fund's successes in the Supreme Court encouraged the creation of organizations concerned with discrimination on grounds other than race, groups that proliferated from the 1960s on.

The groups in the third category represent broad ideological positions or more specific issue positions rather than the interests of a specific segment of society. Here the prototype is the American Civil Liberties Union (ACLU).[34] Established in 1920 to protect civil liberties, the ACLU involves itself in virtually every area of civil liberties law. The ACLU also has created special projects to undertake concerted litigation campaigns in specific areas of concern, such as women's rights, capital punishment, and national security. Other groups that work to achieve liberal policy goals include Earthjustice, which litigates on environmental issues, and the Planned Parenthood Federation of America,

---

A Sampling of Groups
Submitting Amicus Curiae Briefs
to the Supreme Court in the 2008 Term

Economic Groups: Business and Occupational

ABC Television Affiliates Association
American Medical Association
Commercial Fishermen of America
Maine State Employees Association
National Association of Manufacturers
R.J. Reynolds Tobacco Company
Tennessee Education Association

Noneconomic Interests

American Humanist Association
Boy Scouts of America
Japanese American Citizens League
Mexican American Legal Defense and Educational Fund
National Women's Law Center

Ideological and Issue Groups

Criminal Justice Legal Foundation
Lawyers' Committee for Civil Rights Under Law
Morality in Media, Inc.
National Wildlife Federation
Washington Legal Foundation

Governments and Governmental Groups

City of Casper, Wyoming
Florida House of Representatives
Former Commissioners of the Federal Trade Commission
National School Boards Association
State of Oregon

---

for which abortion is a primary concern. The National Association of Criminal Defense Lawyers frequently submits amicus briefs on behalf of defendants.

Issue and ideological groups that favor conservative positions were slower to involve themselves in litigation, but many such groups are now active. Some focus primarily on economic issues. The Institute for Justice, for instance, litigates against government intervention in the economy. Others give primary attention to civil liberties issues. The Center for Individual Rights has engaged in a long-term campaign against affirmative action programs, one that led to the Supreme Court's split decisions in 2003 on the use of affirmative action in college admissions.[35] Several litigating groups represent conservative religious interests.[36] One is the American Center for Law and Justice (ACLJ), which participates in a wide range of cases involving religious activities and values.

The final category consists of governments, sets of governments, and groups of government officials. Governments regularly appear as interest groups in the Court. The federal government is a special case, discussed later in this section. State and local governments often come to the Court as litigants, and they frequently file amicus briefs. It has become standard practice for many or most states to join in a brief to emphasize their strong shared interest in a case.

Group Strategies and Tactics. Any interest group that engages in litigation must make strategic and tactical decisions. At the strategic level, groups that are not set up solely to litigate must decide how much of their energy and resources to devote to litigation rather than other forms of political action. Groups must also decide what kinds of issues to emphasize in their litigation work and how to coordinate their efforts with other groups that have similar interests. At the tactical level, a group's lawyers consider whether initiating a specific case or supporting a litigant in an existing case would serve the group's goals.[37] They sometimes have a choice among different geographical areas in which to initiate cases or between federal and state courts. And like other lawyers, they have to choose which arguments to make in the cases in which they participate.

Many considerations affect these decisions, including the views of group members and the availability of resources. Perhaps the most fundamental consideration is a group's perceptions of the courts in general and the Supreme Court in particular. It is not surprising that conservative groups have become more active in Supreme Court litigation since the 1970s as the Court has grown more receptive to conservative arguments. Similarly, choices of specific cases and arguments reflect judgments about potential responses from the justices.

Some groups establish long-term litigation strategies in which they seek to shape legal policy over time. When groups are skilled and their goals align with the Supreme Court's disposition, they can win major victories. The NAACP Legal Defense Fund successfully attacked racial segregation in education in a series of cases that culminated in *Brown v. Board of Education* (1954). The ACLU's Women's Rights Project won most of the cases it brought to the Supreme Court in the 1970s, as the Court gave governments a strong burden of proof when they treated women and men differently. But such successes are not easy to achieve, and many other litigation campaigns have done less well. As the Court has become more conservative, some conservative groups have developed strategies to establish new principles of constitutional law. They have achieved some major successes, but they have also suffered significant defeats on such issues as affirmative action. None of these groups has yet won a series of favorable decisions from the Court.

The Significance of Interest Groups. Interest groups can affect what the Supreme Court does in several ways; here, I focus on their influence on whether cases get to the Court. In this respect, cases may be placed in three categories.

The largest category includes the cases that come to the Court without any participation by interest groups. The issues in these cases are too narrow to interest any group. They reach the Court because the parties and attorneys have sufficient motivation of their own to seek a Supreme Court hearing and sufficient resources to finance the litigation. These conditions are met when a large business has a substantial financial stake in a case. They are also met when indigent criminal defendants face significant prison terms and need not pay lawyers' fees or other expenses to get a case to the Court.

The second category consists of cases that would have reached the Court without any interest group involvement but in which groups are involved in some way. An interest group may assist one of the parties by providing attorneys' services or financing. And groups frequently submit amicus briefs supporting petitions for hearings by the Court.

The third category includes cases that would not reach the Court without group sponsorship. There are many important legal questions in civil liberties that no individual litigant has the capability or sufficient incentive to take to the Supreme Court. For example, most of the individuals whom the ACLU assists could not go to court without the group's legal assistance.

Because group sponsorship of cases in the Court is relatively rare, only a small proportion of cases brought to the Court fall into this third category. But groups are most likely to sponsor cases that have the potential to be heard by the Court and to produce major legal rulings. Indeed, much of the Court's expansion of legal protections for civil liberties during the twentieth century was made possible by interest group action.[38]

Groups can do more than get cases to the Court; they can help to determine whether those cases are heard and how the Court rules. That influence is discussed later in this chapter and in Chapter 4.

The Federal Government as Litigant

Of all the litigants in the Supreme Court, the federal government appears most frequently. It is a party in a large minority of the cases brought to the Court for consideration. Of the cases actually argued before the Court, the federal government participates as a party or an amicus in a substantial majority. The Court decided seventy-four cases on the merits in its 2007 term; the government presented arguments on its own behalf or as an amicus in fifty-eight of those cases, 78 percent of the total.[39] As a result of its frequent participation, the federal government is the most important interest group in the Court.

In turn, the group of about two dozen lawyers in the Office of the Solicitor General in the Justice Department has more impact on the Court than any other set of attorneys. Those lawyers represent the federal government in the Supreme Court. They decide whether to bring federal government cases to the Court; only a few federal agencies can take cases to the Court without the solicitor general's approval. They also do the bulk of the government's legal work in Supreme Court cases in which it participates, including petitions for hearings, the writing of briefs, and oral arguments.

The solicitor general's office occupies a complicated position.[40] On the one hand, it represents the president and the executive branch, functioning as their law firm. In this role, the office helps to carry out the policies of the president. But the office also has a unique relationship with the Supreme Court, one in which it serves as an adviser as well as an advocate. As Richard Pacelle put it, the solicitor general's office straddles the line "between law and politics."[41]

The unique relationship of the office with the Court rests on the fact that it represents a unique litigant. For one thing, the executive branch and the Supreme Court are both part of the federal government. And because the executive branch is involved in so many potential and actual Supreme Court cases, the solicitor general has the opportunity to build a mutually advantageous relationship with the Court.

One way the solicitor general does so is by exercising self-restraint in requesting that the Court hear cases. The solicitor general's office also seeks to maintain credibility by taking a less partisan stance than other litigants. For instance, the office tries to show that it is above politics by maintaining the position that a prior administration has taken in a case even though the new administration has a different point of view. Thus, the Obama administration adhered to a solicitor general's brief that argued against a constitutional right for prisoners to have access to DNA evidence in order to prove their innocence, even though President Obama's past record suggests that he would have favored the other side.[42]

Elena Kagan, selected by President Obama as solicitor general in 2009. The solicitor general's office is important to the work of the Supreme Court.

In response, the justices give considerable deference to the solicitor general. The office has an extraordinary success rate for its certiorari petitions. And the Court frequently "invites" (in reality, orders) the solicitor general to file amicus briefs in cases that do not affect the federal government directly because the justices are interested in the government's views.[43] In the 2007 term, the solicitor general's office filed amicus briefs in response to twenty-six petitions for hearings—all but two at the Court's invitation. And the solicitor general often participates in oral argument as amicus by invitation or its own request, as it did twenty-five times in the 2007 term. With the occasional exception of state governments, other litigants seldom receive that privilege.

The office's special relationship with the Court leads to a degree of independence from the president and attorney general, who understand the value of maintaining that relationship. But the solicitor general usually is someone who shares the president's general point of view about legal policy. For instance, Barack Obama's solicitor general Elena Kagan spent most of her prior career as a law school teacher and dean, but she also served in the Clinton administration. Further, the office operates in a climate created by the president and attorney general.

Those superiors occasionally intervene in specific cases. In a 2008 case involving the right of investors to sue certain participants in frauds against them, the federal Securities and Exchange Commission recommended that the solicitor general file an amicus brief supporting the investors. But other federal agencies and President Bush argued to the contrary, and the solicitor general ended up filing a brief that supported the other side.[44]

As Pacelle has shown, the impact of a presidential administration on the solicitor general's choices varies with the situation.[45] There are certain positions that the office would take regardless of who the president is. When the federal government is a party to a case, the solicitor general nearly always supports the government's position as a litigant. When the solicitor general participates as amicus, the office necessarily supports government interests such as enforcement of the criminal laws. In many other cases, especially when the solicitor general is invited by the Court to participate, the solicitor general chooses a position without regard to the liberalism or conservatism of the administration. But there are some cases—primarily those involving contentious issues in civil rights and civil liberties—in which the ideological coloration of the administration affects the solicitor general's position. Adding all this together, the solicitor general has considerable independence from the president, an independence that helps to make the office an effective advocate in the Court. However, that independence is most limited on issues that presidents and their administrations care the most about.

Deciding What to Hear: The Court's Role

In its 2007 term the Supreme Court considered nearly eight thousand petitions for hearings. The Court granted certiorari and full consideration to only ninety of those petitions.[46] Of the thousands of other petitions, the great majority were simply denied, allowing a lower-court decision to become final. Some of those cases involved prominent people or powerful institutions. Some raised issues of national importance. Nonetheless, the Court chose not to hear them. In selecting a few dozen cases from the thousands brought to them, the justices determined which legal claims and policy questions they would address.

Options

In screening petitions for hearings, the Court makes choices that are more complicated than simply accepting and rejecting individual cases. To begin with, petitions are not always considered in isolation from one another. The justices may accept a case to clarify or expand on an earlier decision in the same policy area. They may accept multiple cases that raise the same issue to address that issue more fully than a single case would allow them to do. They may reject a case because they are looking for a more suitable case on the same issue.

When the Court does accept a case, the justices can choose which issues they will consider. The Court often limits its grant of certiorari to one issue raised by the petitioner, and it sometimes asks the parties to address an issue that neither had raised. In two cases the Court decided in 2008, it asked the parties to submit briefs on new issues after the oral arguments in the cases.[47] And on rare occasions, the Court decides a case on the basis of an issue that the parties never addressed. In *Mapp v. Ohio* (1961) the Court made a landmark decision on police searches and seizures after the parties had argued the case as one about constitutional limits on the regulation of obscenity.

In accepting a case, the Court also determines what kind of consideration the case will receive. It may give the case full consideration, which means that the Court receives a new set of briefs on the merits from the parties and holds oral argument, then issues a decision on the merits with a full opinion explaining the decision. Alternatively, it may give the case summary consideration. This usually means that the case is decided without new briefs or oral argument; the Court relies on the materials that the parties already submitted.

In most summary decisions, the Supreme Court issues a "GVR" order— that is, granting certiorari, vacating the lower-court decision, and remanding the case to that court for reconsideration. Most of these orders are issued because some event after the lower-court decision, usually a Supreme Court decision, is relevant to the case. The Court struck down the federal sentencing guidelines in *United States v. Booker* (2005), and since then it has reached several decisions that defined allowable sentencing practices for federal judges. After each of these decisions it issued GVR orders in many other cases involving related questions—more than a thousand altogether. In other summary decisions, the Court actually reaches a decision on the merits and issues an opinion of several paragraphs or even several pages. This opinion typically is labeled *per curiam,* meaning "by the Court," rather than being signed by a justice, but it has the same legal force as a signed opinion.

Even after accepting a case, the Court occasionally avoids a decision by issuing what is called a DIG, or Dismissed as Improvidently Granted.[48] A DIG occurs when the parties' briefs on the merits or the oral arguments suggest to the justices that the case is inappropriate for a decision. Like GVRs, DIGs seem routine, but both sometimes draw heated dissents from justices who think they are inappropriate in a particular case or (for GVRs) overused in general.[49]

Screening Procedures

The Court uses a series of procedures to screen petitions for hearing, procedures that are made more complex by two distinctions between types of cases. The first is between the certiorari cases, over which the Court's jurisdiction is discretionary, and the cases labeled appeals, which the Court is required to decide. Few appeals reach the Court. The Court retains, and uses, the option of deciding them without holding oral argument or issuing full opinions. The second distinction, between paid cases and paupers' cases, requires more extensive discussion.

Paid Cases and Paupers' Cases. In recent years only about one-fifth of the requests for hearings that arrive at the Supreme Court have been paid cases, for which the petitioner pays the Court's filing fee of $300 and provides all required copies of materials. The remaining cases are brought *in forma pauperis* by indigent people for whom the fee and the requirement of multiple copies are waived. The great majority of the "paupers'" cases (also called "unpaid") are brought by federal and state prisoners. (A person responding to a petition may also be given pauper status.)

Criminal defendants who have had counsel provided to them in the lower federal courts because of their low incomes are automatically entitled to bring paupers' cases in the Supreme Court. Other litigants must submit an affidavit supporting their motion for leave to file as paupers. The Court has never developed precise rules specifying when a litigant can claim pauper status. However, it has denied many litigants the right to proceed as paupers in particular cases on the grounds that they were not truly paupers or that their petitions were frivolous or malicious. The Court has also gone further, issuing a general denial of pauper status in noncriminal cases to some litigants who have filed large numbers of paupers' petitions. Justice Stevens regularly dissents from such denials because of an experience he had before becoming a judge: he had found "unexpected merit" in the allegations of a repetitive and annoying litigant when he led an investigation of judicial corruption in Illinois in 1969.[50]

A very small proportion of paupers' petitions are accepted for full decisions on the merits—about one-tenth of 1 percent in the 2007 term, compared with 5.6 percent of the paid cases in the same term.[51] The lack of inherent merit in many of these cases and the fact that many litigants have to draft petitions without a lawyer's assistance help to account for the low acceptance rate. It may also be that the Court looks less closely at paupers' petitions than at the paid petitions. Two studies have found evidence that in cases that were similar in other respects, the Court was less likely to accept a pauper's petition than a paid petition.[52] But because there are so many paupers' petitions, even the small proportion that are accepted add up to a significant number of cases—an average of about a dozen a term in recent years—and they constitute an important part of the Court's work on issues of criminal procedure.

Prescreening: The Discuss List. Under its "rule of four," the Court grants a writ of certiorari and hears a case on the merits if at least four justices vote at conference to grant the writ. But petitions for hearings are considered and voted on at conference only if they are put on the Court's "discuss list." The chief justice creates the discuss list, but other justices can and do add cases to it. Cases left off the discuss list are denied hearings automatically. This is the fate of the great majority of petitions.

The discuss list procedure serves to limit the Court's workload. But this procedure also reflects a belief that most petitions do not require collective consideration, because they are such poor candidates for acceptance. A great many petitions raise only narrow issues, and many others make weak legal claims, so it is easy to reject them.

Action in Conference. In conference the chief justice or the justice who added a case to the discuss list opens the presentation of views on the case. In order of seniority, from senior to junior, the justices then speak and usually announce their votes. If the discussion does not make the justices' positions clear, a formal vote is taken, also in order of seniority. Despite the prescreening of cases, a large majority of the petitions considered in conference are denied.

Most cases receive only brief discussion in conference. Some cases receive more consideration, which sometimes extends beyond the initial discussion. In conference, any justice can ask that a case be "redistributed" for a later conference. This step might be taken to obtain additional information, such as the full record of the case in the lower courts. A justice also might ask for redistribution to circulate an opinion dissenting from the Court's tentative denial of a hearing and thereby try to change the Court's decision. Of the cases that the Court accepts for oral argument, probably a majority were redistributed at least once.

Boumediene v. Bush (2008), in which the Court held that prisoners at the Guantánamo Bay Naval Station had a right to petition for habeas corpus, took a very unusual path at the certiorari stage. The Court denied certiorari in April 2007, but three justices dissented and two others (Stevens and Kennedy) issued a statement in which they said they would be inclined to hear the case later if the federal government failed to protect the petitioner detainees' rights adequately. The detainees' lawyers filed a petition for rehearing. After considering the petition at three conferences, the Court belatedly accepted the case. It appeared that Stevens and Kennedy had changed their minds, producing the five votes that are required to accept a case after an initial denial.[53]

When it accepts a case, the Court also decides whether to allow oral argument or to decide the case summarily on the basis of the available written materials. Four votes are required for oral argument. A case that is not given oral argument may be granted a hearing and decided on the merits at the same conference, so the two stages of decision in effect become one.

The Court does not issue opinions to explain its acceptance or rejection of cases. Nor are individual votes announced. But justices occasionally record their dissents from denials of petitions for hearings, sometimes accompanied by dissenting opinions and they sometimes write opinions to explain their reasons for voting against certiorari. Justice Stevens does this most often, usually to make explicit the fact that a denial of certiorari does not necessarily mean the Court endorses the lower-court decision and opinion.[54] In 2008 Stevens used such an opinion to criticize the review of death sentences by the Georgia Supreme Court. Justice Thomas responded with his own opinion to express disagreement with Stevens.[55]

The Clerks' Role. One of the law clerks' primary functions is to scrutinize requests for hearings. From 1990 to 2008 every justice except Stevens was part of the "cert (for certiorari) pool." According to one study of law clerks, Stevens does not participate in the pool because he believes that "he and his clerks provide an important check against potential mistakes."[56] In 2008 Justice Alito left the pool, but he did not announce the reason for that decision.[57] Petitions and other materials on each case are divided among the clerks for the other seven justices. The clerk who has responsibility for a case writes a memorandum, one that typically includes a summary of the case and a recommendation that the petition be granted or denied. Some justices then have their own law clerks examine and react to the memo for each case.

The effect of the law clerks' analyses and recommendations on the justices is difficult to ascertain. Because of the press of time, it is clear that the justices rely heavily on law clerks' analyses. Some justices and other observers have expressed particular concern about the justices' collective reliance on the pool memo.[58] One effect may be to reduce the number of cases that the Court hears. On the whole, clerks who write pool memos are cautious about recommending that the Court hear a case. One reason is that they know that such recommendations will be scrutinized more closely than recommendations to deny. And it would be embarrassing for a clerk to suggest that the Court take a case and have the Court do so, only to have the case DIGged later because the clerk missed an important fact.[59]

Two factors may limit the impact of the pool on certiorari decisions. First, the great majority of petitions would elicit a denial from any justice or clerk. "I would guess," Chief Justice Rehnquist wrote, "that several thousand of the petitions for certiorari filed with the Court each year are patently without merit," so no justice "would have the least interest in granting them."[60] Second, the justices, with help from their own clerks, undertake some independent review of cases. In a substantial proportion of the cases that the Court hears, the pool memo did not recommend that the Court accept the case.[61]

Criteria for Decision

The Supreme Court's decisions to accept some petitions and deny others certainly are not random. Rather, the justices look for cases whose attributes make them desirable to hear. The Court's Rule 10 lists some of those attributes, which are based on the Court's role in enhancing the certainty and consistency of the law. Rule 10 indicates that the Court is more interested in hearing cases if they contain important issues of federal law that the Court has not yet decided, if there is conflict between lower courts on an important legal question or conflict between a lower court's decision and the Supreme Court's prior decisions, or if a federal court of appeals has drastically departed "from the accepted and usual course of judicial proceedings" or allowed a lower court to do so.

The existence of these conditions undoubtedly increases the chances that a case will be accepted, but the list in Rule 10 suggests a conception of the Court's function and of its members' interests that is unrealistically narrow. The Court's pattern of screening decisions and evidence from other sources indicate the significance of several types of considerations.

Technical Criteria. The Court will reject a petition for hearing if it fails to meet certain technical requirements. Some of these requirements are specific to the Court. For example, paid petitions must comply with the Court's Rule 33, which establishes requirements on matters such as the size of print and margins used, type of paper, format and color of cover, and maximum length. The Court has tightened its requirements over the years. Under a 2007 revision to Rule 33, the maximum length of briefs is based on words rather than pages, and lawyers must sign a statement that the brief is no longer than allowed. These requirements are relaxed for the paupers' petitions, but even paupers' petitions may be rejected if they deviate too far from the rules.

The Court also imposes the same kinds of technical requirements that other courts apply. One specific requirement is that petitions for hearing be filed within ninety days of the entry of judgment in the lower court, unless the time has been extended in advance. The Court routinely refuses to allow the filing of petitions that are brought after the deadline. In 2006 a lawyer who frequently participates in Supreme Court cases missed the deadline because he misunderstood when the lower court had decided his case. Two former solicitors general submitted a brief on behalf of his motion to file the case late, but the Court denied the motion.[62]

More fundamental are the requirements of jurisdiction and standing. The Court cannot accept a case for hearing that clearly falls outside its jurisdiction. For example, the Court could not hear a state case in which the petitioner raised no issues of federal law in state court.

The rule of standing holds that a court may not hear a case unless the party bringing the case is properly before it. The most important element of standing is the requirement that a party in a case have a real and direct legal stake in its outcome. This requirement precludes hypothetical cases, cases brought on behalf of another person, "friendly suits" between parties that are not really adversaries, and cases that have become "moot" (in effect, hypothetical) because the parties can no longer be affected by the outcome. For this reason, the Court must dismiss a case if the parties have reached a settlement or if the only party on one side has died. Neither event is rare, and in June 2007 the Court dismissed a case in which it had heard oral arguments and was nearing a decision when it learned that the petitioner had died.[63]

Conflict between Courts. Justice Breyer heartily agrees with Rule 10 on the importance of conflict among lower courts as a basis for accepting cases. "If the lower courts are in agreement," he asked, "why us?"[64] Other justices have expressed the same view. Justice Ginsburg said that "the overwhelming factor" in the granting of certiorari "is the division of opinions in the Circuits."[65]

The depictions of case selection by Breyer and Ginsburg have considerable accuracy.[66] The existence of legal conflict greatly increases the chances that a case will be accepted. And one expert estimated that 80 percent of the cases that the Court accepts involve conflicts between federal courts of appeals.[67] Even so, the Court frequently rejects conflict cases. Rule 10 emphasizes the importance of the issue on which a conflict has arisen, and that criterion undoubtedly affects the justices' choices of cases. Yet the Court occasionally accepts a case to resolve a conflict on a seemingly minor issue, and it sometimes turns down cases involving fairly serious conflicts among several courts.

It is not always clear whether two lower courts actually have reached conflicting decisions on a legal issue, but the existence of conflict is easier to determine than most other criteria that the Court applies in choosing cases. For this reason, law clerks who write memos for the cert pool seem to give even greater weight to intercourt conflict than the justices do. Thus the clerks may help to account for the high proportion of conflict cases that the current Court hears.[68]

Importance of the Issues. Whether or not a case involves conflict between lower courts, the significance of the issues in a case has considerable influence on the Court's willingness to hear it. The primary reason is simple: the best way for the Court to maximize its impact is to decide the cases that affect the most people and that raise the most important policy questions.

This consideration in itself eliminates most petitions for certiorari, petitions in which the "questions presented" at the beginning of the petition are narrow and limited in their impact. Frequently, they ask only whether the case was wrongly decided. The petitioners in these cases may have suffered an injustice, but the justices typically see little reason to address an issue that will have little or no effect on anyone but the litigants themselves.

Importance is a more subjective matter than conflict between courts, so different justices may assess the importance of a case quite differently. In general, justices look for cases in which a decision would have a broad effect on courts, government, or society as a whole. In some of the cases that meet this criterion, the issues are dramatic. In others, the issues are technical but nonetheless important. Even the justices may find such cases unexciting. Chief Justice Rehnquist noted that the Court hears a steady stream of cases under the federal Employee Retirement Income Security Act (ERISA). "The thing that stands out about them is that they're dreary," he said, and the Court takes such cases as a matter of "duty, not choice."[69]

Just as the Court rejects some cases that involve conflicts between lower courts, it also rejects some important cases. The primary reason is the same: the number of meritorious cases is considerably larger than the number the Court is willing and able to hear. Justices sometimes have more specific reasons to vote against cases with significant issues. To take two examples, they may agree with the lower-court decision or want to delay before tackling a difficult issue.

Occasionally, an issue is so consequential that the justices are virtually compelled to hear a case on that issue. Between 2003 and 2006 several states enacted laws requiring that voters provide certain kinds of identification in order to cast a ballot, laws that were quickly challenged as violations of legal protections for voting rights. The Court probably had little choice but to rule on one of these challenges in order to provide guidance to the states before the 2008 presidential election. Indeed, the Court did accept a case, upholding Indiana's photo identification requirement in April 2008.[70] But few cases have that urgency, no matter how significant the issues.

Policy Preferences. Rule 10 does not mention justices' personal conceptions of good policy as a criterion for accepting or rejecting cases, but those conceptions have considerable effect on the Court's choices. Because the Court's agenda largely determines the scope of its work as a policymaker, members of the Court inevitably use the agenda-setting process to advance their own policy goals.

Justices can act on their policy goals primarily in two ways. First, they may vote to hear cases because they disagree with the lower-court decision that they are reviewing: seeing what they believe was an error by the lower court, they want to correct it. Second, they may act strategically by voting to hear a case when they think the Court would reach a decision they favor if it decided the case on the merits and voting against certiorari when they think the Court would reach what they consider the wrong decision.

The justices' use of the first approach is made clear by the Court's decisions on the merits. The Court overturns the lower court altogether or in part in more than two-thirds of its decisions. The comparable rate for the federal courts of appeals, which lack the Court's power to screen the cases brought to it, is under 10 percent.[71] One reason for the Court's reversal rate is that it accepts so many cases in order to resolve conflicts between lower courts; in those cases, there is something like a 50–50 chance that the Court will overturn the decision it hears. Even so, the reversal rate could not be nearly as high as it is if the justices were not inclined to hear cases in which they have doubts about the validity of the lower court's decision.

The justices sometimes use the second approach as well. Among justices and clerks, votes not to hear a case when a justice fears that the Court would make the "wrong" decision have been sufficiently common that they gained the label of "defensive denials" of certiorari.[72] However, scholars who study this issue disagree about how often the justices act strategically in their certiorari votes.[73] Justices probably concentrate their strategic calculations on the relatively small proportion of petitions that are good candidates for acceptance on other grounds. They may also be more inclined to take the Court's prospective decisions into account when they are part of the Court's ideological minority, because members of the minority have the most reason to worry about what the Court might decide.

These two ways of acting on policy goals are likely to have the most powerful impact when they reinforce each other. Justice Stevens complained in three 2006 decisions on state criminal procedure that the Court should not have accepted those cases because its decisions would have only a narrow impact. In his view, the Court had heard the three cases "in order to make sure that a State's highest court has not granted its citizens any greater protection than the bare minimum required by the Federal Constitution."[74] If Justice Stevens's surmise was accurate, more conservative colleagues had voted to review what they saw as undesirable decisions by state supreme courts when they could be confident that the Court would reach what they regarded as the correct result. And even if the individual cases were relatively unimportant, the cumulative effect of deciding them would be to advance a general policy that the Court's majority favored.

Identities of the Participants. Every petition for certiorari involves at least two competing parties. In most paid cases and many paupers' cases, the petitioner is represented by a lawyer. And in some cases, the petitioner is supported by one or more interest groups in amicus briefs. The identities of those participants might have an impact on the Court's decisions whether to grant certiorari.

One participant, the federal government, stands out for its success in winning hearings from the Court. Over the five terms from 2003 through 2007, the Court accepted more than two-thirds of the government's requests to hear cases.[75] That success rate is enormously high in light of the low overall rate of success for petitioners.

This impressive record reflects the solicitor general's special relationship with the Court, discussed earlier in the chapter. As representative of the federal government and as the most frequent litigant in the Court, the solicitor general's office is viewed differently from other participants in litigation. The large number of potential and actual cases that the office handles provides it with three more specific advantages.

First, the solicitor general's staff chooses cases to bring to the Court from a large pool of cases that are eligible for Court consideration. In the Court's 2007 term, the federal government asked the Court to hear seventeen cases, compared with four thousand requests for hearings from parties that opposed the government in litigation. Although the government loses fewer cases in the courts of appeals than its opponents lose, the primary reason for this difference is the solicitor general's willingness to forgo possible petitions for certiorari. The staff can select the cases that are the most likely to be accepted, and almost any litigant who could be so selective would enjoy a fairly high rate of success in getting its cases accepted.

Second, the solicitor general's selectivity earns both gratitude and credibility from the justices. If the federal government brought petitions to the Court at the high rates that other litigants bring them, the Court's caseload would be much heavier than it is. The justices reciprocate for this restraint by viewing the government's petitions in a favorable light. Further, the justices know that the government takes to the Court only the cases that its lawyers deem most worthy, so the justices also are inclined to view those cases as worthy.

Finally, the attorneys in the solicitor general's office handle a great many Supreme Court cases, and they develop considerable expertise in dealing with the Court. Few other lawyers learn as much about how to appeal to the justices' interests. As a result, the government can do more than most other litigants to make cases appear worthy of acceptance.

Other lawyers who frequently appear in the Supreme Court have an opportunity to develop some of the solicitor general's advantages: they can develop a high level of skill in writing petitions for certiorari, and they can gain credibility with the justices. Indeed, there is some evidence that these lawyers and the large firms in which most of them practice fare considerably better than the average lawyer when they petition for hearings from the Court.[76] In a 2008 oral argument, Justice Souter suggested to Carter Phillips, a leading Supreme Court advocate, that he could bring a case involving a particular issue to the Court. Phillips replied, "I wish it were that easy to get this Court to grant review of everything that I bring up here in the first place." Justice Stevens responded, "You don't have any trouble."[77]

Amicus briefs on behalf of petitioners improve the chances that a petition will be accepted. As one leading Supreme Court advocate has pointed out, an amicus brief indicates the significance of a case beyond the parties themselves.[78] Some specific interest groups may have special credibility with at least some of the justices. Credibility may derive from taking an unexpected position. In 2004 a prisoner's petition was supported by an amicus brief that was signed by a former federal prosecutor, two retired court of appeals judges, and a former head of the FBI. The Court accepted the case. However, in 2006 the Court denied certiorari to a criminal defendant despite a supportive amicus brief from 145 people, including four former U.S. attorneys general, more than two dozen former federal judges, and a long list of former federal prosecutors.[79] That outcome underlines the justices' control over their agenda: their choices of cases can be influenced by participants in those cases, but ultimately the justices can turn down any case they want.

Avoiding Problematic Cases. One effect of the justices' control over their agenda is that they can reject cases that have the potential to embroil the Supreme Court in controversy. Some denials of certiorari suggest that the justices may have had that consideration in mind. In 2005, for instance, the Court refused to hear three cases challenging President Bush's temporary "recess" appointment of a federal judge whose confirmation had been blocked by Senate Democrats. The justices may have been influenced by the desire to avoid stepping into the heated battle between the parties over the selection of federal judges.[80] Another example may have been a 2006 case in which the plaintiffs alleged that a major fifty-year-old decision by the Court had resulted from fraudulent conduct by the federal government. Other considerations aside, the justices would not have wanted to hear a case that had the potential to embarrass the executive branch and, more specifically, the solicitor general's office.[81]

A striking example of caution on the part of the justices was the Court's refusal to rule on whether it was constitutional for the United States to participate in the war in Vietnam without a declaration of war. Few issues brought to the Court have been so important, but the Court refused to hear the cases that raised this question between 1967 and 1972. Undoubtedly, some justices wanted to avoid injecting the Court into the most important and most disputed issue of national policy in that era.

Yet the Court agrees to hear a good many cases that involve controversial matters, cases in which the Court's decision is likely to arouse strong negative reactions no matter what it decides. It accepts cases about abortion, the death penalty, and religious observances in public schools. It also hears cases that pit Republicans and Democrats against each other. At least four justices voted to hear *Bush v. Gore* despite their recognition that the Court's intervention in the 2000 presidential election was certain to make many people unhappy.

Sometimes the Court sidesteps a troublesome issue only temporarily. It may reject a case on that issue only to address the issue later, when a more appropriate case comes to it or the issue has "percolated" in the lower courts. If an issue recurs often enough and has considerable importance, the justices may feel a degree of pressure to address it at some point.

Summary. When Supreme Court justices vote on petitions for hearings by the Court, their choices reflect their goals and perspectives. Each justice acts on a complex set of considerations. Inevitably, justices with different priorities and perspectives respond differently to petitions. Some give a higher priority to resolving conflicts among lower courts than others. They assess the importance of cases in various ways. And they act on quite different sets of policy preferences.

It follows that the Court's selection of cases to decide fully, like everything else it does, is affected by its membership at any given time. The great majority of petitions are unlikely to be accepted no matter who is on the Court. But the composition of the cases the Supreme Court actually accepts in a term strongly reflects the identities of the justices who serve during that term.

Setting the Size of the Agenda

Since 1986, the year that William Rehnquist became chief justice, the number of petitions for certiorari per year has doubled. During the same period, the number of cases that the Supreme Court accepts for full consideration has been cut in half. Why have those trends run in opposite directions?

An answer to that question requires some historical perspective. The number of cases brought to the Court went up dramatically over the years, in a trend that culminated in the 1960s. That growth seemed to have several sources. Outside the Court, these sources included an apparent increase in "rights consciousness," which led people to bring more legal claims; the development of interest groups that assisted litigants in carrying cases through the courts; and massive growth in the activities of the federal government, which produced new laws and legal questions. The Court itself contributed to the growth in its caseload. In particular, its sympathy for claims that government actions violated civil liberties encouraged people who felt that their rights had been violated to bring cases to the Court.

By the 1970s, observers of the Court and the justices themselves argued that the larger number of cases had created problems for the Court and for federal law. For the Court, the perceived problem was that the justices' ability to do their work well was compromised by the increased volume of work. For federal law, the concern was that the Court was accepting a smaller proportion of petitions as their numbers grew, so important issues were going unresolved. But proposals to remedy these problems, including the creation of a new court to help the Supreme Court with its work, did not succeed.

After a period of relative stability in the Court's caseload, a second period of rapid growth began in the late 1980s and has continued since then. This new period of growth is quite different from the earlier one. As Figure 3-1 shows, it is limited to the paupers' petitions. The number of paid petitions per term has been fairly stable since the early 1970s, and it has actually declined since the late 1990s. In contrast, the number of paupers' petitions, which hovered around 2,000 per term from the late 1960s to the mid-1980s, grew to the point that there was an average of about 6,500 per term in the 2003–2007 terms—almost four times the number of paid petitions.

The preponderance of paupers' petitions come from prisoners, and the number of adults in prison more than quadrupled between 1980 and 2005.[82] This trend accounts for most if not all of the increase in paupers' cases. Indeed, this growth has occurred even though other factors that affect criminal petitions have worked in the opposite direction. The Court has become less favorable to the claims brought by criminal defendants since the 1960s, and more recently both Congress and the Court have limited the use of habeas corpus actions to challenge criminal convictions.

The pattern of growth in the Court's caseload over the last two decades helps to explain why the Court is not hearing more cases than it did in the mid-1980s. Paupers' petitions are always accepted at relatively low rates, and a Court that has become less sympathetic to claims by prisoners would not find many of those petitions worthy. But why would the Court hear only half as many cases as it did before?

Commentators and the justices themselves have offered several answers.[83] Some of these answers lie outside the Court. Acting at the justices' behest, Congress in 1988 greatly reduced the range of cases that are classified as appeals (rather than petitions for certiorari), which the Court is required to decide, and the Court now hears twenty to thirty fewer appeals each term than it did before 1988. Chief Justice Roberts and former solicitor general Paul Clement have cited a dearth of major new legislation from Congress and a declining number of conflicts between lower courts in

FIGURE 3-1

*Paid and Paupers' Cases Filed in the Supreme Court per Term,
by Five-Year Averages, 1958–2007 Terms*

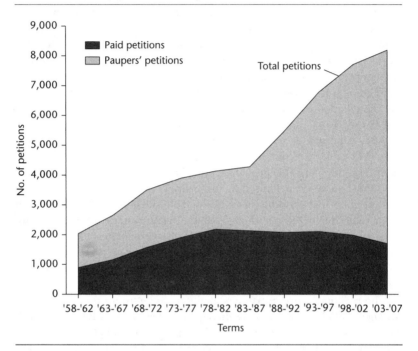

Sources: Gerhard Casper and Richard A. Posner, *The Workload of the Supreme Court* (Chicago:
American Bar Foundation, 1976), 34; "Statistical Recap of Supreme Court's Workload During
Last Three Terms," *United States Law Week,* various years; Supreme Court docket sheets.

their interpretations of legal questions, each reducing the need for the
Court to hear cases.[84] In recent years the solicitor general's office, with its
high rate of success in winning hearings for its petitions, has been bringing fewer cases to the Court. The overall number of paid petitions has
declined somewhat in recent years.

Other possible answers to this question lie within the Court. Two justices who were more inclined than most of their colleagues to accept
cases, Byron White and Harry Blackmun, left the Court in the mid-1990s.
And some observers think that the justices simply like having fewer cases
to decide, so that deciding cases takes less of their time. Even the justices
have lent some credence to that last explanation. When asked whether
the reduction in the number of Supreme Court decisions was good for the
legal system, Justice Scalia responded, "Well, it's good for me."[85] Justice
Stevens said in 2007 that the Court might be "taking fewer cases than we

Case files in the office of the Supreme Court's clerk. In recent years the Court has received an average of about eight thousand petitions for hearings per term. It has given full consideration to fewer than one hundred cases each term.

should. But if the rate was at a level of 150 cases a year, as it was in the past, I would have left the Court long ago."[86]

Although the validity of specific explanations can be debated, it seems clear that the decline in the number of cases that the Court decides reflects multiple factors. Overall, the justices themselves are probably a more important factor than conditions outside the Court.[87] The biggest cuts in the number of cases accepted came long before the number of paid petitions and petitions from the solicitor general declined. And even if there are fewer major statutes and fewer conflicts between lower courts than there were in the past, there is no shortage of cases that the Court reasonably could decide.

Justice Stevens raised the question of whether the Court should be accepting more cases than it does. As far back as the 1970s, there was a concern that with the Court accepting a smaller proportion of petitions as their numbers grew, important issues were going unresolved. And in 1987, before the Court drastically cut the number of cases it accepted, Chief Justice Rehnquist said that the Court was failing to hear some cases involving important legal questions that it would have heard thirty years earlier.[88] Yet not everyone agrees that there is a problem today. In 2003, for instance, Justice Kennedy said that the number of cases heard by the Court "frankly, is too low" but added that the Court was deciding the cases that merited its review.[89]

In any event, the difficulty of gaining a hearing in the Supreme Court has increased. In its 1985 term, the Court accepted for full consideration about 1 in 12 of the paid petitions filed with it. In the 2007 term that rate was 1 in 18. For paupers' petitions the decline was precipitous, from an already low 1 in 108 in 1985 to a spectacularly low 1 in 702 in 2007.[90] Given the worsening odds and the significant costs of filing a petition for those who use lawyers' services, it is not surprising that the number of paid petitions declined.

Conclusion

Like other courts, the Supreme Court can decide only the cases that come to it. For that reason, people and institutions outside the Court have a great effect on the Court's agenda. Ultimately, however, the Court determines which cases it hears. From the wide variety of legal and policy questions brought to the Court, the justices can choose the few that they will address fully. They can also choose which issues in a case they will decide. And the justices help determine which cases are brought to them by suggesting in their opinions what kinds of legal claims they will view favorably in future cases.

The Court is often criticized for its choices of cases to hear and turn aside, and in recent years it has also been criticized for the small number of cases it accepts each term. Whatever the validity of these criticisms may be, the justices employ their agenda-setting powers rather well to serve their purposes. They accept and reject cases on the basis of individual and collective goals, such as avoiding troublesome issues, resolving legal conflicts, and establishing policies that the justices favor. The justices' selection of cases for full decisions helps them shape the Court's role as a policymaker. They also use that process to limit their workloads.

After the Court selects the cases to hear, it decides those cases. In the next chapter, I examine the Court's decision-making process and the forces that shape its choices.

NOTES

1. This summary of the distribution of litigants across categories is based in part on Gregory A. Caldeira and John R. Wright, "Parties, Direct Representatives, and Agenda-Setting in the Supreme Court" (paper presented at the annual meeting of the Midwest Political Science Association, Chicago, April 1989).
2. The description of the *Glenn* case is based primarily on briefs and opinions in the case. The quotation is from Christopher S. Rugaber, "Court to Hear Case That Could Help Workers Claims Benefits," Associated Press, April 23, 2008.
3. The description of this case is based on stories in the news media, primarily Marcia Coyle, "Legal Trio Looks Ahead to High Court Gun-Ban Review," *National Law Journal,* November 26, 2007, 6; and Adam Liptak, "Carefully Plotted Course Propels Gun Case to Top," *New York Times,* December 3, 2007, A17; and on Brian Doherty, "How the Second Amendment Was Restored," *Reason* 40, (December 2008): 52–60.
4. Joseph Margulies, "A Prison beyond the Law," *Virginia Quarterly Review* 80 (fall 2004): 39.
5. Sacha Pfeifer, "Professor Leads Small Group in Battle with Legal Giants," *Boston Globe,* March 2, 2006, D1. The case was *DaimlerChrysler Corp. v. Cuno* (2006).
6. Tony Mauro, "Help Offered for High Court Criminal Cases," *Legal Times,* May 8, 2006, 1, 8.
7. Richard J. Lazarus, "Advocacy Matters Before and Within the Supreme Court: Transforming the Court by Transforming the Bar," *Georgetown Law Journal* 96 (May 2008): 1487–1564; Tom Goldstein, "The Expansion of the 'Supreme Court Bar,'" Scotusblog, March 2, 2006, at www.scotusblog.com/wp/. Mahoney's work is discussed in Marcia Coyle, "Latham Advocate Was a High Court Leader," *National Law Journal,* December 17, 2007, 16.
8. Marcia Coyle, "Justices Listen to a Key Voice," *National Law Journal,* April 7, 2008, 1, 17.
9. Maureen Groppe, "80% Success Rate at Supreme Court," *Indianapolis Star,* July 2, 2007.
10. Noam Scheiber, "The Hustler," *New Republic,* April 10, 2006, 14–19.
11. Brent Kendall, "Supreme Court—The Hottest Docket in Town," *Daily Journal of California,* April 22, 2008, available at http://pda-appellateblog.blogspot.com/2008_04_01_archive.html#4085373736375258215. The case was *Jimenez v. Quarterman* (2009).
12. Katie Mulvaney, "State, Town Can't Agree on Who Argues Tribal Land Case," *Providence Journal,* October 9, 2008; Tony Mauro, "Ted Olson Wins Supreme Court Showdown," The BLT: The Blog of Legal Times (http://legaltimes.typepad.com/), October 31, 2008. The case was *Carcieri v. Salazar* (2009).
13. Tony Mauro, "After a Year on the Court, Alito Holds Forth," *Legal Times,* February 12, 2007, 12.
14. Brent Kendall, "Getting on Scalia's Good Side," *Daily Journal* Newswire article, May 12, 2008, available at http://pda-appellateblog.blogspot.com/2008_05_01_archive.html#4396419852952598031.
15. "Stepping Back from the Fray," *Legal Times,* August 9, 2004, 24.

16. Tony Mauro, "Grapes of Wrath: Lawyers Locked in Fee Fight," *Legal Times,* April 10, 2006, 1.

17. Meg Kinnard, "Attorney: Jailhouse Lawyer Under Investigation for Legal Help," *The State* (Columbia, S.C.), February 26, 2008. The case was *Burgess v. United States* (2008).

18. Walter Dellinger, "Why Me?" *Journal of Appellate Practice and Process* 5 (spring 2003): 95.

19. "Wilmer Cutler Scores a High Court Hat Trick," *National Law Journal,* June 30, 2008, 3. The cases were, respectively, *Rothgery v. Gillespie County* (2008), *Dada v. Mukasey* (2008), and *Boumediene v. Bush* (2008).

20. Vesna Jaksic, "Firms Help Clinics Get Students to High Court," *National Law Journal,* April 7, 2008, S7; Pamela S. Karlan, Thomas C. Goldstein, and Amy Howe, "Go East, Young Lawyers: The Stanford Law School Supreme Court Litigation Clinic," *Journal of Appellate Practice and Process* 7 (fall 2005): 207–230.

21. Lazarus, "Advocacy Matters," 1491.

22. *Exxon Shipping Company v. Baker* (2008).

23. Bara Vaida, "Supreme Court Spinners," *National Journal,* October 21, 2006, 52–54. The case was *eBay v. MercExchange* (2006).

24. See Paul M. Collins Jr., *Friends of the Supreme Court: Interest Groups and Judicial Decision Making* (New York: Oxford University Press, 2008), 24–28.

25. This discussion of the *Kelo* case is based in part on materials on the Institute for Justice Web site, at www.ij.org.

26. On the use of amicus briefs, see Collins, *Friends of the Supreme Court,* 28–74.

27. These figures include only briefs submitted after a case was accepted for oral argument. The figures were compiled from docket sheets on the Supreme Court Web site, at www.supremecourtus.gov/docket/docket. html. Because of the way the docket sheets note briefs, the figures may be slight underestimates.

28. Lazarus, "Advocacy Matters," 1513–1514.

29. The discussion in this paragraph is based in part on Marcia Coyle, "Court Hears Many Voices in One Case," *National Law Journal,* May 1, 2000, A1, A12, A13. See Thomas G. Hansford, "Information Provision, Organizational Constraints, and the Decision to Submit an Amicus Curiae Brief in a U.S. Supreme Court Case," *Political Research Quarterly* 57 (June 2004): 219–230.

30. Marcia Coyle, "Amicus Briefs Are Ammo for Gun Case," *National Law Journal,* March 10, 2008, 1, 17.

31. Tony Mauro, "How 'Winning' Cases Took a Wrong Turn," *Legal Times,* July 4, 2005, 8.

32. The pre-2007 figures are from Joseph D. Kearney and Thomas W. Merrill, "The Influence of Amicus Curiae Briefs on the Supreme Court," *University of Pennsylvania Law Review* 148 (January 2000): 754n26. See also Ryan J. Owens and Lee Epstein, "Amici Curiae during the Rehnquist Years," *Judicature* 89 (November–December 2005): 127–132.

33. Adam Chandler, "Cert.-Stage Amicus Briefs: Who Files Them and to What Effect?" Scotusblog, September 27, 2007, at www.scotusblog.com/wp/.

34. See Samuel Walker, *In Defense of American Liberties: A History of the ACLU,* 2d ed. (Carbondale: Southern Illinois University Press, 1999).

35. *Grutter v. Bollinger* (2003); *Gratz v. Bollinger* (2003). See Shira Kantor, "Conservative Crusaders Target Affirmative Action in Court," *Chicago Tribune,* January 19, 2003, sec. 1, p. 10.

36. Steven P. Brown, *Trumping Religion: The New Christian Right, the Free Speech Clause, and the Courts* (Tuscaloosa: University of Alabama Press, 2002); Hans J. Hacker, *The Culture of Conservative Christian Litigation* (Lanham, Md.: Rowman and Littlefield, 2005).
37. Hansford, "Information Provision."
38. Charles R. Epp, *The Rights Revolution: Lawyers, Activists, and Supreme Courts in Comparative Perspective* (Chicago: University of Chicago Press, 1998), 44–70.
39. Most of the data on the federal government's participation that are discussed here and later in the chapter were provided by the Office of the Solicitor General.
40. This discussion is based in part on Richard L. Pacelle Jr., *Between Law and Politics: The Solicitor General and the Structuring of Race, Gender, and Reproductive Rights Litigation* (College Station: Texas A&M University Press, 2003).
41. Ibid.
42. Tony Mauro, "SG Won't Disavow Bush Position in Controversial DNA Case," The BLT: The Blog of Legal Times (http://legaltimes.typepad.com/), February 20, 2009. The case was *District Attorney's Office v. Osborne* (2009).
43. See David C. Thompson and Melanie F. Wachtell, "An Empirical Analysis of Supreme Court Certiorari Petition Procedures: The Call for Response and the Call for the Views of the Solicitor General," *George Mason Law Review* 16 (2009): 270–296.
44. Susan Beck, "Ensnared by Stoneridge," *The American Lawyer* 29 (September 2007): 71–73. The case was *Stoneridge Investment Partners v. Scientific-Atlanta* (2008).
45. Richard L. Pacelle Jr., "Amicus Curiae or Amicus Praseidentis? Reexamining the Role of the Solicitor General in Filing Amici," *Judicature* 89 (May–June 2006): 317–325.
46. These data were based on analysis of the Court's reports of decisions for the 2007 term.
47. The cases were *Dada v. Mukasey* (2008) and *Hall Street Associates v. Mattel* (2008).
48. See Michael E. Solimine and Rafael Gely, "The Supreme Court and the DIG: An Empirical and Institutional Analysis," *Wisconsin Law Review* 2005 (2005): 1421–1478.
49. See *Youngblood v. West Virginia* (2006) (GVR), and *Roper v. Weaver* (2007) (DIG).
50. John Paul Stevens, foreword, in Kenneth A. Manaster, *Illinois Justice: The Scandal of 1969 and the Rise of John Paul Stevens* (Chicago: University of Chicago Press, 2001), xi.
51. These figures are based on analysis of the Supreme Court's reports of decisions.
52. Wendy L. Watson, "The U.S. Supreme Court's Selection of Petitions *In Forma Pauperis*" (Ph.D. diss., Ohio State University, 2004), chap. 5; Ryan C. Black and Christina L. Boyd, "Litigant Status and Agenda Setting on the U.S. Supreme Court" (paper presented at the annual meeting of the Midwest Political Science Association, Chicago, April 2007).
53. Lyle Deniston, "Court Switches, Will Hear Detainee Cases," *Slate Magazine*, at www.slate.com, June 29, 2007. The Court's treatment of the case is chronicled by its official docket sheet at the Supreme Court's Web site, at www.supremecourtus.gov/docket/docket.html.

54. Examples include *Joseph v. United States* (2007) and *Frazier v. Ohio* (2008).
55. *Walker v. Georgia* (2008).
56. Artemus Ward and David L. Weiden, *Sorcerers' Apprentices: 100 Years of Law Clerks at the United States Supreme Court* (New York: New York University Press, 2006), 126.
57. Adam Liptak, "'Cert. Pool,' a Longtime Custom among the Justices, Loses One of Them," *New York Times*, September 26, 2008, A21.
58. Tony Mauro, "Roberts May Look to Stay Out of the Pool," *Legal Times*, August 15, 2005, available at www.legaltimes.com.
59. David R. Stras, "The Supreme Court's Gatekeepers: The Role of Law Clerks in the Certiorari Process," *Texas Law Review* 85 (2007): 972–976; Elizabeth Francis Ward, "Clerks Avoid Getting Their DIGs In," *American Bar Association Journal* 93 (March 2007): 12–13.
60. William H. Rehnquist, *The Supreme Court*, new ed. (New York: Alfred A. Knopf, 2001), 233.
61. Barbara Palmer, "The 'Bermuda Triangle?' The Cert Pool and Its Influence Over the Supreme Court's Agenda," *Constitutional Commentary* 18 (2001): 111; Stras, "Supreme Court's Gatekeepers," 976–980.
62. *Northwest Airlines v. Spirit Airlines* (2006). See Tony Mauro, "Friends in High Court Places," *Legal Times*, September 18, 2006, 10.
63. The case was *Claiborne v. United States* (2007).
64. Tom Miller, "Breyer Speaks to Bar Convention," *Alaska Bar Rag*, May–June 2001, 10.
65. "Judicial Conference, Second Judicial Circuit of the United States," 178 *Federal Rules Decisions* 210, 282 (1997).
66. This discussion draws from Arthur D. Hellman, "Never the Same River Twice: The Empirics and Epistemology of Intercircuit Conflicts," *University of Pittsburgh Law Review* 63 (fall 2001): 81–157.
67. Thomas Goldstein, "One Plugged, Thousands to Go," *Legal Times*, November 18, 2002, 68.
68. Stras, "Supreme Court's Gatekeepers," 980–985.
69. Tony Mauro, "Court Aces," *Legal Times*, July 14, 2003, 11.
70. *Crawford v. Marion County Election Board* (2008).
71. The proportion for the Supreme Court is based on data in the Supreme Court Database, compiled by Harold Spaeth, available at www.cas.sc.edu/poli/juri/sctdata.htm. The proportion for the courts of appeals is based on data in Administrative Office of the United States Courts, *Judicial Business of the United States Courts: Report of the Director, 2007* (Washington, D.C.: Administrative Office of the U.S. Courts, n.d.), 113, and the same report for earlier years.
72. H. W. Perry Jr., *Deciding to Decide: Agenda Setting in the United States Supreme Court* (Cambridge: Harvard University Press, 1991), 198–207; quotation, 200.
73. Gregory A. Caldeira, John R. Wright, and Christopher J. W. Zorn, "Sophisticated Voting and Gate-Keeping in the Supreme Court," *Journal of Law, Economics, and Organization* 15 (October 1999): 549–572; Saul Brenner and Joseph Whitmeyer, *Strategy on the United States Supreme Court* (New York: Cambridge University Press, 2009), chap. 5.
74. *Washington v. Recuenco*, 548 U.S. 212, 223 (2006). The other cases were *Kansas v. Marsh* (2006) and *Brigham City v. Stuart* (2006).
75. This figure, based on data supplied by the solicitor general's office, does not include cases that the office asked the Court to hold pending a

decision in another case or cases in which the Court granted certiorari and
immediately remanded the case to the lower court.

76. Lazarus, "Advocacy Matters," 1515–1517, 1522–1528.
77. Oral argument, *Vaden v. Discover Bank,* docket number 07-773, 45.
78. John J. Bursch, "Petitions for Certiorari: Understanding the Hidden
    Process," *Appellate Issues* 7 (February 2008) available at www.abanet.org/
    jd/ajc/calnewsletters/200708/article6.pdf.
79. The 2004 case was *Banks v. Dretke.* See Lee Hockstader, "Ex-FBI Chief,
    Judges Take Interest in Texas Execution," *Washington Post,* March 10, 2003,
    A2. The 2006 case was *Angelos v. United States.* The list of signers in the
    Angelos case was taken from "Brief of Amicus Curiae 145 Individuals …,"
    Angelos v. United States, docket number 06-26.
80. Charles Lane, "Court Declines to Wade into Battle on Judge," *Washington
    Post,* March 22, 2005, A15. The cases were *Evans v. Stephens* (2005),
    Miller v. United States (2005), and *Franklin v. United States* (2005).
81. The case was *Herring v. United States* (2006); the earlier decision was *United
    States v. Reynolds* (1953). See Barry Siegel, *Claim of Privilege: A Mysterious
    Plane Crash, a Landmark Supreme Court Case, and the Rise of State Secrets* (New
    York: HarperCollins, 2008).
82. U.S. Census Bureau, *Statistical Abstract of the United States: 2008* (Washington,
    D.C.: U.S. Government Printing Office, 2008), 211.
83. Linda Greenhouse, "Case of the Dwindling Docket Mystifies the Supreme
    Court," *New York Times,* December 7, 2006, A1 A30; Robert Barnes, "Justices
    Continue Trend of Hearing Fewer Cases," *Washington Post,* January 7,
    2007, A4.
84. Robert Barnes, "Roberts Supports Court's Shrinking Docket," *Washington
    Post,* February 2, 2007, A6; "Solicitor General: Supreme Court's Shrinking
    Caseload Due to Fewer Laws Enacted by Congress, More Harmony in
    Circuit Courts," available at www.law.harvard.edu/news/2007/11/02soli-
    citor.php.
85. M. R. Kropko, "Justice Scalia Says Smaller Docket Leads to Better Opinions,"
    Associated Press, January 10, 2007.
86. Pamela A. MacLean, "9th Circuit Reversal Rate Is Misleading," *National
    Law Journal,* July 30, 2007, 14.
87. Kevin M. Scott, "Shaping the Supreme Court's Federal Certiorari Docket,"
    Justice System Journal 27 (2006): 191–207.
88. "Chief Justice Urges National Appeals Court, Repeal of Court's Mandatory
    Jurisdiction," *Third Branch,* July 1987, 1, 5.
89. U.S. House of Representatives, *Departments of Commerce, Justice, and State, the
    Judiciary, and Related Agencies Appropriations for 2004: Hearings before a
    Subcommittee of the Committee on Appropriations,* 108th Cong., 1st sess, April 9,
    2003, 253.
90. These figures are based on data in "Statistical Recap of Supreme Court's
    Workload during Last Three Terms," *United States Law Week,* various years,
    and analysis of the Court's reports of decisions for the 2007 term.

Chapter 4

Decision Making

O nce the Supreme Court determines which cases to hear, the justices get to the heart of their work: reaching decisions in those cases. This chapter examines how and why the Court makes its decisions.

Components of the Court's Decision

A Supreme Court decision on the merits has two components: the immediate outcome for the parties to the case and a statement of general legal rules. In cases that the Court fully considers, it nearly always presents the two components in an opinion. In the great majority of cases, at least five justices subscribe to this opinion. As a result, it constitutes an authoritative statement by the Court.

Opinions for the Court vary in form, but an opinion usually begins with a description of the background of the case. The opinion then turns to the legal issues in the case, with a discussion of the opposing views on those issues and a description of the Court's conclusions about them. A summary of the outcome for the parties ends the opinion.

Except in the few cases the Court hears under its original jurisdiction, the Court describes the outcome in relation to the lower-court decision it is reviewing. The Court can affirm the lower-court decision, leaving that court's treatment of the parties undisturbed. Alternatively, it can modify or reverse the lower-court decision. In general, a reversal overturns the lower-court decision altogether or nearly so, and modification is a more limited, partial overturning. Frequently the Court "vacates" (makes void) the lower-court decision, an action whose effect is similar to that of reversal.

When the Court does disturb a lower-court decision, it sometimes makes a final judgment. More often, it remands the case to the lower court, sending it back for reconsideration. The Court's opinion provides guidance on how the case should be reconsidered. For example, the opinion in a tax case may say that a court of appeals adopted the wrong interpretation of the federal tax laws and that the lower court should reexamine the case on the basis of a different interpretation. The Court's opinion in a 2008 case used typical language: "The judgment of the Court of Appeals is vacated, and the case is remanded for further proceedings consistent with this opinion."[1]

In most cases, the outcome has little impact beyond the parties themselves. Rather, what makes most decisions consequential is the statement of general legal rules that apply to the nation as a whole. When the Court's opinion resolves the legal issues in a case, it is not just providing guidance to a specific lower court in a specific case. It is also laying down rules that any court must follow in a case to which they apply and that can affect the behavior of people outside of court. As a result, decisions that directly affect only a few people may have a substantial indirect effect on thousands or even millions of other people.

The Court has choices about which legal rules it establishes in a case, just as it does about the outcome for the parties. A ruling for one of the parties often could be justified on any of several grounds, and the ground chosen by the Court helps to determine the long-term impact of its decision. If the Court overturns the death sentence for a particular defendant, it might base that decision on an unusual error in the defendant's trial, so that its decision would affect few other defendants. Alternatively, the Court could declare that the death penalty is unconstitutional under all circumstances and thereby make a fundamental policy change.

The Decision-Making Process

When the Court accepts a case for a decision on the merits, it initiates the decision-making process for that case. That process varies from case to case, but it typically involves several stages.

Presentation of Cases to the Court

The written briefs that the Court receives when it considers whether to hear a case usually give some attention to the merits of the case. Once a case has been accepted for oral argument and decision, attorneys for the parties submit new briefs that focus only on the merits. In the preponderance of cases that reach this stage, interest groups submit amicus curiae briefs stating their own arguments on the merits.

Most of the material in these briefs concerns legal issues. The parties muster evidence to support their interpretations of relevant constitutional provisions and statutes. In their briefs they frequently offer arguments about policy as well, seeking to persuade the justices that support for their position constitutes not only good law but good public policy.

Debo Adegbile of the NAACP Legal Defense and Education Fund arguing before the Supreme Court in 2009. Oral argument allows justices to probe issues in a case and try to influence their colleagues' views about the case.

Material in the briefs is supplemented by attorneys' presentations in oral argument before the Court. Attorneys for the parties to a case sometimes share their time with the lawyer for an amicus, usually the federal government. In most cases, each side is provided half an hour for its argument. When time expires a red light goes on at the attorneys' lectern. Chief Justice Rehnquist enforced the time limit strictly, but Chief Justice Roberts is sometimes more lenient. In an unusually complex case that was argued in 2007, the argument went twenty-six minutes longer than the scheduled one hour.[2] Lawyers and the justices who question them typically use all the time available. But in a 2008 case a lawyer who was arguing her first case for the federal government sat down after seven minutes. Apparently she thought there was no need to say any more, and if so she was right: three weeks later the Court issued a unanimous ruling for the government.[3]

Lawyers' presentations are often interrupted by questions and comments from members of the Court. As one observer said, "The lawyers show up with a big notebook full of speaking points, and the justices make it their business to make sure they never get to the second one."[4] In one argument John Paul Stevens told a lawyer that he wanted to hear a list of six arguments that the lawyer had promised, "without interruption from all of my colleagues."[5] Antonin Scalia is the most active questioner, but several other justices participate frequently. Samuel Alito has said that because of the barrage of questions from his colleagues, he finds it "extremely difficult to get a question in."[6] For his part, Clarence Thomas seldom asks questions during oral argument. One reason, he has said, is that "these people only have 30 minutes. Let them talk a little bit. We're not there to debate with them."[7] In a speech he put the same idea more simply: "My colleagues should shut up!"[8]

Oral argument gives attorneys a chance to support their cases by supplementing and highlighting the material in their briefs. For the justices, the argument has two broad functions. First, it allows them to gather information about the strengths and weaknesses of the parties' positions and about other aspects of the case that interest them. In part to serve this function, justices often raise new ideas and arguments in their questions to the lawyers.[9]

Second, oral argument provides a forum in which justices try to shape their colleagues' perceptions of a case. Justice Alito has reported that the justices seldom discuss cases with each other prior to oral argument,[10] so the argument gives them the first good opportunity to communicate their views to their colleagues. In particular, justices try to expose weaknesses in the arguments of the other side. Before he joined the Court, Chief Justice Roberts noticed what scholars have documented: justices tend to ask more questions of the side they ultimately vote against.[11]

Justice Scalia stands out for his use of oral argument to support the side he favors. Reporter Dahlia Lithwick wrote after one argument that her "choice for best oral advocate *ever* to appear before the U.S. Supreme Court is Associate Justice Antonin Scalia. While Scalia is a distinguished jurist, I'm not sure he always gets the credit he deserves on those days, like today, when he actually finds himself both hearing and arguing a case at the same time." Scalia asks tough questions of lawyers, but he also tries to help attorneys on the side he favors. Lithwick described Scalia as "co-counsel" to one lawyer who was arguing a case.[12] In a 2008 argument, Stephen Breyer asked a question of one of the lawyers. Before the lawyer could say anything, Scalia told him, "You want to say yes." When the lawyer did get a chance to answer, he said, "The answer is yes, as Justice Scalia noted."[13]

Tentative Decisions

After oral argument the Court discusses each case in one of its conferences later the same week. The chief justice begins the discussion of a case, which continues with the other justices from most senior to most junior. The justices indicate their vote in the case and the reasons for their positions.

Chief Justice Rehnquist enforced tight limits on conference discussion of cases. Those limits reflected his view that discussion would have little impact, since the justices typically come to the conference with strong views about the cases. He concluded that "it is very much the exception" for justices' minds to be changed in conference.[14]

Justice Stevens reports that "I think we take a little more time under Chief Justice Roberts than we did with Bill Rehnquist. But it's essentially the same."[15] One similarity is that the discussion remains structured. As Roberts describes it, "one of the strict rules ... is that nobody gets to speak twice until everyone has spoken once."[16]

After each two-week sitting, the writing of the Court's opinion in each case is assigned to a justice. If the chief justice voted with the majority, the chief assigns the opinion. In other cases, the most senior associate justice in the majority makes the assignment.

Reaching Final Decisions

The justice who was assigned the Court's opinion writes an initial draft, guided by the views expressed in conference. The justice's clerks often do most of the drafting. Once this opinion is completed and circulated, justices in the original majority usually sign on to it.[17] Sometimes, however, justices hold back rather than signing on, either because they have developed doubts about their original vote or because they disagree with some of the language in the draft opinion. The language is important, because justices are reluctant to sign on to an opinion when they disagree with its reasoning. Indeed, Justice Scalia reported in 2003 that he could not recall any instance in which he had done so.[18] Members of the original minority also read the draft opinion for the Court. They might decide to sign on to the opinion because their view of the case has changed, or they might see a possibility of signing on if the opinion is modified.

Justices who do not immediately sign on may indicate fundamental disagreement with the opinion. Exaggerating somewhat, Justice Thomas has described such responses: "Dear Clarence, I disagree with everything in your opinion except your name. Cheers."[19] But justices often indicate that they would be willing to join an opinion if certain changes are made. Justices who voted with the majority are especially likely to ask for changes. Their memos initiate a process of explicit or implicit negotiation in which the assigned justice tries to gain the support of as many colleagues as possible. At the least, that justice wants to maintain the original majority for the outcome supported by the opinion and to win a majority for the language of the opinion, so that it becomes the official statement of the Court.

In this effort, the justice who was assigned the Court's opinion often competes with other justices, who write alternative opinions supporting the opposite outcome or arguing for the same outcome with a different rationale. Most of the time, assigned justices succeed in winning a majority for their opinions, although sometimes with substantial alterations. More often than not, however, they fail to win the unanimous support of their colleagues. As shown in Table 4-1, which lists several attributes of the Court's decisions in the 2007 term, such unanimity was achieved only 21 percent of the time.

TABLE 4-1

Selected Characteristics of Supreme Court Decisions, 2007 Term

Characteristic	Number	Percentage
Number of decisions	70	NA
Vote for Court's decision[a]		
Unanimous	22	31
Nonunanimous	48	69
Support for Court's opinion		
Unanimous for whole opinion	15	21
Unanimous for part of opinion	3	4
Majority but not unanimous	47	67
Majority for only part of opinion	2	3
No majority for opinion	3	4
One or more concurring opinions[b]	31	44
One or more dissenting opinions[c]	48	69
Total number of opinions		
Concurring	45	NA
Dissenting	66	NA

Source: The decisions included are those listed in the front section of *United States Supreme Court Reports, Lawyers' Edition*, vols. 169–171, and information on cases is taken from that source.

Note: NA = not applicable.

a. "Decision" refers to the outcome for the parties. Partial dissents are not counted as votes for the decision.
b. Opinions labeled "concurring and dissenting" are treated as dissenting opinions.
c. Some concurring opinions are in full agreement with the Court's opinion.

Occasionally, no opinion gains the support of a majority. That occurred three times in the 2007 term, and in two other cases there was a majority for only a portion of an opinion. (In one case in the preceding term, Justice Ginsburg failed to win a majority for her full opinion because three colleagues disagreed with one of her footnotes.)[20] Without a majority opinion, there is no authoritative statement of the Court's position on the legal issues in the case. The opinion on the winning side with the greatest support—the "plurality opinion"—may, however, specify the points for which majority support exists.

On rare occasions the justices find themselves unable to reach a final decision in a case before the term ends. They then schedule the case for a second set of oral arguments, usually in the following term. The Court took this route in both *Brown v. Board of Education* (1954) and *Roe v. Wade* (1973). It also heard rearguments in three cases that were originally heard early in the 2005 term. In each case Justice O'Connor had been part of a 5–4 majority, but Justice Alito succeeded her before the Court's work on the case was completed. Left with a 4–4 tie in each case, the Court held a second argument so that Alito could participate. In all three cases, as expected, Alito ended up as part of a 5–4 majority.[21]

Concurring and Dissenting Opinions

In most cases, an opinion gains a majority but lacks unanimous support. Disagreement with the majority opinion can take two forms. First, a justice may cast a dissenting vote, which expresses disagreement with the result reached by the Court as it affects the parties to a case. If a criminal conviction is reversed, for example, a justice who believes it should have been affirmed will dissent. Second, a justice may concur with the Court's decision, agreeing with the result in the specific case but differing with the rationale expressed in the Court's opinion. Both kinds of disagreement are common. As Table 4-1 shows, dissenting votes are especially common, appearing in a majority of decisions.

A justice who disagrees with the majority opinion nearly always writes or joins in a dissenting or concurring opinion. Because they are individual expressions rather than statements for the Court, both types of opinions can vary a great deal in length, form, and tone. For the same reason, they usually reveal more about the author's views, and often express those views in more colorful language, than do majority opinions.

When the conference vote is not unanimous, the senior dissenting justice assigns the dissenting opinion. This opinion is written at the same time as the assigned opinion for the majority, and one aim often is to persuade enough colleagues to change their positions that a minority becomes a majority.

After the Court reaches its final decision, this aim is no longer relevant, but issuing a dissenting opinion can serve several purposes. For one thing, dissenting opinions give justices the satisfaction of expressing unhappiness with the result in a case and justifying their disagreement. Dissenting opinions sometimes have more concrete purposes as well. Through their arguments, dissenters may try to set the stage for a later Court to adopt their view. In the short term, a dissenting opinion may be intended to subvert the Court's decision by pointing out how lower courts can interpret it narrowly or by urging Congress to overturn the Court's reading of a statute. This is one reason that majority opinions sometimes respond to dissents.

When more than one justice dissents, the dissenters usually join in a single opinion—most likely the one originally assigned. But often there are multiple dissenting opinions, each expressing the particular view of the justice who wrote it but sometimes indicating agreement with another opinion.

As noted earlier, a concurring opinion can disagree with the majority opinion on the rationale for a decision. This kind of opinion is labeled a "special concurrence." Sometimes this disagreement on doctrine is virtually total, in that the majority and concurring opinions agree on nothing other than the outcome of the case. In some other cases the disagreement is quite limited.

Another type of concurring opinion, a "regular concurrence," is written by justices who join the majority opinion, indicating that they agree with both the outcome for the litigants and the legal rules that the Court establishes. Under those circumstances, why would justices write separate opinions? Most often, they offer their own interpretation of the majority opinion as a means to influence lower courts and other audiences as well as the Court itself in future cases. For example, Justice Alito wrote in a 2008 concurrence, "I join the Court's opinion because I do not understand it to hold that a defendant is entitled to the assistance of appointed counsel as soon as his Sixth Amendment right attaches."[22] Occasionally, as in a 2007 opinion by Justice Thomas, a regular concurrence addresses the arguments in a dissenting opinion.[23]

Announcing the Decision

The decision-making process for a case ends when all the opinions have been put in final form and all justices have determined which opinions they will join. The Supreme Court is unusual in that it announces its decisions in a court session, in what one commentator called "ceremonial showtime."[24] Typically, the justice who wrote the majority opinion reads a portion of the opinion. Occasionally—on average, about four times a term between 1994 and 2008—the authors of dissenting opinions also read portions of their opinions.[25] They sometimes add biting remarks, such as Justice Stevens's 2008 admonition about a majority opinion that Justice Scalia had announced: "Do not accept the summary you have just heard."[26]

The length of time required for a case to go through all the stages from filing in the Court to the announcement of a decision can vary a good deal. The cases that the Court decided after full consideration in June 2008 were filed as early as November 2006 and as late as October 2007. The Court's decision often comes long after the incident that triggered the case. In 1989 a ship ran aground off the Alaskan coast, causing a massive oil spill. The Court ruled in *Exxon Shipping Company v. Baker* (2008) that the punitive damages awarded against Exxon were excessive. That decision came nineteen years after the oil spill, fourteen years after the trial verdict in which the damages were awarded.

After the Court decides a case—or declines to hear it—the losing party may petition for a rehearing. Such petitions are rarely granted. In *Kennedy v. Louisiana* (2008), a death penalty case, none of the briefs on the merits had informed the Court of a federal law that had some relevance to the case, so the Court did not take the law into account. When the federal law came to light after the decision, Louisiana—supported by the federal government—asked the Court to rehear the case and take the federal law into account. The Court denied the petition, although two of the original four dissenters in the case did vote for a rehearing.

Influences on Decisions: Introduction

Of all the questions that might be asked about the Supreme Court, the one that has intrigued people most is how the Court's decisions are best explained. Cases present the justices with choices: which party to support, what rules of law to establish. On what bases do they make their choices?

This question is difficult to answer. Like policymakers elsewhere in government, Supreme Court justices act on the basis of several considerations, and those considerations are mixed together. Because of this complexity, people who study the Court disagree sharply about how best to explain the Court's decisions.

The rest of this chapter is devoted to this question. No conclusive answer is possible, but some insight into the bases for the Court's decisions can be gained by examining four broad forces that shape those decisions: the state of the legal rules the Court interprets, the justices' personal values, interaction among the justices, and the Court's political and social environment. The sections that follow each consider one of these forces.

The State of the Law

Every case requires the Supreme Court to interpret the law, usually in the form of constitutional provisions or federal statutes. In this sense a justice's job is different from that of a legislator: justices interpret existing law rather than write new law. For this reason, the state of the existing law is a good starting point for an explanation of the Court's decisions.

The Law's Significance in Decisions

Judges and justices are servants of the law, not the other way around. Judges are like umpires. Umpires don't make the rules; they apply them. The role of an umpire and a judge is critical. They make sure everybody plays by the rules. But it is a limited role. Nobody ever went to a ball game to see the umpire.[27]

In his opening remarks before the Senate Judiciary Committee in 2005, Chief Justice nominee John Roberts articulated one view about the role of the law in Supreme Court positions. In effect, Roberts was saying that

Umpire Dan Iassogna calls Orlando Cabrera of the Angels safe in a game against the Yankees in 2007. At his confirmation hearing in 2005, Chief Justice John Roberts said that "judges are like umpires," who apply rules rather than making them. Some commentators disagree with this description of the Supreme Court's work.

the law is the *only* explanation of what the Court does, that its decisions simply reflect the provisions of law it is called upon to interpret and the appropriate rules for interpreting those provisions. Other justices have taken the same position. In 2007, for instance, Justice Clarence Thomas offered a similar analogy: "We're like referees. We're neutral. And we use the rules given to us."[28]

But this description of the justices' work evokes considerable disagreement. For instance, federal judge and legal scholar Richard Posner has argued that Roberts's conception of judges as umpires is highly unrealistic.[29] Scholars have pointed to two realities that conflict with Roberts's view of decision making on the Supreme Court.

One reality is what might be called the legal ambiguity of the cases the Court decides. In at least the great majority of cases the Court chooses to hear, the proper interpretation of the Constitution or a federal statute is uncertain—often quite uncertain. As a result, a good case can be made for either side on the basis of the applicable legal rules.

A second reality is that justices care about more than the law. In particular, they often hold strong preferences about the policy issues involved in cases. Understandably, they are happier if their position in a case is consistent with their policy preferences than if their position conflicts with their conception of good policy. Thus, unlike umpires, members of the Supreme Court have rooting interests in the cases they decide.

Facing ambiguous legal issues and caring about the policy issues in the case, justices may act consciously to reach decisions that accord with their policy preferences. But even if justices try only to interpret the law properly, they will tend toward the interpretation that is most consistent with their policy preferences. One of Justice Frankfurter's law clerks described that process well in talking about Frankfurter.

He felt very intensely about lots of things, and sometimes he didn't realize that his feelings and his deeply felt values were pushing him as a judge relentlessly in one direction rather than another. I'm sure that you can put these things aside consciously, but what's underneath the consciousness you can't control.[30]

Thus, it is understandable that in most cases the justices disagree among themselves about the outcome for the litigants, the legal rules to adopt, or both. The primary reason for those disagreements is that the ambiguity of the law causes justices with different preferences to reach different conclusions.

Because of this reality some observers of the Court take a position directly opposite to that of Chief Justice Roberts and Justice Thomas, arguing that the state of the law has essentially no impact on the justices' choices.[31] This argument certainly can be defended, but there is good reason to conclude that legal considerations do have an impact on the justices' choices. Even if decisions on either side of a case could be justified under the law, the law may weigh more heavily on one side than the other. If the justices care about making good law, they will be drawn toward the side that seems to have a stronger legal argument.

And there is excellent reason to think that justices do care about making good law. They have been trained in a tradition that emphasizes the law as a basis for judicial decisions. They are evaluated informally by a peer group of judges and legal scholars who care about their ability to reach well-founded interpretations of the law. Perhaps most important, they work in the language of the law. The arguments they receive in written briefs and oral arguments are primarily about the law. The same is true of arguments they make to each other in draft opinions and memoranda.[32]

Indeed, some aspects of the justices' behavior indicate that the law does affect their choices.[33] Sometimes they take positions that seem to conflict with their conceptions of good policy. In a 2008 opinion, for instance, Justice Stevens voted to uphold New York's system for election of judges but cited former justice Thurgood Marshall's aphorism that "the Constitution does not prohibit legislatures from enacting stupid laws."[34] Sometimes the justices in the majority are sufficiently unhappy with their interpretation of a statute that they ask Congress to consider rewriting the statute to override their decision—that is, to establish a policy that the justices feel powerless to adopt themselves because of their reading of the law.[35]

Means of Interpretation

The role of the law in the Court's decisions can be probed further by considering the techniques that the justices use to interpret provisions of the law, and these techniques are also important in themselves. Most fit into a few broad approaches.

Plain Meaning. In the most basic approach, judges analyze the literal meaning of the words in the law. Nearly everyone agrees that interpretation of a legal provision should begin with a search for what is called the "plain meaning" of constitutional and statutory provisions. Some judges, such as Justice Antonin Scalia, strongly emphasize the text of the law they are interpreting as a basis for their decisions.

The plain meaning of a legal provision is not always obvious, and this is especially true in the cases that the Supreme Court considers. Many of the Court's decisions involve interpretation of the Constitution, and the Constitution is written in broad language that often has no plain meaning. This is true, for instance, of the "due process of law" clause in the Fourteenth Amendment. The First Amendment states that "Congress shall make no law ... abridging the freedom of speech," but justices and commentators have disagreed about the meaning of "freedom of speech" and even of "speech."

Federal statutes are typically less vague than the Constitution, but often their provisions as well are unclear in their meaning. The statutory cases that the Court decides tend to involve issues on which Congress has not spoken clearly. In these cases justices can do their best to ascertain the most reasonable interpretation of the words in a statute, but there may be considerable room for disagreement.

Even when a legal provision seems to have a clear meaning, the justices do not always adhere to it. That is especially true in constitutional law. Over time the Court has accepted several interpretations of the Constitution that depart from the language of its provisions. The due process clause of the Fifth Amendment requires only that the federal government follow proper procedures in taking "life, liberty, or property," but the Court interprets it to prohibit discrimination.[36] It interprets the same language in the Fourteenth Amendment as a protection of freedom of expression and freedom of religion.[37] And for more than a century the Court has read the Eleventh Amendment's prohibition of lawsuits against states "by citizens of another state" to prohibit most lawsuits against a state by the state's own residents as well.[38]

Why have the justices adopted and adhered to these seemingly inaccurate interpretations? The primary reason is that doing so advances values that are important to them, values such as protecting freedom of speech. The general acceptance of these "constitutional fictions" shows that no justice always adheres to the plain meaning of the law.

Intent of Framers or Legislators. When the plain meaning of a legal provision is unclear, justices can seek to ascertain the intentions of those who wrote the provision. Evidence concerning legislative intent can be found in congressional committee reports and floor debates, which constitute what is called the "legislative history" of a statute or a constitutional amendment. For provisions of the original Constitution, similar evidence is found in records of the Constitutional Convention of 1787.

Sometimes the intent of Congress or the framers of the Constitution is fairly clear. Frequently, however, it is not. The body that adopted a provision may not have spoken on an issue; the members of Congress who wrote the broad language of the Fourteenth Amendment could hardly indicate their intent concerning all the issues that have arisen under that amendment. And evidence about intent may be contradictory, in part because of conflicting efforts to influence the courts. Committee reports, seemingly a good indication of what members of Congress had in mind, often represent the views of congressional staff more than those of the members.

There is currently a heated debate on the Court about the use of legislative intent in interpreting statutes. The leading opponent is Justice Scalia, who views legislative history as illegitimate: he argues that it is the language of the statute, not legislators' intent, that governs. Further, he sees legislative history as an uncertain and easily distorted guide to congressional intent. Accordingly, Scalia does not refer to legislative history himself and distances himself from its use by his colleagues. In *Hall Street Associates v. Mattel* (2008), for instance, he joined the Court's majority opinion except for a footnote that analyzed the legislative history of the statute in question.

Scalia has gained some support for his view from colleagues, primarily other conservatives, and the Court's use of legislative history declined after he joined the Court.[39] But some justices—most vocally, Justice Stevens—continue to favor the use of legislative history. In a 2006 decision, Scalia's dissenting opinion criticized Stevens's majority opinion in very strong terms for its reliance on legislative history to interpret a statute. Stevens responded by criticizing Scalia for ignoring what Stevens saw as the clear evidence of the statute's meaning in the legislative history.[40]

A somewhat different debate about interpretation of the Constitution involves plain meaning as well as legislative intent. Some people argue that the Court should adhere to the meaning of constitutional provisions at the time they were adopted, a meaning reflected in how words in the Constitution were understood at that time. Others believe the Court should interpret the Constitution according to the current meaning of its language and its underlying values. Taking the first position, Justice Scalia criticized judges and justices who "have invented this notion of a living Constitution, where the interpretation of the Constitution could change." Taking the second position, Justice Ginsburg argued that "no one would say that the Constitution means today what it meant when it was written."[41]

To a considerable extent this is an ideological debate, with liberals wanting the freedom to adopt broad interpretations of constitutional rights. The debate has been especially heated on capital punishment. The Court's decisions prohibiting the death penalty for people who are mentally retarded (in 2002), for murders committed when the defendant was not yet eighteen years old (in 2005), and for sexual assaults of children (in 2008) were based on the majority's view that the prohibition of "cruel and unusual punishments" in the Eighth Amendment should be interpreted on the basis of current values. The conservative dissenters in each case gave greater emphasis to the meaning of "cruel and unusual" when the Eighth Amendment was written and strongly criticized the majority for its approach to interpretation of the Constitution.[42]

Precedent. The Supreme Court's past decisions, its precedents, provide another guide to decision making. A basic doctrine of the law is *stare decisis* (let the decision stand). Under this doctrine a court is bound to adhere to the rules of law established by courts that stand above it. No court stands above the Supreme Court, but *stare decisis* includes an expectation that courts will generally adhere to their own precedents.

Technically, a court is expected to follow not everything stated in a relevant precedent but only the rule of law that is necessary for decision in that case—what is called the holding. In *District of Columbia v. Heller* (2008), the Court ruled that the Second Amendment protects the right of individuals to possess guns and struck down a Washington, D.C., law on the ground that it infringed that right. That was the holding of the case. The Court's opinion also described types of gun regulations that were "presumptively lawful." Because those regulations were not involved in this case, that part of the Court's opinion was "dictum," which has no legal force. The distinction between holding and dictum is not always so clear, however, and one federal judge has complained that the courts—including the Supreme Court—increasingly fail to distinguish between them.[43]

The rule of adhering to precedent would not eliminate ambiguity in legal interpretation even if the justices followed it strictly. Most cases before the Supreme Court concern issues that are at least marginally different from those decided in past cases, so precedents do not lead directly to a particular outcome. Indeed, justices often "distinguish" a precedent, holding that it does not govern the current case. They may also narrow a precedent without overturning it altogether. Since the 1970s, the Court has used both methods to limit the reach of major Warren Court decisions on issues such as the rights of criminal defendants.

The Court explicitly abandons some precedents, and it has done so at an unusually high rate since 1960. By one count, the Court overruled only ninety-four precedents in its history through 1959 but issued eighty-four overrulings in the twenty years from 1960 through 1979. The pace has slowed since then, but the fifty-nine overrulings between 1980 and 2008, about two per year, is still a much higher rate than in the period prior to 1960.[44]

In the current era, every justice votes to overrule some precedents. Clarence Thomas is especially inclined to do so, because he believes there is no reason to maintain a specific precedent or a line of Court doctrine if it is faulty. Exaggerating somewhat, Justice Scalia has said of Thomas that "he does not believe in *stare decisis,* period."[45] Indeed, Thomas has written a good many opinions in which he argues that a precedent in constitutional law should be overruled or at least reconsidered. Scalia has joined some of these opinions and authored similar ones himself.

Inevitably, justices' reactions to precedents are affected by their evaluations of those precedents as legal policy. Most of the time, justices continue to reject a precedent that they opposed when it was originally established.[46] By the same token, the ideological content of a precedent affects justices' responses to it. For instance, conservative justices are more willing to overrule liberal precedents than are their liberal colleagues. In 2007 the Court overruled a century-old precedent that made it easier to prove a violation of the Sherman antitrust law under certain circumstances.[47] The Court's vote was 5–4. Liberals tend to favor broad interpretations of antitrust laws, and the dissenters in the 2007 case were the four most liberal justices. As a result of this tendency, the Court is most likely to weaken or overturn precedents after changes in its membership shift its collective ideological position.[48]

All this may suggest that precedents carry no weight. Yet justices have a degree of reluctance—some more than others—to overturn precedents directly. The Court as a whole adheres to a good many precedents that no longer accord with the majority view among the justices. And justices sometimes announce in an opinion that they are following a relevant precedent even though they disagree with it—as Scalia and Thomas did in a 2008 case about limits on punitive damages in lawsuits.[49] Further, there is evidence that precedents do shape the justices' positions in cases, in part by establishing analytic frameworks that the justices use.[50]

If the Court is not fully bound by its own precedents, it is not at all bound by interpretations of law from other courts. However, the justices frequently cite lower-court decisions in support of their positions. In recent years several justices have also cited decisions of courts outside the United States, most often in rulings that broaden constitutional rights. Justice Scalia and Justice Thomas have argued against this practice. It has also attracted strong criticism from conservatives outside the Court, including some members of Congress.

As for the Court's own precedents, the extent of their influence on the justices' positions in cases is uncertain and a matter of dispute among commentators. However, precedents clearly have some effect. The rule of *stare decisis* does not control the Court's decisions, but it does structure and influence them. The same is true of the law in general: it channels the justices' choices, often in subtle ways, but it also leaves them considerable freedom in making those choices.

Justices' Values

If the law leaves justices free to make choices largely on other bases, the most likely basis is their own values. And of those values, the most salient are the justices' policy preferences.

The importance of policy preferences is reflected in the process of selecting justices. Presidents and their advisers work hard to identify nominees who share the administration's views on major issues of legal policy. Interest groups support or oppose nominees on the basis of their perceived values. And senators ask questions intended to ferret out nominees' attitudes toward issues that they would face as justices. All these people act on the assumption that justices' policy preferences have a fundamental impact on the votes they cast and the opinions they write.

The Influence of Policy Preferences

It is difficult to ascertain the actual effect of justices' policy preferences on their behavior as decision makers, simply because their preferences cannot be observed directly. But some evidence strongly suggests that preferences exert a strong influence on the justices' choices. There is considerable consistency between the justices' expressions of personal views outside the Court and their votes and opinions in cases. Certainly this is true of the justices who speak and write most frequently about judicial issues, such as Stephen Breyer, Antonin Scalia, and Clarence Thomas. Similarly, the justices' positions on the Court tend to be consistent with the positions they took on similar issues before their appointment.

Some scholars argue that the justices' policy preferences are essentially a complete explanation of the Court's decisions.[51] In contrast, I think that the justices' preferences exert their effects in combination with other important forces, such as the political environment—and, for that matter, the law. But policy preferences provide the best explanation for differences in the positions that the nine justices take in the same cases, because no other factor varies so much from one justice to another.

Justices' attitudes on policy issues result from the same influences that shape political attitudes generally. Family socialization, religious training, and career experiences all can shape the values of people who become Supreme Court justices. Justice John Paul Stevens, for instance, has described the impact of experiences such as his military experience in World War II and the criminal conviction of his father for embezzlement (later overturned by the Illinois Supreme Court) on his attitudes toward issues of legal policy. And in a 2007 opinion Stevens brought his childhood recollection of Prohibition in Illinois to bear on the "war on drugs."[52] In part because justices have different backgrounds and learn different things from those backgrounds, each brings a particular set of attitudes to the Court.

The justices' behavior on the Court could reflect their policy preferences in two different ways. Justices might simply take positions in cases that best reflect their views of good policy. Or they might act strategically, adjusting their positions where doing so could advance the policies they favor. In Chapter 3, I discussed strategy in decisions on whether to accept cases: justices might vote whether to hear cases on the basis of their predictions about how the Court would rule on those cases. In decisions on the merits, strategic justices might write opinions that do not fully reflect their own views in order to win the support of other justices. Or the Court collectively could modify its position in a case to reduce the chances that Congress will override the Court's decision and substitute a policy that most justices would want to avoid.

It is not clear to what extent the justices behave strategically and what forms their strategies take.[53] But it appears that strategic considerations seldom move justices very far from the positions they most prefer. For this reason, the impact of justices' policy preferences can be considered initially without taking strategy into account. In two sections later in this chapter, I consider strategy aimed at other justices and at the Court's political environment.

The Ideological Dimension

On most issues that come to the Court, the opposing positions can be labeled as liberal and conservative. For this reason justices' preferences, and the votes and opinions that reflect those preferences, may be understood in ideological terms.

Defining Liberal and Conservative Positions. The positions from which justices can choose are most easily defined on civil liberties issues. In this field the position more favorable to legal protection for liberties is typically considered liberal. Thus, the liberal position gives relatively great weight to people's right to equal treatment by government and private institutions, procedural rights of criminal defendants and others who deal with government, and substantive rights such as freedom of expression and privacy. In contrast, the conservative position gives relatively great weight to values that compete with these rights, such as the capacity to fight crime effectively and to maintain national security.

On economic issues, liberal and conservative positions are often more difficult to define. But the liberal position is basically more favorable to economic "underdogs" and to government policies that are intended to benefit underdogs. In contrast, the conservative position is more favorable to businesses in conflicts with labor unions and less favorable to government regulation of business practices.

Some cases that come before the Supreme Court, such as boundary disputes between two states, do not have obvious liberal and conservative sides. On some other issues, especially in the field of economic policy, ideological lines in American society and thus in the Court have become more complicated. Still, most issues that the Court decides do have clearly defined conservative and liberal sides.

Ideology and the Justices' Positions. If opposing positions in most cases can be identified as liberal or conservative, the justices' voting patterns can be described in terms of the frequency with which they support the conservative side and the liberal side. Table 4-2 shows the ideological patterns of votes for the justices in the 2006 and 2007 terms. The table shows that every justice cast a good many votes on both sides. But the justices also differed considerably in their ideological tendencies: the three most liberal justices (Stevens, Ginsburg, and Souter) supported the liberal side more than twice as often as their two most conservative colleagues (Scalia and Thomas).

When justices respond differently to the same cases, the primary reason is differences in their policy preferences. Thus one can conclude from Table 4-2 that Justice Thomas is considerably more conservative than Justice Stevens. One piece of evidence for this conclusion is that the relative positions of the justices on a liberal-conservative scale tend to remain fairly stable from term to term. It is also true that the justices' relative positions tend to be similar across different issues. This similarity, however, is far from absolute. A justice who has one of the most liberal voting records on conflicts between business and labor might have a relatively conservative record on criminal justice.

TABLE 4-2
Percentages of Liberal Votes
Cast by Justices, 2006–2007 Terms

Justice	Liberal votes
Stevens	70.1
Ginsburg	68.6
Souter	67.9
Breyer	66.7
Kennedy	48.5
Alito	38.2
Roberts	36.8
Scalia	34.3
Thomas	28.1

Source: U.S. Supreme Court Database, compiled by Harold Spaeth, Michigan State University, at www.cas.sc.edu/poli/juri/sctdata.htm.

Note: Cases are included if they were decided on the merits with full opinions and if votes could be classified as liberal or conservative. Criteria for classifying votes are those used in the database.

The justices' relative ideological positions are reflected in the frequency with which they join the same opinions in a case. In the Court's 2007 term, the mean rate of agreement on opinions between pairs of justices was 62 percent. The mean rate of agreement among the four most liberal justices was 72 percent; for the four most conservative justices, it was 76 percent. The highest rate of agreement, 84 percent, was between the like-minded Scalia and Thomas. The lowest rate, 36 percent, was between the justices at the opposite ends of the Court's ideological spectrum, Stevens and Thomas.[54] To a degree, rates of agreement on opinions may reflect self-conscious alliances or personal relationships, but similarity in policy preferences is the key factor.

The general patterns of agreement and disagreement between the justices are reflected in the lineups of justices in individual cases. In the 2007 term, for instance, eight of the twelve 5–4 decisions found either the four most liberal justices or the four most conservative justices dissenting, with Justice Kennedy joining one side or the other to create the majority in each case.[55] But there are numerous exceptions to the rule; for example, in one 5–4 decision, *United States v. Santos* (2008), which involved interpretation of a federal criminal law, the majority consisted of the Court's three most liberal justices (Stevens, Souter, and Ginsburg) and the two most conservative justices (Scalia and Thomas), with the justices in between them dissenting.

Observers of the Court regularly label the justices not just in relative terms but in absolute terms as well: Justice Thomas is called a conservative, Justice Stevens a liberal. Because the justices' votes in cases reflect several different forces, this conclusion does not follow directly from the patterns of votes. This is especially true because the proportions of liberal and conservative votes that a justice casts in a particular period reflect the mix of cases that the Court decides in that period. A justice who had a strongly liberal voting record in one era might not have as liberal a record in a different era.

Still, the role of the justices' policy preferences in their votes and opinions is sufficiently strong that those ideological labels seem appropriate. A justice who casts a preponderance of votes that can be characterized as conservative almost surely holds conservative views on most issues. Indeed, most justices who were perceived as strongly liberal or strongly conservative at the time of their appointment establish records on the Court that are consistent with those perceptions.[56]

Court Policy and Policy Change

If the positions of individual justices reflect their policy preferences, the collective decisions of the Court must also reflect the mix of preferences among the justices. A Court composed primarily of conservatives will tend to make conservative decisions and move legal doctrine in a conservative direction.

The balance between liberalism and conservatism in the Supreme Court's decisions and in its most visible decisions fluctuates from term to term. Observers of the Court often make a good deal of those changes, but most of the time they just reflect the particular mix of cases that the Court decides each term rather than a shift in the Court's collective position. Sometimes, however, that collective position does change, in the sense that the Court would decide the same cases differently. As a result, there is change in the Court's policies in a specific policy area or in a broader field, such as civil liberties.

If the Court's collective positions reflect the policy preferences of individual justices, the primary source of changes in Court policies must be a shift in the preferences of the justices as a group. These shifts could come from change in the preferences of people already serving on the Court or from change in the Court's membership. In practice, both are significant.

Changes in Individual Preferences. Close observers of the Supreme Court often try to predict how the Court will decide a pending case; typically, they do rather well in their predictions. The primary reason is that individual justices tend to take stable positions on the issues that arise in various policy areas, positions that largely reflect their policy preferences. The views that a justice expressed in past cases about when cars can be searched or when mergers of companies violate the antitrust laws are a good guide to the justice's stance in a future case. In turn, the Court's collective position on such issues generally remains stable as long as its membership remains unchanged.

But as members of the Court, justices are exposed to new influences and confront issues in new forms. The result may be to modify their policy preferences. Small changes are common, and more fundamental changes sometimes occur. The possibility of such changes affects the selection of justices as presidents and their aides seek to identify nominees whose preferences are so deeply held that they seem unlikely to shift.

Individual issues aside, most justices do retain the same basic ideological position throughout their career. The liberal Ruth Bader Ginsburg and the conservative Clarence Thomas are good examples. When a justice's position shifts relative to that of the Court as a whole, it is usually because new appointments have shifted the Court's ideological center while the justice has retained the same general views. This seems to be true of John Paul Stevens, who was initially near the center of the Court but now has the most liberal record of any justice.

Justice Harry Blackmun was one of the few justices whose basic views seemed to shift fundamentally. Blackmun came to the Court in 1970 as a Nixon appointee, and early in his tenure he aligned himself chiefly with the other conservative justices. He and Chief Justice Warren Burger, boyhood friends from Minnesota, were dubbed the "Minnesota Twins." In the 1973 term, Blackmun agreed with Burger on opinions in 84 percent of the Court's decisions, and with liberal William Brennan in only 49 percent.[57] Blackmun gradually moved toward the center of the Court, and from the 1980 term on he usually had higher agreement rates with Brennan than with Burger—in 1985, Burger's last term, 30 percentage points higher. In the last few terms before his 1994 retirement, Blackmun had become one of the two most liberal justices on the Court.

This shift to the Court's left resulted in part from the replacement of liberal colleagues with conservatives, but Blackmun's own positions clearly became more liberal. Although the reasons for this change are uncertain, it appears that his experiences in dealing with cases that came to the Court—especially *Roe v. Wade,* in which he wrote the Court's opinion— were important.[58]

Perhaps more common than individual shifts are changes in the views of the justices as a group on a particular issue. These changes typically result from developments in American society that shape the views of the justices along with those of other people.

One example concerns the legal status of women. The liberal Warren Court gave unprecedented support to the goal of equality under the law, but it did not strike down legal rules that treated women and men differently. In contrast, the more conservative Burger and Rehnquist Courts handed down a series of decisions promoting legal equality for men and women. Today, even the most conservative justices use a fairly rigorous standard to evaluate laws that treat women and men differently, a standard that no justice supported in the 1960s. The most fundamental cause of this change was the direct and indirect effect of the feminist movement on the Court's agenda and, even more, on justices' views about women's social roles. This example underlines the potential for significant changes in justices' collective views on policy issues.

Membership Change. Dissenting from a 2007 decision, Justice Stevens expressed his "firm conviction that no Member of the Court that I joined in 1975 would have agreed with today's decision."[59] In doing so, he underlined the importance of membership change, probably the most important source of change in the Court's policies. If those policies are largely a product of the justices' preferences, and if those preferences tend to be stable, then change will come most easily when one justice is succeeded by a new justice who has a different set of policy preferences.

Change in the Court's membership often alters its positions on specific issues. The overturning of a recent precedent usually results from the replacement of justices who helped create that precedent with others who disagree with it. Even when the Court maintains a precedent, a shift in membership may result in a narrower interpretation of the precedent. Retired justice Sandra Day O'Connor has said that the law "shouldn't change just because the faces on the court have changed,"[60] but frequently it does.

More broadly, shifts in the Court's overall ideological position through new appointments typically lead to change in the general content of its policies. The Court's civil liberties policies since the 1950s demonstrate this effect of membership change. Table 4-3 shows the proportions of decisions favorable to parties with civil liberties claims during successive periods in the 1958 to 2007 terms. Because changes in the content of civil liberties cases can make these proportions misleading, the table also shows civil liberties support with an adjustment for the content of cases based on a statistical technique.

The early Warren Court was closely divided between liberals and conservatives; from 1958 until 1961 there was a relatively stable division between a four-member liberal bloc and a moderate to conservative bloc of five. By the standards of the 1920s and 1930s, the Court's decisions were quite liberal, but the table shows that parties with civil liberties claims won only a little more than half their cases between 1958 and 1961.

President Kennedy's 1962 appointments created a liberal majority; a law clerk during the 1962 term referred to it as "a turning point in the modern

TABLE 4-3

Proportions of Supreme Court Decisions Favoring Parties with Civil Liberties Claims and Changes in Court Membership, 1958–2007 Terms

Terms	Proportions of pro–civil liberties decisions		New justices (appointing presidents) and justices leaving the Court
	Actual	Adjusted[a]	
1958–1961	60.1	60.1	NA
1962–1968	75.3	77.6	*New:* White, Goldberg (Kennedy); Fortas, Marshall (Johnson). *Leaving:* Whittaker, Frankfurter, Goldberg, Clark.
1969–1974	48.8	55.9	*New:* Burger, Blackmun, Powell, Rehnquist (Nixon). *Leaving:* Warren, Fortas, Black, Harlan.
1975–1980	42.0	51.6	*New:* Stevens (Ford). *Leaving:* Douglas.
1981–1985	40.0	51.5	*New:* O'Connor (Reagan). *Leaving:* Stewart.
1986–1989	42.4	46.1	*New:* Scalia, Kennedy (Reagan). *Leaving:* Burger, Powell.
1990–1992	42.7	35.4	*New:* Souter, Thomas (Bush). *Leaving:* Brennan, Marshall.
1993–2004	46.6	43.9	*New:* Ginsburg, Breyer (Clinton). *Leaving:* White, Blackmun.
2005–2007	44.0	39.7	*New:* Roberts, Alito. *Leaving:* Rehnquist, O'Connor.

Source: Based on data in the U.S. Supreme Court Database, compiled by Harold Spaeth of Michigan State University, at www.cas.sc.edu/poli/juri/sctdata.htm.

Note: NA = not applicable.

a. Adjusted using a statistical technique to control for changes in the content of civil liberties cases decided by the Court. The technique is described in Lawrence Baum, "Measuring Policy Change in the U.S. Supreme Court," *American Political Science Review* 82 (September 1988): 905–912.

history of the Supreme Court."[61] The Johnson appointments later in the decade maintained that majority. The 1962 through 1968 terms were probably the most liberal period in the Court's history. The Court established strikingly liberal positions in a variety of policy areas, and the proportion of pro–civil liberties decisions increased substantially.

Between 1969 and 1992, every appointment to the Court was made by a Republican president, and all but Ford sought to use their appointments to make the Court more conservative. Thus, the Court gained a distinctly more conservative set of justices. The effect of these membership changes on the Court's civil liberties policies was somewhat ambiguous. The Court adhered to some policies of the Warren Court and even took new liberal directions on such issues as women's rights. Yet, on the whole, the Burger Court was distinctly less supportive of civil liberties than was the Court of the 1960s, and the early Rehnquist Court was even less supportive than the Burger Court.

Table 4-3 shows the effect of these Republican appointments on the proportion of decisions favorable to civil liberties. The Nixon appointments reduced that proportion from about three-quarters to about one-half. The replacement of the highly liberal William Douglas with the moderately liberal John Paul Stevens further reduced the level of support for civil liberties. If the content of cases is taken into account, another major decline in support occurred after David Souter and Clarence Thomas replaced the Court's two remaining strong liberals in the early 1990s.

Ruth Bader Ginsburg and Steven Breyer were the first appointees of a Democratic president since 1967. Best characterized as moderate liberals, they did not change the Court's ideological balance a great deal. The proportion of pro–civil liberties decisions did increase somewhat after they joined the Court, but the Rehnquist Court remained distinctly more conservative in its decisions and doctrines than the Warren and Burger Courts.

President Bush's appointments of John Roberts and Samuel Alito moved the Court somewhat to the right, with the adjusted proportion of liberal decisions declining by 4 percentage points. By this measure the early Roberts Court was not quite as conservative as the Court of the early 1990s, but it was far less favorable to civil liberties claims than the Warren Court of the 1960s. That difference underlines the ability of presidents to shape the Supreme Court through the selection of justices.

Role Values

Policy preferences are not the only values that can affect the Court's decisions. Justices may also be influenced by their role values, their views about what constitutes appropriate behavior for the Supreme Court and its members. In any body, whether it is a court or a legislature, members' conceptions of how they should carry out their jobs structure what they do and affect their policy decisions.

A variety of role values can shape the justices' behavior. Their views about the desirability of unanimous decisions help determine the frequency of dissent in the Court's decisions. Their judgments about the legitimacy of "lobbying" colleagues on decisions may determine the outcomes of some cases. But the role values that could have the greatest impact concern the considerations that justices take into account in reaching their decisions and the desirability of active intervention in the making of public policy.

It is clear that several different forces shape the justices' votes and opinions. The relative weight of these forces depends in part on what justices think they ought to do. In particular, justices have to balance their strong policy preferences on many issues with the expectation of others (and themselves) that they will seek to interpret the law accurately.

Some evidence suggests that justices differ in the relative weight they give to these legal and policy considerations.[62] However, these differences are not as sharp as they sometimes appear. For example, at any given time, some justices are more willing than others to uproot some of the Court's precedents. But the justices' attitudes about maintaining precedent in general are less important than their attitudes toward the policies embodied in particular precedents. As noted earlier, justices are more inclined to vote to overrule a precedent when the precedent runs counter to their general ideological position.

Active intervention in policymaking is often viewed negatively. Justices who seem eager to engage in that intervention are criticized as "activists," and those who seem less prone to do so are praised as "restrained." But activism, like the treatment of precedent, does not seem to differ all that much among justices.

The most visible form of active intervention in policymaking is striking down federal statutes, which is often controversial as well. The historical patterns are illuminating. During the 1920s and early 1930s, the laws that the Court struck down were primarily government regulations of business practices. Conservative justices were the most willing to strike down such laws, and liberals on the Court and elsewhere argued for judicial restraint. In contrast, in the 1960s and 1970s, the Court struck down primarily laws that conflicted with civil liberties. Liberals were most likely to act against these laws and conservatives to call for judicial restraint.

Since the 1980s the Court has overturned a wide variety of federal laws. No justice has stood out for a willingness to strike down laws or an unwillingness to do so. Rather, the justices have responded to the ideological content of the statutes in question. The same is true of the decisions in which the Court strikes down state laws on constitutional grounds.[63] In this respect the justices' decisions whether to declare laws unconstitutional are similar to their decisions whether to overrule precedents.

All this is not to say that the justices' role values have no impact on their behavior. Undoubtedly, such values help to structure the ways in which justices perceive their jobs. But justices' conceptions of good public policy have a more fundamental impact on their choices.

Group Interaction

In the preceding section, I treated the justices as individuals who act on their own. But when justices make choices, they do so as part of a Court that makes collective decisions and as part of American government and society. Justices who seek to make good policy might act strategically by taking their colleagues and other institutions into account. Whether or not justices act strategically, they can be influenced in a variety of ways by other justices and by their political and social environment. This section examines the justices as a group, and the next section considers the Court's environment.

A Quasi-Collegial Body

In historical accounts of the Supreme Court, some of the most dramatic events concern interactions among the justices in major cases. Newly appointed Chief Justice Earl Warren, engaging in what Justice Douglas called "a brilliant diplomatic process," moved the Court from sharp division to a unanimous decision in *Brown v. Board of Education* (1954).[64] The Court's decision in *Planned Parenthood v. Casey* (1992) reflected close collaboration among three justices on a joint opinion that determined the Court's position, with one of the three shifting position after the Court's initial vote and thereby preventing the Court from overturning *Roe v. Wade*.[65] In *Bush v. Gore* (2000), which ensured that George W. Bush would become president, the Court's decision came after intense interplay among the justices over the short period in which the Court considered the case.[66]

Those episodes are consistent with the image of the Court that many people hold, one in which justices constantly lobby each other over the cases before them and decisions reflect the persuasive powers of certain justices. For the most part, however, that image is false. For one thing, except for oral argument and conferences, there is only limited face-to-face interaction among the justices in the decision-making process. According to Justice Breyer, "Things take place in writing because that is a mode through which appellate judges are most comfortable communicating."[67]

More fundamentally, the justices' influence on each other occurs within constraints—constraints that result from their strongly held views on many issues. When they apply their general positions on an issue to a specific case, the resulting judgment about that case may be too firm for colleagues to sway. As Justice Rehnquist wrote early in his tenure, when justices who have prepared themselves "assemble around the conference table on Friday morning to decide an important case presenting constitutional questions that they have all debated and written about before, the outcome may be a foregone conclusion."[68] Thus, he concluded some years later, the Court is dominated chiefly "by centrifugal forces, pushing toward individuality and independence."[69]

But the justices' independence should not be overstated. They have powerful incentives to work with each other, even if doing so requires them to adopt positions that depart from the positions they most prefer. One reason is institutional: justices want to achieve opinions that at least five members endorse so that the Court is laying down authoritative legal rules. And to give more weight to the Court's decisions, they generally would like to reach greater consensus. According to Justice O'Connor, "Neither my colleagues nor I make a practice of joining opinions with which we do not agree." Unanimity "does not overwhelm our other goals." Still, "we all greatly prefer the Court to be unanimous or almost so whenever possible, and we work to make that happen."[70]

The justices' interest in winning majority support for their positions creates an even stronger incentive to work together. Justices prefer to have the Court support the legal rules they favor, and at least some justices get satisfaction simply from being on the winning side. Thus justices have good reason to engage in efforts at persuasion. They also have reason to be flexible in the positions they take in cases, because flexibility may help them to win colleagues' support for rules that are at least close to the ones they prefer.

These incentives are reflected in the negotiation that was described in the first section of this chapter.[71] The most common course of events in a case is for a justice to write a draft opinion for the Court and then gain the support of a majority for that opinion with no difficulty. But other justices frequently ask for changes in the draft opinion, and most of the time justices who make these requests indicate that they cannot join the opinion unless the changes are made. The opinion author usually makes these changes. During the seventeen years of the Burger Court, requests for changes in the draft opinion occurred in 32 percent of all cases, and more often in important cases. Seventy percent of the time, the opinion was modified to make the requested change.[72]

Pamela Corley's analysis of Justice Harry Blackmun's papers from the late 1980s provides a sense of how this process works.[73] Blackmun's drafts of opinions for the Court frequently attracted memos from other members of the conference majority who disagreed with something in the draft. Blackmun nearly always made changes in the opinion in response to those memos. As a result, the colleagues who requested changes in the original draft usually joined Blackmun's final opinion; they wrote concurring opinions in only about 20 percent of those cases. The negotiations sometimes got complicated. In one case, Blackmun received conflicting suggestions from Antonin Scalia and Anthony Kennedy, and ultimately Scalia and Kennedy came up with a compromise that they and Blackmun could all accept. Not surprisingly, Blackmun was considerably less willing to accommodate colleagues when he had already secured majority support for his opinion.

Whether or not colleagues request changes in opinions for the Court, those opinions frequently are revised during the decision process. In the Burger Court, slightly more than half of all cases had at least three drafts of the Court's opinion circulated by the author.[74] Although successive drafts may differ only on minor matters, they sometimes differ considerably in the legal rules they proclaim.

Beyond the content of opinions, the votes of individual justices on the case outcome can shift during the decision process. In the Burger Court, 7.5 percent of the justices' individual votes to reverse or affirm were switched from one side to the other, and at least one such switch occurred in 37 percent of the cases. Most vote switches increase the size of the majority, as the Court works toward consensus. During the Burger Court, the justices who initially voted with the majority switched their votes 5 percent of the time, but those who initially voted with the minority switched 18 percent of the time.[75] Occasionally, however, shifts of position turn an initial minority into a majority. This occurred in about 7 percent of the cases decided by the Burger Court.[76]

The effects of interactions among the justices should not be exaggerated. After all, in the great majority of cases, the side that won in the Court's first vote on the merits of the case wins in the final vote as well. Most of the majority opinions that the Court issues look similar to the original drafts of those opinions. But votes and opinions do change; the Court's decisions are often more than simply an adding together of the positions with which each justice begins.

The similarity between the original draft and the final opinion in most cases suggests that the majority opinion author largely determines the legal rules that the Court lays down in its opinion. But sometimes the opinion changes a good deal as a result of interactions among justices, and even the original draft reflects the author's recognition of what other justices will find acceptable. Thus it might be that the majority opinion author has little more influence than other justices over the Court's doctrinal position in a case. Research on this issue so far has reached different conclusions, but as a whole it supports the view that most observers of the Court hold: the opinion author does have special influence over the content of the Court's opinion, but that influence falls well short of complete control.[77]

The group life of the Court affects its decisions more broadly and subtly than do shifts of position in individual cases. Interactions among the justices create general patterns of influence within the Court, and the extent of conflict among its members affects its ability to reach consensus. Both of these effects merit consideration.

Patterns of Influence

The capacity of any justice to exert influence over other justices is inherently limited. Justice O'Connor said, "I work with eight very strong-willed colleagues. I don't think that any of us exerts much power over the others."[78] Other members of the Court have expressed similar views.

Within these limits, however, the justices do influence each other. It follows that some are more influential than others. In general, the primary requisites for influence are the same as in any other group: an interest in exerting influence and skill in doing so.

Justice William O. Douglas, who served for a record thirty-six years between 1939 and 1975, had relatively little influence because he did little to achieve it. Certainly, he devoted some efforts to winning support for his positions, especially in the cases that concerned him most. But in contrast with some other justices, whom he called "evangelists," he generally preferred to go his own way.[79] According to William Rehnquist, "At the Court conferences we sometimes had the impression that he was disappointed to have other people agree with his views in a particular case, because he would therefore be unable to write a stinging dissent."[80] Douglas's isolation was symbolized by his speedy departures from Washington at the end of the Court terms or, on occasion, even earlier.

Douglas's long-time colleague Felix Frankfurter actively sought influence over his colleagues, and his eminence as a legal scholar should have put him in a good position to persuade his colleagues to his position. But his weak interpersonal skills worked against him. Justice Potter Stewart said that Frankfurter "courted" him, but "Felix was so unsubtle and obvious that it was counterproductive."[81] Further, Frankfurter's arrogance caused him to lecture to colleagues, and he reacted sarcastically to opinions with which he disagreed. At one Court conference he "had taken a printed draft opinion by Justice Tom Clark and first verbally and then physically torn it to shreds, contemptuously tossing the sheets of paper all over the ornate private room."[82] Such behavior had an inevitable impact on Frankfurter's influence within the Court.

William Brennan, who served from 1956 to 1990, had a strong interest in exerting influence. As a liberal he worked hard to gain support from more conservative colleagues, both in individual cases and over the long term. But unlike Frankfurter, Brennan had a warm personal style and an ability to work with his colleagues. "Everybody got along with him," according to one observer, "even those who bitterly opposed him from a doctrinal view."[83] Brennan was also perceptive about how to win majorities; one commentator said that he could "accurately judge his colleagues and figure out what is doable."[84] These qualities helped Brennan in his efforts to forge a liberal majority for the expansion of civil liberties in the Warren Court and to limit the Court's conservative shift in the Burger Court.

Brennan's influence should not be exaggerated. According to one account, he alienated Sandra Day O'Connor and exerted little impact on her positions in cases.[85] And in discussing Brennan, John Paul Stevens alluded to the limits on the influence of any justice: "I was very fond of Bill Brennan—loved the guy and had great admiration for him. But it's simply not right to say that he was able to craft the majority. He just had five votes on his side!"[86]

Influence can arise in another way, through a justice's position on the ideological spectrum. The vote of a "swing" justice at the ideological center of the Court often will determine which side wins in cases that closely divide the Court along ideological lines. In itself, this does not mean that the swing justice is influential: every justice in a 5–4 majority contributes to that result with one vote.

Still, swing justices do have a degree of influence because their positions are seen as relatively unpredictable and their support as crucial to the outcome of many cases. Lawyers work to devise arguments that appeal to the swing justice, and colleagues also work hard to win their favor. Justice O'Connor was the closest thing to a swing justice during most of her tenure on the Court, and she gained those advantages. As her biographer Joan Biskupic has described her, O'Connor made the most of her pivotal position, because she had the same determination and skills as William Brennan. As a result, it appears, she *was* one of the most influential justices.[87] (In 2009, when O'Connor appeared on "The Daily Show," she corrected host Jon Stewart when he said she had been the swing justice on the Court. "We don't use that word swing," she said. Stewart rephrased his thought and called O'Connor "the most principled justice." O'Connor responded, "There you go. Much better. Much better.")[88]

Since 2006, when O'Connor retired, Anthony Kennedy has clearly been the swing justice, because four justices are well to his ideological left and four others well to his right. On a series of major decisions involving issues such as abortion and the death penalty, he has created liberal or conservative majorities with his vote. As a result, lawyers and colleagues show considerable deference to him. Briefs and opinions quote his statements in prior cases in an effort to appeal to him.[89] In a 2007 case the majority and dissenting opinions argued about the implications of a little-known precedent that Kennedy had mentioned in oral argument.[90] Reporting on another oral argument, an observer reported that "as Kennedy speaks, Breyer nods so vigorously, I want to call in a chiropractor."[91]

The descriptions of Justice Kennedy's power sometimes exaggerate the reality. A satirical blog claimed in 2007 that the Supreme Court had "agreed Friday to eventually decide 5–4 that Guantánamo Bay detainees may not go to federal court to challenge their indefinite confinement." According to the story, "Justices Alito, Roberts, Thomas, and Scalia could not be reached for immediate comment, as they were taking Justice Kennedy out for a really nice dinner at his favorite steakhouse."[92] As it turned out, the blog predicted the Court's decision inaccurately: in

Boumediene v. Bush (2008), the Court ruled that Guantánamo detainees did have the right to seek writs of habeas corpus. But the blog was right about Kennedy's decisive position, in that his vote for the detainees created a 5–4 decision in their favor. Whatever may be the influence of a swing justice, that justice at least has the benefit of being on the winning side more often than anyone else.

The Chief Justice

The chief justice has both advantages and limitations in seeking to influence colleagues. One limitation stems from administrative duties, which reduce the time that the chief can spend on cases. More fundamental is the difficulty of leading colleagues who strongly resist control. When a reporter asked, "You can't tell Justice Scalia what to do?" Chief Roberts responded, "You know, I don't think anybody can tell Justice Scalia what to do." More broadly, Roberts has said that "the chief's ability to get the Court to do something is really quite restrained."[93] Balanced against these limitations are the chief's formal powers, which provide at least a moderate advantage over other justices in exerting influence.

The Chief Justice's Powers. The chief presides over the Court in oral argument and in conference. In conference the chief can direct discussion and frame alternatives, roles that may shape the outcome of the discussion. Most important, the chief ordinarily speaks first on a case in conference. Another power involves the discuss list, the set of petitions for hearing that the Court considers fully. The chief, aided by clerks, makes up the initial version of the discuss list. This task gives the chief the largest role in determining which cases are set aside without group discussion.

Opinion Assignment. Perhaps the most important power of the chief justice is opinion assignment. The chief is in the majority and thus assigns the Court's opinion in the preponderance of cases, a little over 80 percent in the period from 1953 to 1990.[94] In making assignments, chief justices balance different considerations.[95]

Administrative considerations relate to spreading the workload and opportunities among the justices. Chief justices generally try to make sure that each colleague gets about the same number of opinions for the Court, taking into account assignments from senior associate justices. And as Chief Justice Roberts put it, "You want to make sure everyone has their fair share of interesting cases and has their fair share of what we call the dogs, the uninteresting cases."[96] Chiefs may also take into account the workload of opinion writing that a justice already faces at a given time, a consideration that was especially important to Chief Justice Rehnquist. He wrote in 2001, "As the term goes on I take into consideration the extent to which

Chief Justice John Roberts. As Roberts has suggested, even an effective chief justice has limited ability to influence other members of the Court.

the various justices are current in writing and circulating opinions that have previously been assigned."[97]

Other considerations relate to the substance of the Court's decisions. As discussed earlier, the legal rules proclaimed by the Court may depend in part on who writes its opinion. For this reason, chief justices tend to favor themselves and colleagues who have similar ideological positions when assigning opinions in cases they consider especially important. The chief might also act to help the conference majority remain a majority. When the conference majority is slim, the chief is likely to assign opinions to a relatively moderate member of that majority, even if the assigned justice is ideologically distant from the chief. This practice stems from the belief, accurate or not, that a moderate has the best chance to write an opinion that will maintain the majority and perhaps win over justices who were initially on the other side.

Because chief justices favor ideological allies in assigning important opinions, in effect they reward the justices who vote with them most often. They might also use the assignment power more directly to reward and punish colleagues. Chief Justice Roberts said in 2006 that "you can always give all the tax opinions to a justice, if you want to punish them."[98] Roberts added that he had not yet taken that kind of action. But according to Justice Blackmun, Chief Justice Burger might assign one of the "crud" opinions "that nobody wants to write" to a justice who was "in the doghouse" with Burger.[99]

Variation in Leadership. What particular chief justices make of their formal powers and the strength of their leadership vary a good deal. These differences result from several conditions, including the chief's interest in leading the Court, the chief's skill as a leader, and the willingness of the associate justices to be led.

Warren Burger was ambitious for leadership. He achieved some success in securing administrative changes in the federal courts and procedural changes in the Court itself. But he was not especially influential within the Court itself.

To a considerable extent, Burger's limited impact on the Court's decisions stemmed from his own qualities and predilections. Colleagues chafed at what they considered a poor style of leadership in conference, and they disliked Burger's occasional practice of casting "false" votes so that he could assign the Court's opinion.[100] He was also accused of bullying his colleagues. One scholar concluded that Potter Stewart "loathed" Burger,[101] and other colleagues also disliked his leadership style. Apparently, they were not alone; Justice Marshall's messenger said that when Burger retired, "it was just like Christmas morning."[102] But Burger also faced obstacles that were beyond his control. Perhaps most important, as a strong conservative he had the disadvantage of standing near one end of the Court's ideological spectrum.

William Rehnquist became chief justice in 1986 after serving on the Court for fifteen years. He brought important strengths to the position, especially his well-respected intellectual abilities and a pleasant manner of interaction with people. For these reasons, his promotion was welcomed by colleagues and other Court personnel.[103]

Having served in the Burger Court as an associate justice, Rehnquist learned—in one observer's words—"how *not* to be Chief Justice."[104] In any case, Rehnquist seems to have been an effective chief justice, and his leadership was widely praised even by justices who did not share his conservative views on most judicial issues.[105] Reflecting his views, the Court's discussions of cases at conference were shorter and tighter than they had been in the recent past. Rehnquist's leadership was one source of the sharp decline in the number of cases accepted by the Court. In decision making he enhanced his influence by taking strong positions with an affable style.

John Roberts's effectiveness as chief justice will become clear only with time. Still, both colleagues and observers of the Court have already attested to his strengths. Justice Stevens, for instance, described Roberts's fairness and effectiveness in leading the Court's conference.[106] Already respected as an advocate by his colleagues, Roberts has impressed them as a chief.

Yet Roberts's tenure thus far underlines the limits to the influence of the chief justice. From the start, he has emphasized his goal of achieving greater consensus in the Court's decisions, with more unanimous decisions and fewer separate opinions.[107] But this is a difficult task because justices are accustomed to expressing their own views and feel reluctant to join opinions that diverge from those views. Justice Alito expressed agreement with Roberts's desire for unanimity, but not if it meant "endorsing something you don't believe in." [108] Justice Scalia's reaction was more pointed: "Lots of luck." [109] Indeed, in Roberts's first three terms the proportion of unanimous decisions was about the same as the proportion in the Rehnquist Court, and the proportion of 5–4 and 5–3 decisions was a bit higher. [110] Even the most effective chief justice can achieve only limited influence over a set of highly independent colleagues.

Harmony and Conflict

In the Supreme Court, as in other work groups, some conditions favor harmonious relations among the justices but other conditions foster conflict. Harmony makes the Court a more pleasant place to work, and it also helps the justices to achieve consensus in decisions. And justices who seek the support of colleagues for the positions they prefer want to maintain good relations with those colleagues. Still, all the sources of strife that exist in other groups can operate in the Court as well. The justices care a great deal about many of the issues they address in their decisions, issues on which they disagree with each other, and they often work under considerable pressure.

The justices' interest in achieving harmony is reflected in some of the ways that the Court operates. Stephen Breyer said in a television interview, "I have never heard a voice raised in anger in that conference room. I have never heard one member of the court say something insulting about another even as a kind of joke." [111] Even if Breyer exaggerated, he was describing one means that the justices use to limit conflict.

Yet conflict among the justices certainly exists. Anger sometimes becomes apparent when the justices announce their dissents from decisions, and some dissenting opinions are written in strong language. That language does not necessarily stem from personal animosity, but it sometimes reflects (or creates) friction among the justices.

Relationships among the justices on the current Court differ from those on some of its predecessors. In 2007 commentator Jeffrey Toobin described that difference.

The justices are polite to and respectful of each other.... Yet there are few real friendships among them, either. They spend little time together outside of the Court. They do not shoot the breeze in each others' offices. This was not true at other times in the Court's history. There were times when several justices hated each other, and there were times when there were close friendships; neither has been true over the last two decades at the Court. [112]

There does seem to be at least one close friendship, between Antonin Scalia and Ruth Bader Ginsburg, a friendship that is noteworthy because of the ideological distance between them.[113] But Toobin's overall characterization of the Court accords with the perceptions of other observers. It may be that the personal distance among justices today helps to limit personal conflict. In any event, the current Court is more harmonious than several past Courts, in which some pairs of justices were actually unable to work with each other. The absence of such deep conflicts undoubtedly improves the functioning of the Court.

The Court's Environment

Compared with Congress, the Supreme Court is more isolated from the world around it and more insulated from the influence of that world. The isolation is reflected in the relatively limited contact between the justices and other participants in politics, such as members of Congress and representatives of interest groups. The insulation is primarily a result of the justices' life terms: no matter whom they displease, they can be removed from office only through impeachment proceedings, an unlikely occurrence.

But the Court's isolation and insulation are far from total. The justices interact regularly with people outside the Court, and they are aware of events and developments in American society. The recent increase in the justices' public appearances and media interviews underlines their interest in the world outside the Court. They also have reasons to care about what people think of them and their Court, reasons that range from concern about the Court's effectiveness as a policymaker to an interest in their personal standing in the legal community. As a result, the Court's environment might shape the justices' thinking about cases and issues, and the potential influence of that environment merits consideration.

Mass Public Opinion

In *Hall Street Associates v. Mattel, Inc.* (2008), Justice Souter's opinion for the Court summarized the issue and decision: "The Federal Arbitration Act provides for expedited judicial review to confirm, vacate, or modify arbitration awards. The question here is whether statutory grounds for prompt vacatur and modification may be supplemented by contract. We hold that the statutory grounds are exclusive."[114]

It is doubtful that many people knew of this case or would have cared about the Court's decision had they known of it. On the issue in this case, as on many issues that come before the Court, there is no public opinion to speak of.

But a few individual decisions, such as the Court's major rulings on gun control and the rights of suspected terrorists, are highly visible and controversial. Many other decisions, not very visible in themselves, address issues that much of the public does care about, issues such as crime and civil rights. On these cases and issues, it is possible that public opinion or potential public reactions influence the justices.

Such influence may seem unlikely, because the justices do not depend on public approval to keep their jobs. But at least some justices see public support for the Court as a resource, helping to protect the Court from negative actions by the other branches and improving compliance with its decisions. And even though most justices are fairly obscure, they still might seek public approval for its own sake.

Indeed, some justices clearly care about the public. Sandra Day O'Connor, who had held elective office and who was the best-known justice, wrote books for a general audience and made frequent appearances before groups other than lawyers and judges. She received a great deal of mail from the public, and early in her tenure on the Court she tried to answer it all.[115]

Whether the justices need to worry about the consequences of public disapproval for the Court and its decisions is uncertain. On constitutional questions, one scholar concluded, "on the rare occasions" that the Court "has been even modestly out of line with popular majorities, it has gotten into trouble." But another scholar responded that lack of public interest in the Court and the Constitution leaves "the Court substantial leeway to put in place its vision of the Constitution."[116]

If the justices do seek public support for personal or institutional reasons, their interest in that support might affect their decisions. It is true that the justices' votes and the Court's decisions seldom have much effect on their individual and collective public approval. Even the Court's controversial decision resolving the 2000 presidential election in *Bush v. Gore* did not change its public standing appreciably.[117] But the justices still might want to avoid actions that could jeopardize this standing.

If so, one possible effect is that the justices avoid highly unpopular decisions. The Court certainly does make some decisions on controversial issues that conflict with majority views in the public. One example is the Court's rulings limiting religious exercises in public schools and the display of the Ten Commandments in public places. But perhaps concern with public opinion keeps some justices from acting contrary to the views of the public in some other cases.

Another possible effect of public opinion is to move the Court's overall ideological stance. As the public moves to the political left or right, so may the Court. Scholars have disagreed about whether the Court's mix of liberal and conservative decisions or the mix of votes by individual justices tracks ideological trends among the public, but some have found evidence of this relationship.[118]

Even if the Court's decisions track public opinion or the justices refrain from making highly unpopular decisions, they are not necessarily responding directly to the public. The kinds of decisions that most people strongly dislike usually run contrary to the justices' own preferences. It is noteworthy that on issues for which opinion surveys are available, the Court's decisions agree with the majority of the public more often than not.[119] But that agreement may reflect a similarity of attitudes between the public and Court rather than public influence on the Court.

By the same token, the social forces that move public opinion to the left or right may have a similar effect on the justices. To take one example, since the 1980s the Court has addressed a wide range of cases involving conflicts between individual liberties and the government's interest in controlling illegal drugs. For the most part, the Court has approved the government policies in question. One example was *Morse v. Frederick* (2007), in which the Court held that schools could suppress speech by students that might promote the use of illegal drugs. Perhaps the justices have sought to align themselves with a public that was highly supportive of the government's "war on drugs." But it is at least as likely that most justices simply shared the views of the public.

Perhaps the primary effect of public opinion is to help shape the justices' values and perceptions of reality. That effect could be substantial. But the justices' absence of worries about reelection reduces the influence of the public on them, giving them greater freedom to follow their own course than elected officials enjoy.

Elite Opinion: Friends and Acquaintances, the Legal Community, and the News Media

Whether or not the justices respond to public opinion, they can be influenced by more specific sets of relevant people. One set is the justices' personal friends and acquaintances. We would expect the justices, like other people, to give attention to the perspectives and reactions of those who are most important to them. Two other groups that may be relevant are the legal community and the mass media.

The legal community is important as a professional reference group. Justices draw many of their acquaintances from this community. Most justices interact a good deal with practicing lawyers, law professors, and lower-court judges, and most of the justices' public appearances are before legal groups. Lawyers are also the primary source of expert evaluations of the Court, often presented in the law reviews that law schools publish. Scrutiny by the legal community helps to make legal considerations important to the justices in reaching decisions. And if a particular view of legal issues is dominant among

Justice Anthony Kennedy, speaking at a meeting of the American Bar Association in San Francisco in 2007. The legal community is one of the audiences that might shape the justices' positions on issues that the Court decides.

lawyers or in a segment of the bar with which a justice identifies, that justice may be drawn toward the dominant view.

The law reviews can have another kind of impact as well. Because law review articles are often discussed in briefs, they constitute one source of the information that enters into the Court's decisions. Justices frequently cite law review articles in support of their positions, and on occasion the material in articles may affect their positions.

Most justices maintain a degree of distance from the news media. They talk to reporters less than do their counterparts in the other branches of government, and they give relatively few on-the-record interviews about their work. But there have always been some justices who interacted a good deal with reporters, and in recent years the justices as a whole have become more willing to give interviews.

Whether or not the justices talk with reporters, the news media are important to the Court. The media are the public's primary source of information about the Court, so they can shape public attitudes toward the justices. And even if the news media have no effect on public views of the Court, justices understandably prefer to be depicted positively rather than negatively in news reports. For these reasons, justices pay attention to coverage of the Court. Justice Thomas, with a "near-photographic memory," "can recall the dates of unflattering articles written about him, and the names of the reporters who wrote them."[120] In 2006 Justice Kennedy criticized newspaper editorial writers for their coverage of the Court, asking members of a legal group to suggest "that they read the opinions before they write their editorials."[121]

Most of the people in the justices' personal circles, the legal community, and the news media are from elite groups in American society. To the extent that these elites have a distinctive point of view, they may move justices toward that point of view. Indeed, in the current era some conservative commentators have argued that the desire to win praise from legal scholars, reporters who write about the Court, and other elites causes some Republican appointees to the Court to become more liberal over time.[122] Whether or not this effect occurs, almost surely those people who are especially salient to the justices have greater potential to influence them than does the public as a whole.

Litigants and Interest Groups

Simply by bringing cases to the Supreme Court, litigants, interest groups, and the lawyers that represent them have an effect on the Court's policies. Once the Court has accepted a case, litigants and interest groups may influence its decision on the merits. Because communications to the Court must go through formal channels, any such influence comes primarily through advocacy in written briefs and oral arguments.

Certainly, justices pay attention to the material provided by litigants and interest groups. Opinions for the Court address the arguments raised by the parties to the case, they make use of language in the parties' briefs,[123] and they often refer to amicus briefs. Controlling for other factors, the number of amicus briefs on each side has a meaningful effect on the outcome of cases. One reason is that the new arguments raised by amici sometimes persuade the justices.[124] When justices question lawyers closely during oral argument, they are often looking for responses to strong arguments by the other side. Therefore, the way lawyers frame arguments in a case can affect the justices' thinking and ultimately their decisions.

Further, the quality of advocacy on the two sides of a case has an impact. Justice Blackmun graded the performance of attorneys in oral argument. Using those grades, one study found that the relative strength of the advocacy for the two sides affected their likelihood of victory.[125]

Justices may react to the identities of the litigants or amici themselves rather than just the arguments they present. Individual justices may have positive or negative attitudes toward groups such as the ACLU or toward particular companies, but the federal government is probably in the best position to benefit from favorable perceptions on the part of the justices. The government enjoys a high rate of success as a party and amicus in the

Court's decisions on the merits, 75 percent in the 2003–2007 terms.[126] In part, that success rate reflects the agreement of conservative justices with the government's positions on issues such as criminal justice. Another source of the government's success is the expertise of the advocates in the solicitor general's office. But the justices' sympathies for the government's interests may also play a part.

Thus, the identities of the participants in cases may influence the Court, and the arguments they make certainly have an effect. But neither influence is as strong as the justices' preexisting attitudes toward the issues they address. Whatever influence the federal government has over the Court, the government wins the justices' support far more often when its arguments accord with their ideological positions than when the two conflict.[127]

Congress and the President

Policymakers elsewhere in government affect the Court and its policies. Because of this effect, the justices may take those policymakers into account when they reach decisions. The president and Congress are especially important to the Court, so they have the greatest potential for influence on the Court's decisions.

Congress. Congressional powers over the Court range from reversing the Court's interpretations of statutes to controlling salary increases for the justices. Because of this array of powers, the justices have some reason to think about congressional reactions to their decisions. Relations with Congress can affect their prestige and their comfort. And justices who think strategically in a broad sense, who care about the impact of the Court's policies, want to avoid congressional actions that undercut those policies.

If the justices do act strategically toward Congress, one likely form of strategy involves decisions that interpret federal statutes. These decisions are more vulnerable than the Court's interpretations of the Constitution because Congress and the president can override them simply by enacting a new statute. Indeed, Congress considers such overrides quite frequently, and it actually enacts them into law fairly often.

For this reason, justices might try to calculate whether their preferred interpretation of a statute would be sufficiently unpopular in Congress to produce an override. If so, justices would modify their interpretation to avoid that result. By making this implicit compromise with Congress, the justices could get the best possible result under the circumstances: not the interpretation of a statute that they favor most, but one that is closer to their preferences than the new statute that Congress would enact to override the Court's decision.

It may be, however, that most justices do not care that much whether Congress overrides their decisions. For one thing, overrides do not necessarily involve serious conflicts between the branches.[128] Or justices might find it so difficult to predict overrides and their content that there is little to be gained by trying to make those predictions. In any case, it is not yet clear how often justices pursue this strategic approach.[129] One possibility is that the justices do so selectively, when they perceive that a decision disfavored by Congress is a good candidate for an override. If so, the justices might be wary of handing down highly conservative statutory decisions on issues such as civil rights as long as the president is a Democrat and both houses of Congress have solid Democratic majorities.

Occasionally, a conflict between the Court and Congress goes much deeper than disagreement over the meaning of statutes. During a few periods in the Court's history, its general line of policy aroused so much dissatisfaction in Congress that it generated a serious threat of concrete action against the Court itself. It may be that at least some justices take care to avoid precipitating such conflicts. It is more likely that justices act to reduce the threat of negative congressional action in periods when serious conflicts actually arise.

The first such period was the early nineteenth century, when John Marshall's Court faced congressional attacks because of its policies. Marshall, as the Court's dominant member, was careful to limit the frequency of decisions that would further anger its opponents. As discussed in Chapter 1, in the late 1930s the Court's shift from opposition to support of New Deal legislation may have reflected an effort by one or two justices to avoid a serious confrontation with the other branches. In the late 1950s, members of Congress reacted to the Court's expansions of civil liberties by seeking to override its policies and limit its jurisdiction. A few justices shifted their positions on some contentious issues. As a result, the Court reversed some of its collective positions and thereby helped to quiet congressional attacks on the Court.

There have been no clear retreats of this sort since the 1950s. Indeed, the Court has engaged in considerable resistance to congressional pressures. Members of Congress have attacked the Court for its positions on a variety of civil liberties issues, including school desegregation, legislative districting, abortion, school prayer, and flag burning. On each of these issues, members have tried to overturn the Court's decisions, to limit its jurisdiction over the issue, or both. In the face of these attacks, the Court has adhered to many of its unpopular policies, and it changed others only when new appointments made the Court more conservative. Perhaps the key reason is that there has been insufficient support in Congress for strong measures against the Court to make such measures likely. The justices may be willing to accept strong criticism as long as congressional action goes no further than criticism.[130]

The President. Presidents have multifaceted relationships with the Supreme Court, and these relationships provide several sources of potential influence. Two of these sources, discussed in earlier chapters, are the power to appoint justices and the government's major role in Supreme Court litigation. The appointment power gives presidents considerable ability to determine the Court's direction. The president helps to shape the federal government's litigation policy and affects the Court's decisions through appointment of the solicitor general and occasional intervention in specific cases.

Presidents may have other ways to influence the justices. One stems from personal relationships between justices and presidents. In past periods some members of the Court were close associates of the presidents who later selected them, and some interacted regularly with presidents while serving on the Court. Such relationships hardly compel justices to support the president's position in litigation, but they might affect a justice's responses to cases that concern the president.

Another potential source of influence derives from the president's impact on other institutions. Because of their visibility and prestige, presidents might shape the public's view of the Court and its decisions. They also affect responses to the Court's decisions by Congress and the federal bureaucracy. For these reasons, justices have an incentive to keep the peace with the president.

Even with all these means to exert influence, presidents frequently suffer defeats in the Supreme Court cases they care most about. And as one scholar has argued, there are signs that the Court has become less deferential to the president in the past quarter century.[131] During that time the Court has favored presidential power in some decisions, but its decisions limiting that power are noteworthy. For instance, in *Clinton v. City of New York* (1998) the Court struck down the statute that gave the president power to veto individual items in budget bills. Two of its rulings have overruled presidential policies relating to the procedural rights of suspected terrorists, and a third overturned a statute the president had secured on that issue.[132] These decisions are a reminder that the president's influence over the Court, like that of Congress, has limits.

Conclusion

Of all the considerations that could influence the Supreme Court's decisions, I have given primary emphasis to the justices' policy preferences. The application of the law to the Court's cases is usually ambiguous, and constraints from the Court's environment are generally weak. As a result, the justices have considerable freedom to take positions that accord with their own conceptions of good policy. For this reason, the Court's membership and the process of selecting the justices have the greatest impact on the Court's direction.

If justices' preferences explain a great deal, they do not explain everything. The law and the political environment rule out some possible options for the Court, and they influence the justices' choices among the options that remain. The group life of the Court affects the behavior of individual justices and the Court's collective decisions. In particular, the justices regularly adjust their positions to win support from colleagues and help build majorities. Factors other than policy preferences are reflected in results that might seem surprising: strikingly liberal decisions from conservative Courts and the maintenance of precedents even when most justices no longer favor the policies they embody.

Thus, what the Court does is a product of multiple, intertwined forces. These forces can be discussed one at a time, but ultimately they operate together in complicated ways to shape the Court's decisions. Those who want to understand why the Court does what it does must recognize the complexity of the process by which justices make their choices.

NOTES

1. *Meacham v. Knolls Atomic Power Laboratory,* 171 L. Ed. 2d 283, 297 (2008).
2. Linda Greenhouse, "Case of Texas Murder Engrosses Supreme Court," *New York Times,* October 11, 2007, A24. The case was *Medellín v. Texas* (2008).
3. Tony Mauro, "A Trifecta and a Sprint at the Supreme Court," *BLT: The Blog of Legal Times,* March 24, 2008, at http://legaltimes.typepad.com/ blt/2008/03/page/5/. The case was *Burgess v. United States* (2008).
4. Joe Bob Briggs, "Joe Bob Briggs Goes to the Supreme Court," *Washingtonian,* December 2003, 63.
5. *Medellín v. Texas,* transcript of oral argument, October 10, 2007, 48.
6. Tony Mauro, "Alito Reflects on His Role on the Court," *Legal Times,* August 13, 2007, 1.
7. Charles Lane, "A Private Hearing, of Sorts, for Anti-War Activists," *Washington Post,* May 6, 2002, A19.
8. Paul Bedard, "This Is Not Perry Mason," *Washington Whispers* (blog of *U.S. News & World Report*), November 29, 2007, at www.usnews.com/blogs/ washington-whispers/2007/11/29/.
9. Timothy R. Johnson, *Oral Arguments and Decision Making on the United States Supreme Court* (Albany: State University of New York Press, 2004).
10. Mauro, "Alito Reflects on His Role."
11. Tony Mauro, "All about Harry," *Legal Times,* July 9, 2007, 10; Sarah Levien Shullman, "The Illusion of Devil's Advocacy: How the Justices of the Supreme Court Foreshadow Their Decisions during Oral Argument," *Journal of Appellate Practice and Advocacy* 6 (fall 2004): 292; Lawrence S. Wrightsman, *Oral Arguments before the Supreme Court: An Empirical Approach* (New York: Oxford University Press, 2008), 127–146.

12. Dahlia Lithwick, "Nino's Chain Gang," *Slate Magazine,* at www.slate.com, April 17, 2002.
13. *District of Columbia v. Heller,* transcript of oral argument, March 18, 2008, 53.
14. William H. Rehnquist, *The Supreme Court,* new ed. (New York: Knopf, 2001), 258.
15. "An Interview with Supreme Court Justice John Paul Stevens," *The Third Branch* 39 (April 2007), at www.uscourts.gov/ttb/2007-04/interview/index.html.
16. Jan Crawford Greenburg, "Interview with Chief Justice Roberts," *Nightline,* ABC News, November 15, 2006, at http://abcnews.go.com/Nightline/print?id=2661589.
17. The process of responding to draft majority opinions is described in Forrest Maltzman, James F. Spriggs II, and Paul J. Wahlbeck, *Crafting Law on the Supreme Court: The Collegial Game* (New York: Cambridge University Press, 2000), 62–72.
18. Ralph A. Rossum, *Antonin Scalia's Jurisprudence: Text and Tradition* (Lawrence: University Press of Kansas, 2006), ix.
19. Kevin Merida and Michael A. Fletcher, "Thomas v. Blackmun: Late Jurist's Papers Puncture Colleague's Portrait of a Genteel Court," *Washington Post,* October 10, 2004, A15.
20. *Microsoft Corporation v. AT&T Corp.* (2007).
21. The cases were *Garcetti v. Ceballos* (2006); *Kansas v. Marsh* (2006); and *Hudson v. Michigan* (2006). See Charles Lane, "Justices to Rehear Speech Case from October," *Washington Post,* February 18, 2006, A15.
22. *Rothgery v. Gillespie County,* 171 L. Ed. 2d 366, 383 (2008).
23. *Parents Involved in Community Schools v. Seattle School District No. 1* (2007).
24. Walter Dellinger, "Showtime for the Supremes," *Slate Magazine,* June 28, 2004, at www.slate.com.
25. William D. Blake and Hans J. Hacker, "The Brooding Spirit of the Law: Supreme Court Justices Reading Dissents from the Bench" (typescript, University of Texas and Arkansas State University, 2008), table 2.
26. Tony Mauro, "Supreme Court: Scalia and Stevens Duke it Out," *BLT: The Blog of Legal Times,* June 26, 2008, at http://legaltimes.typepad.com/blt/2008/06/page/2/.
27. U.S. Senate, *Confirmation Hearing on the Nomination of John G. Roberts, Jr. to be Chief Justice of the United States,* 109th Cong., 1st sess., September 12, 2005, 55.
28. Chris Dickerson, "Thomas Talks Courts, Sports at Marshall," *West Virginia Record,* September 12, 2007.
29. Richard A. Posner, *How Judges Think* (Cambridge: Harvard University Press, 2008), 78–81.
30. Norman I. Silber, *With All Deliberate Speed: The Life of Philip Elman* (Ann Arbor: University of Michigan Press, 2004), 51.
31. Jeffrey A. Segal and Harold J. Spaeth, *The Supreme Court and the Attitudinal Model Revisited* (New York: Cambridge University Press, 2002), chap. 2.
32. Walter Murphy, *Elements of Judicial Strategy* (Chicago: University of Chicago Press, 1964), 44n*. See Jack Knight and Lee Epstein, "The Norm of *Stare Decisis,*" *American Journal of Political Science* 40 (November 1996): 1018–1035.
33. Additional evidence is discussed and presented in Stefanie A. Lindquist and David E. Klein, "The Influence of Jurisprudential Considerations on Supreme Court Decisionmaking: A Study of Conflict Cases," *Law & Society Review* 40 (2006): 135–161.

34. *New York State Board of Elections v. Lopez Torres,* 169 L. Ed. 2d 665, 676 (2008).
35. Lori Hausegger and Lawrence Baum, "Inviting Congressional Action: A Study of Supreme Court Motivations in Statutory Interpretation," *American Journal of Political Science* 43 (January 1999): 162–185.
36. *Bolling v. Sharpe* (1954).
37. *Gitlow v. New York* (1925); *Cantwell v. Connecticut* (1940).
38. *Hans v. Louisiana* (1890).
39. James J. Brudney and Corey Ditslear, "The Decline and Fall of Legislative History? Patterns of Supreme Court Reliance in the Burger and Rehnquist Eras," *Judicature* 89 (January–February 2006): 220–229.
40. *Hamdan v. Rumsfeld,* 548 U.S. 557, 584, 665–667 (2006).
41. Carl Smith, "Quizzing Justice," *The Reflector* (Mississippi State University), January 25, 2008; Sally Friedman, "Supreme Court Justice Ginsburg Advocates Women Pursuing Law," *Philadelphia Bulletin,* March 11, 2008. An apparent typographical error in the Scalia quotation was corrected.
42. The decisions were *Atkins v. Virginia* (2002); *Roper v. Simmons* (2005); and *Kennedy v. Louisiana* (2008).
43. Pierre N. Leval, "Judging under the Constitution: Dicta about Dicta," *New York University Law Review* 81 (October 2006): 1249–1282.
44. Congressional Research Service, *The Constitution of the United States of America: Analysis and Interpretation* (Washington, D.C.: Government Printing Office, 2004), 2392–2399; *2008 Supplement* (Washington, D.C.: Government Printing Office, 2008), 169.
45. Ken Foskett, *Judging Thomas: The Life and Times of Clarence Thomas* (New York: Morrow, 2004), 281.
46. Harold J. Spaeth and Jeffrey A. Segal, *Majority Rule or Minority Will: Adherence to Precedent on the U.S. Supreme Court* (New York: Cambridge University Press, 1999).
47. *Leegin Creative Leather Products, Inc. v. PSKS, Inc.* (2007). See Lori A. Ringhand, "Judicial Activism: An Empirical Examination of Voting Behavior on the Rehnquist Natural Court," *Constitutional Commentary* 24 (2007): 66.
48. See Thomas G. Hansford and James F. Spriggs II, *The Politics of Precedent on the U.S. Supreme Court* (Princeton: Princeton University Press, 2006).
49. *Exxon Shipping Company v. Baker,* 171 L. Ed. 2d 570, 599–600 (2008).
50. Mark J. Richards and Herbert M. Kritzer, "Jurisprudential Regimes in Supreme Court Decision Making," *American Political Science Review* 96 (June 2002): 305–320; Michael A. Bailey and Forrest Maltzman, "Does Legal Doctrine Matter? Unpacking Law and Policy Preferences on the U.S. Supreme Court," *American Political Science Review* 102 (August 2008): 369–384.
51. A good example is Segal and Spaeth, *Supreme Court and the Attitudinal Model Revisited.*
52. Diane Marie Amann, "John Paul Stevens, Human Rights Judge," *Fordham Law Review* 74 (2006): 1582–1583; Ken Kobayashi, "Justice Stevens Recalls War Years in Honolulu," *Honolulu Advertiser,* July 20, 2007; Jeffrey Rosen, "The Dissenter," *New York Times Magazine,* September 23, 2007, 54; *Morse v. Frederick,* 551 U.S. 393, 447–448 (2007).
53. For two competing positions, see Lee Epstein and Jack Knight, *The Choices Justices Make* (Washington, D.C.: CQ Press, 1998); and Saul Brenner and Joseph M. Whitmeyer, *Strategy on the United States Supreme Court* (New York: Cambridge University Press, 2009).

54. Data on rates of agreement are from "The Statistics," *Harvard Law Review* 122 (November 2008): 518.
55. Ibid., 522.
56. Jeffrey A. Segal, Lee Epstein, Charles M. Cameron, and Harold J. Spaeth, "Ideological Values and the Votes of Justices Revisited," *Journal of Politics* 57 (August 1995): 812–823.
57. Figures on agreement between Blackmun and his colleagues are taken from the annual statistics on the Supreme Court term in the November issues of *Harvard Law Review*, vols. 85–100 (1972–1987). See also "The Changing Social Vision of Justice Blackmun," *Harvard Law Review* 96 (1983): 717–736.
58. See Linda Greenhouse, *Becoming Justice Blackmun: Harry Blackmun's Supreme Court Journey* (New York: Times Books, 2005).
59. *Parents Involved in Community Schools v. Seattle School District No. 1*, 551 U.S. 701, 803 (2007).
60. Hope Yen, "O'Connor: Supreme Court Rulings Shouldn't Differ Based on Who Sits on Court," Associated Press, May 20, 2007.
61. Richard A. Posner, "A Tribute to Justice William J. Brennan, Jr.," *Harvard Law Review* 104 (November 1990): 13.
62. Spaeth and Segal, *Majority Rule or Minority Will*, 290–301.
63. Lori A. Ringhand, "Judicial Activism," *Constitutional Commentary* 24 (2007): 48–63.
64. See Richard Kluger, *Simple Justice: The History of* Brown v. Board of Education *and Black America's Struggle for Equality* (New York: Knopf, 1976), 582–699. The quotation is from William O. Douglas, *The Court Years, 1939–1975: The Autobiography of William O. Douglas* (New York: Random House, 1980), 115.
65. David G. Savage, "The Rescue of Roe vs. Wade," *Los Angeles Times,* December 13, 1992, A1, A28, A29.
66. David Margolick, "Bush's Court Advantage," *Vanity Fair,* December 2003, 144–162; Jan Crawford Greenburg, *Supreme Conflict: The Inside Story of the Struggle for Control of the United States Supreme Court* (New York: Penguin Press, 2007), 174–177.
67. Institute of Governmental Studies, "Justice Stephen Breyer Visits IGS for an Informal Talk about the Supreme Court," *Public Affairs Report* 38 (May 1997): 10.
68. William H. Rehnquist, "Chief Justices I Never Knew," *Hastings Constitutional Law Quarterly* 3 (summer 1976): 647.
69. Rehnquist, *Supreme Court,* 222.
70. Sandra Day O'Connor, *The Majesty of the Law: Reflections of a Supreme Court Justice* (New York: Random House, 2003), 119.
71. See Maltzman, Spriggs, and Wahlbeck, *Crafting Law on the Supreme Court.*
72. Sandra L. Wood, "Negotiating on the Burger Court" (paper presented at the annual meeting of the Midwest Political Science Association, Chicago, April 1999), 22–23.
73. Pamela C. Corley, "Bargaining and Accommodation on the United States Supreme Court: Insight from Justice Blackmun," *Judicature* 90 (January–February 2007): 157–165.
74. Maltzman, Spriggs, and Wahlbeck, *Crafting Law on the Supreme Court,* 116.
75. Forrest Maltzman and Paul J. Wahlbeck, "Strategic Policy Considerations and Voting Fluidity on the Burger Court," *American Political Science Review* 90 (September 1996): 587.
76. Segal and Spaeth, *Supreme Court and the Attitudinal Model Revisited,* 286.

77. Chris W. Bonneau, Thomas H. Hammond, Forrest Maltzman, and Paul J. Wahlbeck, "Agenda Control, the Median Justice, and the Majority Opinion on the U.S. Supreme Court," *American Journal of Political Science* 51 (October 2007): 890–905; Jeffrey R. Lax and Kelly T. Rader, "Bargaining Power in the Supreme Court" (Department of Political Science, Columbia University, 2008).

78. O'Connor, *Majesty of the Law,* 195.

79. Douglas, *The Court Years,* 18.

80. Rehnquist, *Supreme Court,* 225–226.

81. James F. Simon, *The Antagonists: Hugo Black, Felix Frankfurter and Civil Liberties in Modern America* (New York: Simon and Schuster, 1989), 249.

82. Charles A. Reich, "Deciding the Fate of *Brown,*" *Green Bag* 7 (winter 2004): 138.

83. Alexander Wohl, "What's Left," *American Bar Association Journal* 77 (February 1991): 42.

84. Nina Totenberg, "A Tribute to Justice William J. Brennan, Jr.," *Harvard Law Review* 104 (November 1990): 37.

85. Greenburg, *Supreme Conflict,* 82–83, 124.

86. Rosen, "The Dissenter," 53.

87. Joan Biskupic, *Sandra Day O'Connor* (New York: HarperCollins, 2005). See also Nancy Maveety, *Queen's Court: Judicial Power in the Rehnquist Era* (Lawrence: University Press of Kansas, 2008).

88. "The Daily Show," Comedy Central, March 3, 2009, at www.thedailyshow.com.

89. Dahlia Lithwick, "A Supreme Court of One," *Washington Post,* July 2, 2006, B1.

90. *Massachusetts v. Environmental Protection Agency* (2007). See Tony Mauro, "Wooing Kennedy on Warming," *The BLT: The Blog of Legal Times,* April 4, 2007, at http://legaltimes.typepad.com/blt/2007/04/page/17/.

91. Dahlia Lithwick, "Button It," *Slate Magazine,* October 11, 2006, at www.slate.com/

92. "Supreme Court to Decide against Gitmo Detainees in 5–4 Decision," *Wonkette,* June 29, 2007, at http://wonkette.com/273658/.

93. Greenburg, "Interview with Chief Justice Roberts"; Jeffrey Rosen, "Roberts's Rules," *Atlantic,* January/February 2007, 105.

94. Forrest Maltzman and Paul J. Wahlbeck, "A Conditional Model of Opinion Assignment on the Supreme Court," *Political Research Quarterly* 57 (December 2004): 555n6.

95. This discussion of criteria for opinion assignment is based largely on the findings for the 1953–1990 period in Maltzman and Wahlbeck, "Conditional Model of Opinion Assignment"; Forrest Maltzman and Paul J. Wahlbeck, "May It Please the Chief? Opinion Assignments in the Rehnquist Court," *American Journal of Political Science* 40 (May 1996): 421–443; and Paul J. Wahlbeck, "Strategy and Constraints on Supreme Court Opinion Assignment," *University of Pennsylvania Law Review* 154 (2006): 1729–1755.

96. Greenburg, "Interview with Chief Justice Roberts."

97. Rehnquist, *Supreme Court,* 260.

98. Greenburg, "Interview with Chief Justice Roberts."

99. Ruth Marcus, "Alumni Brennan, Blackmun Greet Harvard Law Freshmen," *Washington Post,* September 6, 1986, 2.

100. See Timothy R. Johnson, James F. Spriggs II, and Paul J. Wahlbeck, "Passing and Strategic Voting on the U.S. Supreme Court," *Law and Society Review* 39 (June 2005): 349–377.
101. David J. Garrow, *Liberty and Sexuality: The Right to Privacy and the Making of Roe v. Wade* (New York: Macmillan, 1994), 558.
102. John C. Jeffries Jr., *Justice Lewis F. Powell, Jr.* (New York: Scribner's, 1994), 545.
103. This discussion of Rehnquist is based in part on David G. Savage, "The Rehnquist Court," *Los Angeles Times Magazine,* September 29, 1991, 12–16, 38, 40; David J. Garrow, "The Rehnquist Reins," *New York Times Magazine,* October 6, 1996, 65–71, 82, 85; Sue Davis, "The Chief Justice and Judicial Decision-Making: The Institutional Basis for Leadership on the Supreme Court," in *Supreme Court Decision-Making: New Institutionalist Approaches,* ed. Cornell W. Clayton and Howard Gillman (Chicago: University of Chicago Press, 1999), 141–149; and Jeffrey Rosen, "Rehnquist the Great?" *Atlantic Monthly,* April 2005, 79–90.
104. Linda Greenhouse, "How Not to Be Chief Justice: The Apprenticeship of William H. Rehnquist," *University of Pennsylvania Law Review* 154 (2006): 1367, emphasis in original.
105. Rosen, "Rehnquist the Great?" 79–80.
106. "An Interview with Supreme Court Justice John Paul Stevens," *The Third Branch* 39 (April 2007), at www.uscourts.gov/ttb/2007-04/interview/index.html.
107. Rosen, "Roberts's Rules," 105–113.
108. Tony Mauro, "Alito Recaps First Year on High Court," *The Legal Intelligencer,* February 7, 2007, 4.
109. Jan Crawford Greenburg, "Justices Scalia and Breyer: Little in Common, Much to Debate," ABC News, December 6, 2006, at www.abcnews.go.com/Politics/print?id=2704898.
110. These findings are based on analysis of the U.S. Supreme Court Database, compiled by Harold Spaeth, at www.cas.sc.edu/poli/juri/sctdata.htm.
111. "This Week with George Stephanopoulos," ABC News, July 6, 2003.
112. Ben Winograd, "'Ask the Author' with Jeffrey Toobin: Part 2," Scotusblog, September 19, 2007, at www.scotusblog.com/wp/?s=ask+the+author+wit h+jeffrey+toobin.
113. Joan Biskupic, "Justices Strike a Balance," *USA Today,* December 26, 2007, 1D.
114. *Hall Street Associates, L.L.C. v. Mattel, Inc.,* 170 L. Ed. 2d 254, 259 (2008). Citations of statutory provisions and an abbreviation of the statute were omitted from the quoted passage.
115. Jeffrey Rosen, "The O'Connor Court: America's Most Powerful Jurist," *New York Times Magazine,* June 3, 2001, 35.
116. Jeffrey Rosen, *The Most Democratic Branch: How the Courts Serve America* (New York: Oxford University Press, 2006), 185; Neal Devins, "The D'Oh! of Popular Constitutionalism," *Michigan Law Review* 105 (April 2007): 1335.
117. James L. Gibson, Gregory A. Caldeira, and Lester Kenyatta Spence, "The Supreme Court and the U.S. Presidential Election of 2000: Wounds, Self-Inflicted or Otherwise?" *British Journal of Political Science* 33 (2003): 535–556; Stephen P. Nicholson and Robert M. Howard, "Framing Support

for the Supreme Court in the Aftermath of *Bush v. Gore,*" *Journal of Politics* 65 (August 2003): 676–695.

118. See Kevin T. McGuire and James A. Stimson, "The Least Dangerous Branch Revisited: New Evidence on Supreme Court Responsiveness to Public Preferences," *Journal of Politics* 66 (November 2004): 1018–1035; and Micheal W. Giles, Bethany Blackstone, and Richard L. Vining Jr., "The Supreme Court in American Democracy: Unraveling the Linkages between Public Opinion and Judicial Decision Making," *Journal of Politics* 70 (April 2008): 293–306.

119. Thomas Marshall, *Public Opinion and the Rehnquist Court* (Albany: State University of New York Press, 2008).

120. Foskett, *Judging Thomas,* 18.

121. Charles Lane, "Kennedy's Assault on Editorial Writers," *Washington Post,* April 3, 2006, A17.

122. Thomas Sowell, "Blackmun Plays to the Crowd," *St. Louis Post Dispatch,* March 4, 1994, 7B; Michael Barone, "Justices Have Typically Felt Little Compunction about Overturning Laws and Making Public Policy," *Chicago Sun-Times,* July 13, 2005, 55.

123. Pamela C. Corley, "The Supreme Court and Opinion Content: The Influence of Parties' Briefs," *Political Research Quarterly* 61 (September 2008): 468–478.

124. Paul M. Collins Jr., *Friends of the Supreme Court: Interest Groups and Judicial Decision Making* (New York: Oxford University Press, 2008), chap. 4.

125. Timothy R. Johnson, Paul J. Wahlbeck, and James F. Spriggs II, "The Influence of Oral Arguments on the U.S. Supreme Court," *American Political Science Review* 100 (February 2006): 99–113.

126. This percentage is based on data provided by the Office of the Solicitor General.

127. See Rebecca E. Deen, Joseph Ignagni, and James Meernik, "Individual Justices and the Solicitor General: The Amicus Curiae Cases, 1953–2000," *Judicature* 89 (September–October 2005): 68–77.

128. Jason D. Mycoff, Jacquelyn S. Bryan, and Alex G. Stanzione, "Regulatory Statutes, Supreme Court Decisions, and Congressional Overrides" (paper presented at the annual meeting of the Midwest Political Science Association, Chicago, April 2008).

129. For contrasting arguments and evidence, see Segal and Spaeth, *Supreme Court and the Attitudinal Model Revisited,* 326–356; and Mario Bergara, Barak Richman, and Pablo T. Spiller, "Modeling Supreme Court Strategic Decision Making: The Congressional Constraint," *Legislative Studies Quarterly* 28 (May 2003): 247–280.

130. See Neal Devins, "Should the Supreme Court Fear Congress?" *Minnesota Law Review* 90 (May 2006): 1337–1362.

131. David Yalof, "The Presidency and the Judiciary," in *The Presidency and the Political System,* 8th ed., ed. Michael Nelson (Washington, D.C.: CQ Press, 2006), 501–504.

132. These decisions were *Hamdi v. Rumsfeld* (2004); *Hamdan v. Rumsfeld* (2006); and *Boumediene v. Bush* (2008).

Chapter 5

Policy Outputs

———————————

The last two chapters examined the processes that shape the Supreme Court's policies. In this chapter, I consider the substance of those policies by addressing several issues. What kinds of issues does the Court address? How active is the Court as a policymaker? What is the ideological content of its policies? I conclude the chapter by developing an explanation for historical patterns in the Court's outputs.

Areas of Activity: What the Court Addresses

During any given term, the Supreme Court resolves a broad range of issues in fields as varied as antitrust, environmental protection, and freedom of speech. In this sense the Court's agenda is highly diverse. But the Court generally devotes most of its efforts to a few policy fields. To a considerable degree, then, the Court is a specialist.

The Court's Current Activity

The content of the Court's agenda can be illustrated with the cases that it heard in the 2007 term. It is useful to begin by describing the issues in a fairly representative sample of cases decided during that term.

1. In reviewing criminal sentences by federal district judges, are courts of appeals always required to use an "abuse of discretion" standard that favors affirmance of a sentence? (*Gall v. United States,* 2007)

2. When a trust pays fees to an investment adviser, are fees that fall below 2 percent of the trust's adjusted gross income generally deductible from its taxable income? (*Knight v. Commissioner of Internal Revenue,* 2008)

3. Under Section 10b of the Securities Exchange Act, can stock investors sue entities that assisted a company in misleading the investors but that did not actually prepare or disseminate the misleading

financial statement? (*Stoneridge Investment Partners v. Scientific-Atlanta*, 2008)

4. When a state trial judge rejected a defendant's objection to the prosecutor's challenge of a prospective juror, did the judge fail to follow the Supreme Court's rule against peremptory challenges of jurors that are based on race? (*Snyder v. Louisiana*, 2008)

5. Does a state law that requires voters to present government-issued photo identification at the polls violate the equal protection clause of the Fourteenth Amendment? (*Crawford v. Marion County*, 2008)

6. Did police officers violate the Constitution when they made an arrest that was illegal under state law but that was based on probable cause or when they carried out a search after that arrest? (*Virginia v. Moore*, 2008)

7. When an employee alleges that he was fired for complaining that another employee had been fired because of race, can he bring a lawsuit for retaliation under an 1870 civil rights law? (*CBOCS West, Inc. v. Humphries*, 2008)

8. When an immigrant requests voluntary departure from the United States as an alternative to deportation, can that person withdraw the request before the voluntary departure period expires? (*Dada v. Mukasey*, 2008)

9. Is a California law that prohibits employers who receive certain state funds from using the funds to assist or deter union organizing invalid because it is preempted by the National Labor Relations Act? (*Chamber of Commerce v. Brown*, 2008)

10. Does a person who trades drugs for a gun fall under the federal law that sets a mandatory minimum sentence for using a firearm in a drug trafficking crime? (*Watson v. United States*, 2007)

Table 5-1 provides a more systematic picture of the Court's agenda in the 2007 term by summarizing the characteristics of the seventy decisions with full opinions in that term. The Court's decisions were closely connected with the other branches of government. The federal government or one of its agencies was a party in about 40 percent of all cases. State governments were parties in most other cases, so that three in four cases had at least one government party. Moreover, most of the disputes between private parties were based directly on government policy in fields such as environmental protection and civil rights.

Only about one-quarter of the cases were decided on constitutional grounds, a smaller proportion than usual, although several additional cases had constitutional issues in the background. Still, the 2007 term was similar to other recent terms in that the majority of cases involved interpretations of federal statutes. Observers of the Court tend to focus on its

TABLE 5-1

Characteristics of Decisions by the Supreme Court with Full Opinions,
2007 Term

Characteristic	Number	Percentage
Number of decisions	70	NA
Cases from lower federal courts	58	83
Cases from state courts	11	16
Original cases	1	1
Federal government party[a]	27	39
State or local government party[a]	26	37
No government party	17	24
Constitutional issue decided[b]	19	27
No constitutional issue decided	51	73
Civil liberties issue present[c]	34	49
No civil liberties issue	36	51
Criminal cases[d]	28	40
Civil cases	42	60

Source: The cases listed were those included in the front section of *United States Supreme Court Reports, Lawyers' Edition*, vols. 169–171.

Note: NA = not applicable. Consolidated cases decided with one set of opinions were counted once.

a. Cases with both a federal government party and another government party were listed as federal government. Government as party includes agencies and individual government officials.
b. In several additional cases, the parties raised constitutional issues or those issues were present in the underlying case. Cases involving federal preemption of state laws are not treated as constitutional.
c. Includes cases in which the Court did not decide the civil liberties issue directly.
d. Includes actions brought by prisoners to challenge the legality of their convictions but excludes cases concerning rights of prisoners.

interpretations of the Constitution, which often involve fundamental issues about the structure and power of government. However, the Court devotes much of its collective energy to statutory interpretation, adjudicating disputes about the meaning of federal laws.

In the 2007 term, as has been true for several decades, the Court's single biggest area of activity was civil liberties. As in earlier discussions, the term "civil liberties" refers here to three general types of rights: procedural rights of people involved in government proceedings; the right of disadvantaged groups to equal treatment; and certain substantive rights,

Workers at an office of the Internal Revenue Service. The majority of Supreme Court decisions interpret federal statutes such as the tax laws, not provisions of the Constitution.

the most important of which are freedom of expression and freedom of religion. By that definition, about half of the Court's decisions fell into this area.

Related to the Court's civil liberties emphasis is its work in criminal law and procedure. Forty percent of the 2007 decisions resulted from criminal prosecutions. Although in most terms criminal cases are less prominent on the agenda, since the 1950s they have consistently made up a substantial proportion of the Court's cases. In many of the criminal cases, the Court addresses civil liberties issues by interpreting constitutional protections of due process rights.

The list of representative cases from the 2007 term illustrates two other areas in which the Court is active. Outside of civil liberties, the largest number of cases concerns economic issues. Most civil liberties cases are based on constitutional questions, but economic cases generally involve statutory interpretation. Most of these cases arise from government regulation of economic activity, such as labor-management relations, antitrust, and environmental protection.

Another major subject of Court activity is federalism, the division of power between federal and state governments. Federalism overlaps with other categories, and most federalism cases concern economic issues. This subject has been especially prominent in the past fifteen years.

Taken together, civil liberties, economic policy, and federalism cover a large portion of the issues that arise in American government. Still, the Court's emphasis on those issues constitutes something of a specialized focus. Most striking is its concentration on civil liberties. Although civil liberties cases vary considerably, the fact that about half the Court's decisions concern this single kind of issue is an indication of the Court's specialization.

Change in the Court's Agenda

The Court's agenda is hardly static. Even over a few terms, the Court's attention to specific categories of cases sometimes increases or decreases substantially. The shape of its agenda as a whole changes more slowly, but over long periods it may undergo fundamental change.[1]

Changes in Specific Portions of the Agenda. Sometimes an issue that has occupied a very small place on the Court's agenda, or no place at all, becomes more prominent. More often than not, the source is action by Congress. Before federal law prohibited discrimination in employment, for instance, people who felt that they had been subjected to discrimination had little basis for bringing cases to court. The series of federal statutes that were enacted from 1963 on provided that basis, and the resulting cases created a substantial number of legal questions that the Court chose to resolve. It has now heard about one hundred fifty cases on employment discrimination.

Another example concerns employee pension plans. Until 1980 the Court decided few cases involving those issues. Since then these cases have been common. The source of this change is simple: Congress enacted the Employee Retirement Income Security Act of 1974 (ERISA). This regulation of pension plans raised a variety of legal questions that the courts had to address. The justices have seen a need to resolve many of these questions themselves, even though they have limited interest in the complex issues that arise under ERISA. As a result, the Court has heard more than fifty cases interpreting ERISA.

The Court itself can open up new areas on its agenda with decisions that create legal rights or add to existing rights. When the Court ruled in *Roe v. Wade* (1973) that the abortion laws of most states violated the constitutional right to privacy, it ensured that it would have to decide a stream of cases involving challenges to new abortion laws. The Court's decision in *Batson v. Kentucky* (1986) allowed criminal defendants to challenge the use of peremptory challenges by prosecutors on the ground that the challenges were used in a racially discriminatory way. Since then, the Court has decided a series of cases about who has the right to raise a *Batson* claim and how judges are to determine whether a challenge was used with the intent to exclude prospective jurors on the basis of race.

On sentencing guidelines for federal judges, Congress put the issue on the Court's agenda and a Court decision two decades later brought a new set of cases to the agenda. In 1984 Congress set up a system under which district judges would sentence defendants according to a set of guidelines established by a sentencing commission. The Court then decided a series of cases about interpretation of the guidelines. In *United States v. Booker* (2005) the Court ruled that mandatory sentencing guidelines for federal judges were unconstitutional and required that the guidelines be made voluntary. Since then, the Court has already decided several cases on the meaning and implications of the *Booker* decision.

Just as issues can rise on the Court's agenda, they can also recede. Often, a new statute or Court decision raises a series of issues that the Court resolves. Once they are resolved, the Court need not decide as many cases in this area. In *Benton v. Maryland* (1969) the Court ruled that the constitutional protection against double jeopardy for criminal offenses applied to the states. This decision opened the way for state cases involving claims of double jeopardy to reach the Court, and in the 1970s and 1980s the Court decided more than fifty cases in that field. But with so many issues resolved, the Court has heard only occasional double jeopardy cases since then.

Changes in the Agenda as a Whole. Beyond changes in specific areas, the overall pattern of the Court's agenda may change over a period of several decades. The current agenda reflects a fundamental change that occurred between the 1930s and 1960s. In the half century up to the 1930s, the largest part of the Court's agenda was devoted to economic issues. Also important but clearly secondary were cases about federalism. Issues of procedural due process constituted a small proportion of the agenda, and other civil liberties issues were barely present.

Over the next three decades the Court evolved from an institution concerned primarily with economic issues to one that gave most of its attention to individual liberties. The proportion of decisions dealing with civil liberties grew from 8 percent of the agenda in the 1933–1937 terms to 59 percent in the 1968–1972 terms.[2] Issues involving the rights of criminal defendants became far more numerous, and other civil liberties issues such as racial equality took a substantial share of the agenda. At the same time, some kinds of economic cases declined precipitously. In 1933–1937, one of every three cases involved federal taxation or economic disputes between private parties. By 1968–1972, the two areas accounted for only 6 percent of the Court's agenda. Federalism also took a reduced share of the agenda, falling from 14 percent in 1933–1937 to 5 percent in 1968–1972.

Many forces contributed to this change, ranging from public opinion to federal legislation. Interest groups that supported civil liberties cases played a key role by bringing relevant cases to the Court. But actions by the Court itself had the most direct effect. Perhaps most important, the justices became more interested in protecting civil liberties and thus in hearing claims that government policies infringed on liberties. In part because they had to make room for civil liberties cases, the justices gave more limited attention to other fields. They continued to hear a good many cases involving economic issues, but economics declined considerably as part of the Court's work.

The Court's agenda has changed in some respects since then. Within the civil liberties field, cases involving criminal law and procedure have taken a larger share of the agenda, while issues of equality and First Amendment rights have declined. Meanwhile, federalism cases have become more common. But on the whole, the broad contours of the agenda have remained stable. In particular, as the agenda for the 2007 term illustrates, the Court continues to hear more cases in civil liberties than in any other field. Thus, the Court's work still reflects the changes in its agenda that occurred between the 1930s and the 1960s.

A Broader View of the Agenda

If the Supreme Court's current agenda differs from the agendas of previous Courts, it also differs from those of other policymakers. In turn, those differences provide some perspective on the Court's role.

Comparison with Other Institutions. In some respects, the Supreme Court's agenda resembles the agendas of other appellate courts, especially state supreme courts and federal courts of appeals. To a considerable extent, all these courts focus on government parties and government policy. Criminal cases are prominent on the agendas of virtually all appellate courts, and most give substantial attention to economic issues. Except for the rights of criminal defendants, however, civil liberties issues are relatively rare in lower appellate courts. The Supreme Court stands alone in the prominence of issues involving rights to equal treatment and freedom of expression.

Like the Court, the president is something of a specialist. But the president's agenda has its own emphases: foreign policy and maintenance of the nation's economic health. In contrast, the Court makes few decisions about foreign policy, and its decisions on economic policy barely touch the function of managing the economy.

More than the president and the Court, Congress is a generalist, spreading its activity across a large set of issues. One result is that the congressional agenda covers virtually all the types of policy that the Supreme Court deals with. But some of the issues that are central to the Court, especially in civil liberties, receive much less attention from Congress. And Congress gives a high priority to several fields, ranging from foreign policy to agriculture, that are less important to the Court.

The Court's Position. These comparisons of agendas underline the limited range of the Court's work. Its jurisdiction is broad, but the bulk of its decisions are made in only a few policy areas. The Court's specialization affects its role as a policymaker. By deciding as many civil liberties cases as it does, the Court can do much to shape law and policy in this area. In contrast, the Court's more limited activity in some major policy areas severely narrows its potential impact in those fields. Foreign policy is the most striking example.

Even in the areas in which it is most active, the Court addresses only certain types of issues. In criminal justice, the Court does much to define the rights of criminal defendants and the scope of federal criminal statutes. But its cases do not affect funding of criminal justice agencies, and they have little to do with prosecution policies and plea bargaining. In economics, the Court's decisions barely touch the most important government policies—on revenue, spending, and management of the economy.

Because it focuses on a limited set of issues in a few policy areas, the Court does not deal with most of the issues that are high on the agendas of government and of the public. The wars in Iraq and Afghanistan have proceeded with essentially no involvement by the Court. The Court eventually may deal with some issues that relate to revival of the U.S. economy, but the major decisions are being made in the other branches of government.

These realities should caution against the conclusion that the Supreme Court is the most powerful policymaker in the United States. Legal scholar Fred Schauer has argued that we should not "leap from the accurate premise that much of what the Supreme Court does is important to the erroneous conclusion that much of what is important is done by the Supreme Court."[3] Although the importance of the Court's role can be debated, the limited range of the Court's activities inevitably limits its power. The Court could not possibly be dominant as a policymaker except in federalism, civil liberties, and some limited areas of economic policy. For reasons that are discussed in the rest of this chapter and in Chapter 6, even in those areas the Court is far from dominant.

The Court's Activism

The Court's attention or inattention to various areas of policy helps determine where it is likely to play a significant role. But its impact also depends on what it rules in those policy areas. Of particular importance is how much it engages in activism.

The term *judicial activism* has multiple meanings, and people sometimes use the term simply as a negative label for decisions they dislike. What I mean by activism is that a court makes significant changes in public policy, especially in policies that the other branches have established. One form of activism involves the Court's use of judicial review, its power to overturn acts of other policymakers because they violate the Constitution. The Court intervenes in government policy most directly and most clearly when it strikes down the policies of the other branches on constitutional grounds.

Overturning Acts of Congress

The most familiar use of judicial review comes in decisions holding that federal statutes are unconstitutional. Such a ruling represents a clear assertion of power by the Court, because it directly negates a decision by another branch of the federal government.

It can be difficult to count instances in which the Court actually has struck down a statute. By one imperfect count, shown in Table 5-2, by the end of 2008 the Court had overturned 163 federal laws completely or in part.[4] (When different provisions of a statute were struck down in different decisions, each decision is counted once.) This number in itself is noteworthy. On the one hand, it indicates that the Court has made fairly frequent use of its review power—on average, more than once every two years. On the other hand, the laws struck down by the Court constitute a minute fraction of the laws that Congress has adopted. And when the Court rules on whether a federal statute is unconstitutional, in about five times out of six it upholds the statute.[5]

A closer look at the decisions striking down federal laws provides a better sense of their significance.[6] One question is the importance of the statutes that the Court has overturned. The Court has struck down some statutes of major importance. Among these were the Missouri Compromise of 1820, concerning slavery in the territories, which the Court declared unconstitutional in the *Dred Scott* case in 1857, and the New Deal economic legislation that was overturned in 1935 and 1936.[7] In contrast, many of the Court's decisions declaring statutes invalid have been unimportant to the policy goals of Congress and the president, either because the statutes were minor or because they were struck down only as they applied to particular circumstances.

A related question is the timing of judicial review. The Court's decisions striking down federal statutes fall into three groups of nearly equal size: those that came no more than four calendar years after a statute's enactment, those that came five to twelve years later, and those that occurred at least thirteen years later. Congress sometimes retains a strong commitment to a statute from an earlier period. But often few members care much if an older law is overturned: the statute becomes less relevant over time or the collective point of view in Congress becomes less favorable to the provision in question.

For these reasons the Court's frequent use of its power to invalidate congressional acts is somewhat misleading. Any decision that strikes down a federal statute might seem likely to produce major conflict between the Court and Congress, but that is not necessarily the case. Conflict is most likely when the Court invalidates an important congressional policy within a few years of its enactment, but most decisions striking down statutes do not meet both those criteria. Some decisions striking down legislation receive little attention, and others are actually welcomed by presidents and members of Congress.[8]

Another way to gauge the significance of judicial review is by the historical patterns of its use. As Table 5-2 shows, the Court has not overturned federal statutes at a constant rate. Before 1865 it struck down only two statutes. The Court then began to exercise its judicial review power more actively, overturning thirty-five federal laws between 1865 and 1919. Two more increases, even more dramatic, followed: the Court struck down fifteen federal laws during the 1920s, and twelve from 1934 through 1936. Over the next quarter century, the Court used this power sparingly. But between 1960 and 2008, it overturned ninety-one statutes, far more than in any previous period of the same length and more than half of the total for the Court's entire history.

The period of greatest conflict between the Court and Congress was 1918 to 1936, when the Court overturned twenty-nine federal laws. Many of these laws were significant. Between 1918 and 1928, the Court invalidated two child labor laws and a minimum wage law, along with several less important statutes. Then, between 1933 and 1936, a majority of the Court engaged in a frontal attack on the New Deal program, an attack that ended with the Court's 1937 shift in position.

Among all the statutes that the Court declared unconstitutional between 1960 and 1994, a few were of major importance. *Buckley v. Valeo* (1976) and several later decisions invalidated major provisions of the Federal Election Campaign Act on First Amendment grounds and thereby made comprehensive regulation of campaign finance impossible. In *Immigration and Naturalization Service v. Chadha* (1983), the Court struck down a relatively minor provision of an immigration law. But its ruling indicated that the legislative veto, a widely used mechanism for congressional control of the executive branch, violated the constitutional separation of powers. These decisions were exceptions. In general, the laws overturned by the Court in the 1960–1994 period were not nearly as significant as the economic legislation that it struck down in the 1930s. Indeed, most of the Court's decisions striking down federal laws received little attention from the mass media or the general public.

Between 1995 and 2002, the Court invalidated thirty-two federal laws, a record number for an eight-year period. During that period, as in prior periods, most of the laws struck down were relatively minor. One exception was *Clinton v. City of New York* (1998), in which the Court ruled that Congress

TABLE 5-2
*Number of Federal Statutes and State and Local Statutes Held
Unconstitutional by the Supreme Court, 1790–2008*

Period	Federal statutes	State and local statutes
1790–1799	0	0
1800–1809	1	1
1810–1819	0	7
1820–1829	0	8
1830–1839	0	3
1840–1849	0	10
1850–1859	1	7
1860–1869	4	24
1870–1879	7	36
1880–1889	4	46
1890–1899	5	36
1900–1909	9	40
1910–1919	6	119
1920–1929	15	139
1930–1939	13	92
1940–1949	2	61
1950–1959	5	66
1960–1969	16	151
1970–1979	20	195
1980–1989	16	164
1990–1999	24	62
2000–2008	15	34
Total	163	1,301

Sources: Congressional Research Service, *The Constitution of the United States of America: Analysis and Interpretation, 2002 Edition* and *2008 Supplement* (Washington, D.C.: Government Printing Office, 2004, 2008); one 2008 addition to list by the author.

Note: State and local laws include those that the Supreme Court held to be preempted by federal statutes.

could not give presidents the power to veto individual items within budget bills and thereby ended a major innovation in policymaking.

The Court also handed down ten decisions that limited the power of Congress to regulate state governments. In these decisions the Court gave narrow interpretations to the Commerce Clause and the Fourteenth Amendment as bases for federal power while giving a broad interpretation to the Eleventh Amendment as a limit on lawsuits against states. In *Board of Trustees v. Garrett* (2001), for example, the Court ruled that Congress could not authorize disabled individuals to seek monetary damages from states in lawsuits for discrimination. This set of decisions constituted a substantial change in the federal-state balance, but it did not create serious conflict with the other branches, because the Republican majorities in Congress during that period were not inclined to assert federal power against the states in the areas in which the Court limited that power.

The pace of overturnings slowed considerably after 2002. In the six years that followed, the Court issued only five decisions striking down federal laws. In *United States v. Booker* (2005), the Court invalidated the provision that made the federal sentencing guidelines mandatory, thereby overturning the sentencing system that had operated in the federal courts for nearly two decades. The decision in *Boumediene v. Bush* (2008) struck down a 2006 provision denying the right to file habeas corpus petitions to detainees at the Guantánamo Bay Naval Station. The other three of these decisions ruled that various provisions of the Bipartisan Campaign Reform Act of 2002 were unconstitutional, thereby limiting the reach of a second major effort by Congress to regulate funding of political campaigns.[9] With these five decisions, then, the Court had considerable impact on three areas of federal policy.

Overturning State and Local Laws

The Supreme Court's exercise of judicial review over state and local laws has less of an activist element than does its use of that power over federal laws. When the Court strikes down a state law, it does not put itself in conflict with the other branches of the federal government. Indeed, it may be supporting their powers over those of the states. Still, it is invalidating the action of another policymaker. For that reason, this form of judicial review is significant.

From 1790 to 2008, by one count, the Court overturned 1,070 state statutes and local ordinances as unconstitutional. It ruled that another 231 state and local laws were invalid because they were preempted by federal law under the constitutional principle of federal supremacy. As shown in Table 5-2, the total of 1,301 state and local laws struck down is about eight times the number for federal statutes. The disparity is even greater than this figure suggests, because many of the Court's decisions overturning particular state and local laws also applied to similar laws in other states.

As with federal laws, the rate at which the Court invalidates state and local laws has tended to increase over time, and it was far higher in the twentieth century than in the nineteenth. The rate of overturnings was very high between 1909 and 1937, and that rate was even higher from the 1960s through the 1980s. In that period, the Court declared unconstitutional an average of seventeen state and local laws per year. The rate of invalidations has been much lower since 1990, and in the first decade of the twenty-first century it returned to the pace of the late nineteenth century.

Although the Court struck down relatively few state laws before 1860, its decisions during that period were important because they limited state powers under the Constitution. For example, under Chief Justice John Marshall (1801–1835) the Court weakened the states with such decisions as *McCulloch v. Maryland* (1819), which denied the states power to tax federal agencies, and *Gibbons v. Ogden* (1824), which narrowed state power to regulate commerce.

The state and local laws the Court has overturned in more recent periods have been a mixture of the important and the minor. In the aggregate, the Court's decisions have given it a significant role in shaping state policy. During the late nineteenth century and the first third of the twentieth, the Court struck down a great deal of state economic legislation, including many laws regulating business practices and labor relations. The net effect was to turn back much of a major tide of public policy.

Some of the Court's decisions since the mid-1950s have also impinged on major elements of state policy. A series of rulings helped to break down the legal bases of racial segregation and discrimination in southern states. In 1973 the Court overturned the broad prohibitions of abortion that existed in most states, thereby requiring a general legalization of abortion; it has struck down several new laws regulating abortion since then, and its rulings have indirectly invalidated many other abortion laws. And through a long series of decisions, the Court limited state power to regulate the economy in areas that Congress has preempted under its constitutional supremacy. In doing so, the Court shifted power further toward the federal government and away from the states.

Other Targets of Judicial Review

The Supreme Court can declare unconstitutional any government policy or practice, not just laws enacted by legislatures. The number of non-statutory policies and practices that the Court has struck down is probably much larger than the number of laws it has overturned. On constitutional grounds the Court has overruled actions taken by federal cabinet departments, local school boards, and state courts, among others.

The Court is especially active in overseeing criminal procedure under the Constitution, and it frequently holds that actions by police officers or trial judges violate the rights of defendants. In 2008, for instance, the Court declared unconstitutional a county's policy not to provide an attorney for defendants at an early stage in their proceedings, a judge's allowance of a peremptory challenge to a prospective juror, and a judge's admission into evidence of a statement made by a person who was later murdered.[10] And there has been a long series of decisions holding that police searches and questioning of suspects violated constitutional protections under certain conditions.

Of particular interest is the Court's review of presidential orders and policies. Decisions of presidents or officials acting on their behalf can be challenged on the grounds that they are unauthorized by the Constitution or that they violate a constitutional rule. It is difficult to say how frequently the Court strikes down presidential actions as unconstitutional, because it is often unclear whether an action by the executive branch should be considered "presidential." But such decisions by the Court seem to be relatively rare.[11]

The Court has invalidated a few major actions by presidents, however. In *Ex parte Milligan* (1866), it held that President Abraham Lincoln had lacked the power to suspend the writ of habeas corpus for military prisoners during the Civil War. And in *Youngstown Sheet and Tube Co. v. Sawyer* (1952), it declared that President Harry Truman had acted illegally during the Korean War when he ordered the federal government to seize and operate major steel mills because their workers were preparing to go on strike. Between 2004 and 2008, the Court issued four decisions that established procedural protections for Guantánamo detainees. Those decisions did not hold that any decisions by President George W. Bush were unconstitutional, but they overruled some of the president's policies relating to terrorism.[12]

Judicial Review: The General Picture

The Supreme Court's record of judicial review is complicated. The Court has been more activist in some eras than others. On the whole the level of activism has increased over time, in part because of growth in the volume of government activity that can be challenged. The Court has struck down far more state and local policies than federal policies.

Altogether, the justices have made considerable use of the power of judicial review, thereby making the Court a major participant in the policymaking process. Yet the justices also have been quite selective in using their power to strike down laws. Partly as a result, the great majority of public policies at all levels of government have continued without Court interference. Thus, important as judicial review has been, it has not given the Court anything like a dominant position in the national government.

Statutory Interpretation

Historically and currently, most of the Supreme Court's decisions interpret federal statutes rather than constitutional provisions. Statutory interpretation may seem routine, but it can involve activism in at least two senses.

For one thing, the Court's statutory decisions often determine whether an administrative agency has interpreted a statute correctly in the process of implementing it. If the Court concludes that an agency has erred, it strikes down the agency's action as contrary to the statute. More broadly, the Court often puts its own stamp on a statute through its interpretations of that statute over the years. It has done so with its decisions on antitrust, labor relations, and environmental protection. In this way the Court affects national policy in the fields covered by those statutes.

This process is exemplified by Title VII of the Civil Rights Act of 1964, the most important of the federal statutes that prohibit employment discrimination. As with many other statutes, Congress laid out the broad outlines of the law and left it to the other branches to fill in the gaps. Over the years the Court has resolved many major issues. For example, it has established and revised the guidelines that trial courts use to determine whether an employer has engaged in discrimination.[13] It ruled that a company's policies could violate Title VII on the basis of their impact, even if the employer did not intend to discriminate.[14] It held that sexual harassment may constitute sex discrimination under Title VII and set up rules to determine when an employer is legally responsible for harassment.[15] Through these and other rulings the Court has affected the use and effect of Title VII and thus has shaped federal policy concerning employment discrimination.

The Content of Policy

So far, I have examined the areas in which the Supreme Court concentrates its efforts and the extent of its activism. A third aspect of the Court's role as a policymaker is the content of its policies. This content can best be understood in terms of its ideological direction and its beneficiaries. Dividing the Court's history into eras is arbitrary, but it is useful to think of the period since the late nineteenth century as containing three eras.

The 1890s to the 1930s

Over several decades the Supreme Court is certain to shift its position on some broad issues. That was true of the period that began in the 1890s and ended in the 1930s. But in ideological terms, the Court of that era was predominantly conservative. Most of its activism was on behalf of advantaged interests, such as business corporations. In contrast it did little to protect such disadvantaged groups as racial minority groups.

Scrutinizing Economic Regulation. In 1915 the Supreme Court decided *South Covington & Cincinnati Street Railway Co. v. City of Covington.* The company, which ran streetcars between Covington, Kentucky, and Cincinnati, Ohio, challenged several provisions of a Covington ordinance regulating its operations. The Court struck down some provisions on the ground that they constituted a burden on interstate commerce between Ohio and Kentucky.

The Court also declared invalid a regulation stipulating that the temperature in the cars never be permitted to go below fifty degrees Fahrenheit: "We therefore think ... this feature of the ordinance is unreasonable and cannot be sustained"—apparently on the ground that the regulation violated the Fourteenth Amendment by depriving the company of its property without due process of law.

The *South Covington* case illustrates some important attributes of the Court's decisions during the period from the 1890s to the late 1930s. In that period, as discussed earlier, the Court dealt primarily with economic issues. Most important, it ruled on challenges to growing government regulation of business practices.

In these cases the Court frequently ruled in favor of government, rejecting most challenges to federal and state policies and giving broad interpretations to some government powers.[16] But the Court limited government regulatory powers in important respects, and over time its limits on regulation became tighter. This development is reflected in the number of laws involving economic policy that the Court struck down each decade: 43 from 1900 to 1909, 114 from 1910 to 1919, and 133 from 1920 to 1929.[17] The Court's attacks on government regulation peaked in the mid-1930s, when it struck down most of the major statutes in President Franklin Roosevelt's New Deal program to deal with the Great Depression.

The theme of limiting government regulatory powers was reflected in the Court's constitutional doctrines. At the national level, the Court gave narrow interpretations to congressional powers to tax and to regulate interstate commerce. In contrast, the Court read the general limitation on federal power in the Tenth Amendment broadly, using that provision to prohibit some federal actions on the ground that they interfered with state prerogatives. At the same time, the Court limited state powers in the economic sphere. It ruled in 1886 that corporations were "persons" with rights protected by the Fourteenth Amendment.[18] It also interpreted the Fourteenth Amendment requirement that state governments provide due process of law as an absolute prohibition of regulations that interfered unduly with the liberty and property rights of businesses. The Court's ruling against the streetcar temperature regulation was one of many such decisions.

The Court's Beneficiaries. The business community benefited from the Court's policies during this period, and major corporations benefited the most. Of the regulatory legislation that the Court overturned or limited, much was aimed at the activities of large businesses. The railroads were the most prominent example. Although the Court allowed a good deal of government control over railroads, it also struck down a large body of railroad regulation.[19] In the decade from 1910 to 1919, the Court overturned forty-one state laws in cases

An engine of the Erie Railroad in 1903. Railroad companies benefited from the Supreme Court decisions that limited government power to regulate businesses in the early twentieth century.

brought by railroad companies. Major corporations such as railroads might be considered the clientele of the Court from the 1890s to the 1930s.

Large corporations did not simply benefit from the Court's policies; they helped to bring them about.[20] Beginning in the late nineteenth century, the corporate community employed much of the best legal talent in the United States to challenge the validity of regulatory statutes. The effective advocacy of these attorneys helped lay the groundwork for the Court's policies favoring business.

Corporate interests came to the judiciary because of their defeats elsewhere in government. On the whole, Congress and the state legislatures were friendly to business interests, but they did enact a good many regulations of private enterprise. In scrutinizing these regulations closely, the Court served as a court of last resort for corporations in a political sense as well as the legal sense.

Civil Liberties: A Limited Concern. Although the Court decided relatively few civil liberties cases in that era, it gave some attention to that field.[21] Overall, the justices provided much less protection for individual liberties than for the economic rights of businesses. The Court's limited support for racial equality was exemplified by *Plessy v. Ferguson* (1896), in which it promoted racial segregation by ruling that state governments could mandate "separate but equal" facilities for different racial groups. In 1908 the Court held that only a small subset of the procedural rights for criminal defendants in the Bill of Rights was incorporated into the Due Process Clause of the Fourteenth Amendment and thus applicable to proceedings in state courts.[22] Late in that era the Court ruled that the Due Process Clause protected freedom of speech and freedom of the press from state violations. But in a series of decisions it held that the federal government could prosecute people whose expressions allegedly endangered military recruitment and other national security interests.[23]

A Long-Standing Position. The Court's conservatism during that period was not new; the dominant themes of the Court's work in earlier periods were also conservative. The Court provided considerable support for the rights of property holders and much less support for civil liberties outside the economic sphere.

Because of this history, observers of the Supreme Court in the New Deal period had reason to conclude that the Court was a fundamentally conservative body. Indeed, this was the position of two distinguished observers in the early 1940s. The historian Henry Steele Commager argued in 1943 that, with one possible exception, the Court had never intervened on behalf of the underprivileged; in fact, it frequently had blocked efforts by Congress to protect the underprivileged.[24] Two years earlier, Attorney General Robert Jackson, a future Supreme Court justice, reached this stark conclusion: "Never in its entire history can the Supreme Court be said to have for a single hour been representative of anything except the relatively conservative forces of its day."[25] Jackson may have exaggerated for effect, but he captured an important theme in the Court's history.

1937 to 1969

Even before Commager and Jackson described this record of conservatism, however, the Court was beginning a shift in its direction that one historian called "the Constitutional Revolution of 1937." That revolution, he said,

altered fundamentally the character of the Court's business, the nature of its decisions, and the alignment of its friends and foes. From the Marshall Court to the Hughes Court, the judiciary had been largely concerned with questions of property rights. After 1937 the most significant matters on the docket were civil liberties and other personal rights.... While from 1800 to 1937 the principal critics of the Supreme Court were social reformers and the main supporters people of means who were the principal beneficiaries of the Court's decisions, after 1937 roles were reversed, with liberals commending and conservatives censuring the Court.[26]

Acceptance of Government Economic Policy. In the first stage of the revolution, the Court abandoned the limits it had established on government intervention in the economy. That step came quickly. In a series of decisions beginning in 1937, majorities accepted the constitutional power of government—especially the federal government—to regulate and manage the economy. This shift culminated in *Wickard v. Filburn* (1942), in which the Court held that federal power to regulate interstate commerce extended so far that it applied to a farmer who grew wheat for his own livestock.

This collective change of heart proved to be of long duration. The Court consistently upheld major economic legislation against constitutional challenges, striking down only one minor provision of the federal laws regulating business from the 1940s through the 1960s.[27] Supporting federal supremacy in economic matters, the Court struck down many state laws on the ground that they impinged on the constitutional powers of the federal government or that they were preempted by federal statutes. But in other respects it gave state governments more freedom to make economic policy.

The Court continued to address economic issues involving interpretations of federal statutes. In some instances it overrode decisions of regulatory agencies such as the National Labor Relations Board, holding that those decisions misinterpreted statutes. Some of these interventions were significant, but the Court did not challenge the basic economic programs of the federal government.

Support for Civil Liberties. In a 1938 decision, *United States v. Carolene Products Co.*, the Court signaled that there might be a second stage of the revolution. The case was one of many in which the Court upheld federal economic policies. But in what would become known as "footnote 4," Justice Harlan Stone's opinion for the Court argued that the Court was justified in taking a tolerant view of government economic policies while it gave "more exacting judicial scrutiny" to policies that infringed on civil liberties.

This second stage took a long time to develop. The Court gave more support to civil liberties in the 1940s and 1950s than it had in earlier eras, but it did not make a strong and consistent commitment to the expansion of individual liberties. This stage of the revolution finally came to full fruition in the 1960s. Civil liberties issues dominated the Court's agenda for the first time. The Court's decisions expanded liberties in many areas, from civil rights of racial minority groups to procedural rights of criminal defendants to freedom of expression.

As in the preceding era, the Court's policy position was reflected in the constitutional doctrines it adopted. Departing from its earlier view, the Court of the 1960s ruled that nearly all the rights of criminal defendants in the Bill of Rights were incorporated into the Fourteenth Amendment and therefore applied to state proceedings. In interpreting the Equal Protection Clause of the Fourteenth Amendment, the Court held that it would give government policies strict scrutiny if the groups that the policies disfavored were especially vulnerable or if the rights involved were especially important.

The Court's sympathies for civil liberties were symbolized by *Griswold v. Connecticut* (1965), which established a new constitutional right to privacy. A majority of the justices discovered that right in provisions of the Bill of Rights nearly two centuries after those provisions were written.

The Court's direction after 1937 is illustrated by the pattern of decisions declaring laws unconstitutional. Figure 5-1 shows the number of economic statutes and statutes limiting civil liberties that the Court overturned in each decade of the twentieth century. The number of economic laws the Court struck down declined precipitously between the 1920s and the 1940s and fell even lower in the 1960s. In contrast, the number of statutes struck down on civil liberties grounds became significant in the 1940s and 1950s and rose sharply in the 1960s, reflecting the Court's growing liberalism. The reversal of these trends in the 1980s is also noteworthy; I discuss its implications later in this section.

The Court's Beneficiaries. The groups that the Court's policies benefited most were those that gained from expansions of legal protections for civil liberties. Among them were socially and economically disadvantaged groups, criminal defendants, and people who took unpopular political stands. In 1967, during the Court's most liberal period, an unsympathetic editorial cartoonist depicted the Court as a Santa Claus whose list of gift recipients included communists, pornographers, extremists, drug pushers, criminals, and perverts.[28] Whatever may be the accuracy of that characterization, it underlines the change in the Court. Like the Court's policies favoring corporations in an earlier era, this support reflected effective litigation efforts by groups such as the NAACP Legal Defense Fund and the American Civil Liberties Union.

The segment of the population that the Court supported most strongly was black citizens, particularly in the fields of education and voting rights. The Court also made great efforts to protect the civil rights movement when southern states attacked it in the late 1950s and 1960s.

The Court was generally more favorable to liberties than were the other branches of government. Congress did not adopt a strong statute attacking racial discrimination until 1964, ten years after *Brown v. Board of Education.* The Court's support for some other liberties diverged even more from the positions of the other branches. The procedural rights of criminal defendants had few advocates in the executive and legislative branches. Congress

FIGURE 5-1
Number of Economic and Civil Liberties Laws (Federal, State, and Local) Overturned by the Supreme Court by Decade, 1900–2008

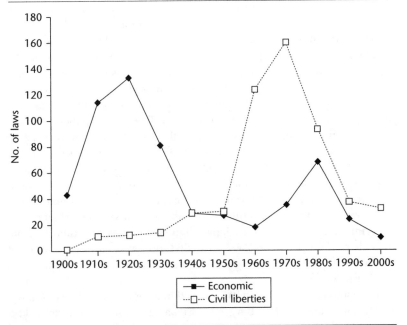

Sources: Congressional Research Service, *The Constitution of the United States of America: Analysis and Interpretation, 2002 Edition* and *2008 Supplement* (Washington, D.C.: Government Printing Office, 2004, 2008).

Note: Civil liberties category does not include laws supportive of civil liberties.

did much to attack leftist political groups such as the Communist Party. As it had done when it favored business interests, the Court provided relief for groups that fared less well elsewhere in government.

The Era since 1969

It is always more difficult to characterize the Supreme Court's policies in the recent past than in more distant eras. That certainly is true of the Burger, Rehnquist, and early Roberts Courts. The Court's policies became more conservative from the 1970s on, but there is considerable disagreement about the extent of the Court's ideological shift. Complaints from political liberals that the Court moved too far to the right have been matched by complaints from conservatives that it did not move far enough.

Uneven Support for Civil Liberties. To some extent in the Burger Court, and to a greater extent since then, the Court has narrowed legal protections for individual liberties. The Court's shift is reflected in the rate of success for parties bringing civil liberties claims, shown in Table 4-3. Since 1969 the Court has ruled in favor of those claims at a considerably lower rate than the Warren Court did. As shown in Figure 5-1, the number of laws struck down on the ground that they violated constitutional protections of civil liberties increased in the 1970s but declined dramatically after that.

The reduction in support for civil liberties came most quickly on the rights of criminal defendants. From the early 1970s on, the Court narrowed the *Miranda* rules for police questioning of suspects and the *Mapp* rule disallowing the use of evidence obtained through illegal searches, although it did not overturn either decision. The Court's policies on capital punishment took a series of twists: the Court struck down existing death penalty laws in *Furman v. Georgia* (1972), upheld a new set of laws in *Gregg v. Georgia* (1976), set some limits on the death sentence while rejecting others, and then ruled that capital punishment could not be imposed for offenses committed by juveniles or the retarded.[29] In conjunction with Congress the Court limited the use of habeas corpus petitions as a means for criminal defendants to challenge their convictions after their original appeals ran out. Between 2004 and 2008, however, it issued a series of decisions supporting the procedural rights of detainees at the Guantánamo Bay Naval Station.

On issues of equality, the Court moved in a conservative direction more slowly and unevenly. The Burger Court was the first to strike down laws under the Equal Protection Clause on the ground that they discriminated against women. It also held that northern-style school segregation, in which schools were not explicitly segregated by law, could violate equal protection. It generally gave broad interpretations to federal laws against discrimination but limited constitutional challenges to discrimination by private institutions that are connected to the government. The Rehnquist and Roberts Courts have interpreted antidiscrimination laws more narrowly across a wide range of issues. The Rehnquist Court also approved the termination of court orders that maintained racial integration of public schools and limited the power of the federal government to enforce antidiscrimination laws against states. However, the Court has continued to strengthen legal protections against sex discrimination in some important respects.

Freedom of expression is the only field in which the Court has directly overruled major Warren Court decisions favoring civil liberties—specifically, on the definition of obscenity.[30] The Burger and Rehnquist Courts narrowed some other First Amendment protections as well. But this is the field in which the Court in the current era has given the greatest support to civil liberties. One example is its protections for commercial speech, such as advertising. The Court struck down much of the congressional scheme for regulation of campaign finance on First Amendment grounds in *Buckley v. Valeo* (1976). It upheld the bulk of a more limited scheme in *McConnell v. Federal Election Commission* (2003) but struck down some provisions of that law in *McConnell* and later decisions.

Conservatism on Economic Issues. In interpreting federal statutes that regulate economic practices, the Courts of the last forty years have taken more conservative positions than the Warren Court. The Court has narrowed the application of antitrust laws to business practices. It has given more support to employers in labor law, and for the most part it has interpreted environmental laws narrowly.

The Burger Court maintained the Court's broad interpretation of government powers under the Constitution to regulate economic activity. In contrast, the Rehnquist Court took some steps to limit those powers. In the economic arena, as in civil liberties, the Rehnquist Court limited federal power over state governments. However, the Court ruled that several state regulations of business practices were preempted by federal laws that allowed those practices. The Roberts Court has continued that trend. It has limited antitrust suits in several decisions. It has also handed down major decisions limiting punitive damage awards and holding that some state lawsuits against manufacturers of medical devices are preempted by federal law.[31]

The Court's Beneficiaries. In some respects, state governments have benefited from the Court's policies in the current era. The Court has narrowed federal power over state governments, and the Rehnquist and Roberts Courts have struck down relatively few state laws. But as the preemption decisions illustrate, the Court's support for the power and autonomy of state governments varies with the issues and interests that are implicated by cases.

The business community has received more consistent support from the Court in this period. Indeed, that community can be considered the chief beneficiary of the Burger and Rehnquist Courts, and thus far it has done very well in the Roberts Court. A leader of the National Chamber Litigation Center, affiliated with the U.S. Chamber of Commerce, concluded that the Court's 2006 term "has been our best Supreme Court term in 30 years."[32] In this era the Court has generally favored business interests across a wide range of fields, from labor law to freedom of speech. As in an earlier era, this favorable record is partly a product of effective litigation by businesses and business groups.[33]

The Court has not been uniformly favorable to business. As in other eras, the Court's recent policies are too mixed in theme to allow easy generalizations. Still, both the Court's major beneficiaries and its dominant ideological direction clearly differ from those of the preceding period.

TABLE 5-3
Summary of the Supreme Court's Policies during Three Historical Periods

Period	Predominant area on agenda	Extent of activism	Content of policy
1890s to 1930s	Economic regulation	Variable, becoming more inclined to strike down legislation	Mixed, primarily conservative
1937 to 1969	Economic regulation, then civil liberties	Initially low, becoming higher, then very high in 1960s	Generally liberal, very liberal in 1960s
1969 to 2009	Civil liberties	High, declining in some respects after the 1970s	Moderate in 1970s, then more conservative

Note: Characterizations of each period are approximate and subject to disagreement. Extent of activism is gauged primarily by striking down of government policies.

Explaining the Court's Policies

In the preceding sections, I described changes over time in the Supreme Court's agenda, the extent of its activism, and the content of its policies. All these changes are summarized in Table 5-3.

The magnitude of these changes underlines the need for explanation. What forces can account for the various elements of the Court's policies? These forces were discussed in earlier chapters, but in this section I pull them together and apply them to the broad patterns described in this chapter.

The Court's Environment

Freedom from External Pressures. The life terms of Supreme Court justices give them considerable freedom from the rest of government and from the general public. This freedom is reinforced by the general reluctance of Congress and the president to use their powers over the Court as an institution. The Court's relative freedom from external pressures distinguishes it from the other branches of government.

The Court's freedom is reflected in some of the positions that it takes in individual decisions. Political realities would not allow a legislative body to support the right to burn the American flag as a form of political protest, nor could it prohibit student-led prayers at football games. But the Court could and did make such decisions.

More important, the Court has adopted some broad lines of policy that run counter to the majority view in the general public and elsewhere in government. To a considerable degree, it resisted the widespread support for regulation of business in the early twentieth century. Even more striking was the Court's expansion of the procedural rights of criminal defendants in the 1960s. No elected body, even a court, could have adopted so many rules that favored so unpopular a segment of society.

Influence from the Other Branches. The Court is not entirely free from external pressure. Congress and the president hold substantial powers over the Court. Although these powers are seldom used, their use is often threatened. The other branches can legislate to raise the justices' salaries or leave them as they are, allow the Court's interpretations of statutes to stand or override them, and control its jurisdiction. They also can shape the implementation of the Court's decisions. Because such threats and criticisms are unpleasant in themselves, and because they might affect the Court's public standing, the justices have an incentive to minimize direct conflicts with Congress.

It is difficult to ascertain the effect of this incentive on the Court's policies. It may be that the other branches of government have little impact on the justices. In at least a few instances, however, the justices seemed to avoid or minimize conflict with the other branches. Examples include the Court's retreat from some of its expansions of civil liberties in the late 1950s and its refusal to decide whether American participation in the Vietnam War was unconstitutional. More broadly, the Court has limited its use of judicial review to strike down significant national policies. It is noteworthy that the Court has struck down far more state laws than federal laws. The activism of the Warren Court in civil liberties was directed primarily at the states, and on the whole that Court was sympathetic to the federal government.[34] The Rehnquist Court's limitations on federal power provoked little conflict with the other branches because members of Congress during that period were largely sympathetic to those limitations.[35]

Societal Influence. The justices are also influenced by developments in society as a whole. Those developments can affect the justices' attitudes toward such issues as women's rights and terrorism. They can exert an influence on their own as well.

One form of influence concerns what might be called a requirement of minimum support: the justices are unlikely to take a sustained policy position that lacks significant support outside the Court, especially support from the segments of society whose judgment is most important to them. Justices may perceive that taking such positions would damage the

Court's institutional position. More fundamentally, the justices may see positions with little support as unreasonable in themselves. Another form of influence derives from the litigation process. The Court acts on the cases that come to it: the Court cannot reshape its agenda without action by litigants and without interest groups that support litigation. In turn, those groups develop from broad social movements.

These influences are reflected in the two most distinctive patterns in the Court's policies during the twentieth century. The Court's resistance to government regulation of the economy before 1937 may have had only minority support in society, but most of the business community and much of the legal community strongly approved that position. Corporations and their representatives engaged in a concerted litigation campaign, bringing to the Court a steady flow of litigation and strong legal arguments against government economic policies.

The Court's expansions of civil liberties from the 1940s to the 1970s also benefited from social support. If these expansions were not always popular, they were favored by significant portions of society as a whole and of political elites and the legal community.[36] Social changes and the work of organizations such as the NAACP and the ACLU allowed civil liberties to take a more prominent place on the Court's agenda and allowed the Court to broaden its interpretations of constitutional rights.[37]

To a degree, the Court's increased conservatism since the 1970s reflects changing attitudes in the general public and a growth in litigation by conservative groups. By the same token, there is probably too little support for the Court to fully reverse its earlier expansions of government regulatory power and protections for civil liberties. The Court has considerable freedom from societal opinion and social trends, but its freedom is not total.[38]

Policy Preferences and the Appointment Power

The freedom the justices do have generally allows them to make their own judgments about the issues they face. Those judgments are based in part on their assessments of cases in legal terms. But because the questions before the Court seldom have clear legal answers, the justices' policy preferences are the primary basis for the positions they take.

The importance of policy preferences suggests that a great deal about the Court's policies can be explained simply and directly: during any given period in the Court's history, its policies have reflected the collective preferences of its members. Most of the justices who served from the 1890s through the early 1930s were political conservatives who generally accepted government restrictions on civil liberties but questioned government regulation of business enterprises. In contrast, the justices who came to the Court from the late 1930s through the mid-1960s were predominantly

President Richard Nixon with his Supreme Court appointees Lewis Powell (left) and William Rehnquist (right). Nixon's appointments of justices between 1969 and 1971 began the Court's movement in a conservative direction.

liberals who supported government management of the economy and, in most instances, broader protections of civil liberties.

For their part, with a few exceptions, the justices joining the Court since 1969 have been more conservative on civil liberties and economic issues than the justices of the preceding period. In 2007 Justice John Paul Stevens underlined how much the Court's membership has changed in ideological terms: "Including myself, every judge who's been appointed to the Court since Lewis Powell," selected in 1971, "has been more conservative than his or her predecessor. Except maybe Justice Ginsburg. That's bound to have an effect on the court."[39]

An explanation of the Court's direction that is based on the justices' policy preferences is not entirely satisfying, because it does not show why certain preferences predominated on the Court during particular periods. One reason is that some values were dominant in the nation during the periods in which justices were developing their attitudes. Another is that the justices came from backgrounds that instilled particular values in them. Most important, the higher-status backgrounds that predominated during most of the Court's history fostered sympathy for the views and interests of higher-status segments of society. Further, the prevailing ideology in elite segments of the legal profession shapes the views of its members, including future Supreme Court justices. The most direct source of the Court's collective preferences, however, is the decisions that presidents make in appointing justices.

Indeed, the predominant pattern of Supreme Court policy at any given time tends to reflect the identities of appointing presidents. If a series of appointments is made by conservative presidents, the Court is likely to become a conservative body. And because vacancies occur on the Court with some frequency—on average, once every two years—most presidents can significantly affect the Court's direction.

Robert Dahl argued that for this reason "the policy views dominant on the Court are never for long out of line with the policy views dominant among the lawmaking majorities of the United States."[40] In Dahl's judgment, the president's power to make appointments has limited the frequency with which the Court overturns major federal statutes: justices generally take the same view of policy as members of Congress and the president, so they seldom upset the policies of these branches. I think there is much to Dahl's argument. But because of several complicating factors, the appointment power produces only imperfect control by "lawmaking majorities."

One factor is time lag. Most justices serve for many years, so the Court usually reflects the views of past presidents and Senates more than those of the current president and Senate. That is why legal scholar Fred Rodell suggested that the aphorism "the Supreme Court follows the election returns" be amended to refer to the returns "of ten or twelve years before."[41]

The lag varies in length, chiefly because presidents have differing opportunities to make appointments. Richard Nixon selected four justices during his six years in office, but Bill Clinton and George W. Bush each chose only two justices in eight years. Jimmy Carter did even worse. The absence of vacancies during his term, combined with his failed reelection bid in 1980, made him the first president to serve at least four years without appointing any justices.

Further, a president's influence on the Court depends on its ideological configuration and on which members leave it as well as the simple number of appointments. Barack Obama's impact on the Court will depend largely on whether any of the conservative justices leave the Court during his time in office.

Another complicating factor is the deviation of justices from presidential expectations. Presidents usually get most of what they want from their appointees, but that is not a certainty. The unprecedented liberalism of the Court in the 1960s resulted largely from Dwight Eisenhower's miscalculations in nominating Earl Warren and William Brennan. The Rehnquist Court would have been more conservative if Sandra Day O'Connor, Anthony Kennedy, and especially David Souter had not diverged from the expectations of the Republican presidents who chose them.

The role of chance in shaping the Court's general direction also deserves emphasis. Chance plays a part in the timing of Court vacancies and in the performance of justices relative to their appointers' expectations. For that matter, the identity of the president who fills vacancies on the Court some-times reflects chance. The close electoral victories of John Kennedy in 1960 and Richard Nixon in 1968 were hardly inevitable. The election of George W. Bush in 2000 was even closer. The Kennedy and Nixon appointments had a major impact on the Court's policies, and Bush achieved a more limited but real impact.

The policy orientations of the Supreme Court between the 1890s and the 1960s reflected the existence of strong lawmaking majorities during two periods: the conservative Republican governments that dominated much of the period from the Civil War to the Great Depression, and the twelve-year tenure of Franklin Roosevelt that was accompanied by heavily Democratic Senates. These orientations also reflected patterns of resigna-tions and deaths, unexpected behavior on the part of justices, and other factors that were a good deal less systematic. By the same token, if these factors had operated differently since 1969, the current Court might be less conservative—or even more so—than the one that actually exists. The forces that shape the Court's policy positions, like so much about the Court, are highly complex.

Conclusion

In this chapter, I have examined several issues relating to the Supreme Court's policy outputs. A few conclusions merit emphasis.

First, in some periods the Court's policymaking has had fairly clear themes. During the first part of the twentieth century, the dominant theme was scrutiny of government economic policies. Later in that century, the primary theme was scrutiny of policies and practices that impinged on indi-vidual civil liberties. In each instance, the theme was evident in both the Court's agenda and the content of its decisions.

Second, these themes and the Court's work as a whole reflect both the justices' policy preferences and the influence of the Court's environment. In large part, the Court's policies are what its members would like them to be. But the Court is subject to external influences that limit the divergence between Supreme Court decisions and the policies adopted by the other branches of government. In a different way, the president's appointment power creates a link between the justices' policy preferences and their political environment.

Finally, the Court's role as a policymaker—although clearly significant—is a limited one. The Court gives considerable attention to some areas of policy but scarcely touches others. Some critical matters, such as foreign policy, are left almost entirely to the other two branches of government. Even in the areas to which the Court gives the most attention, it seldom disturbs the basic features of national policy.

To a considerable degree, the significance of the Supreme Court as a policymaker depends on the impact of its decisions, the subject of Chapter 6. After examining the effect of the Court's decisions, I make a broader assessment of the Court's role in the policymaking process.

NOTES

1. The discussion of agenda change in this section is drawn in part from Richard L. Pacelle Jr., *The Transformation of the Supreme Court's Agenda from the New Deal to the Reagan Administration* (Boulder, Colo.: Westview Press, 1991); Richard L. Pacelle Jr., "The Dynamics and Determinants of Agenda Change in the Rehnquist Court," in *Contemplating Courts,* ed. Lee Epstein (Washington, D.C.: CQ Press, 1995), 251–274; and Drew Noble Lanier, *Of Time and Judicial Behavior: United States Supreme Court Agenda-Setting and Decision-Making, 1888–1997* (Selinsgrove, Pa.: Susquehanna University Press, 2003), chap. 3. Numbers of cases in broad policy areas and involving particular issues were calculated from data collected and presented by Pacelle in his publications and from data in the U.S. Supreme Court Database created by Harold Spaeth, at www.cas.sc.edu/poli/juri/sctdata.htm.
2. These and other data in this paragraph are taken from Pacelle, *Transformation of the Supreme Court's Agenda,* 56–57. The civil liberties category includes cases classified by Pacelle as due process, substantive rights, and equality.
3. Frederick Schauer, "Foreword: The Court's Agenda—and the Nation's," *Harvard Law Review* 120 (November 2006): 8.
4. Because of ambiguities, different people have obtained different numbers of federal and state laws that the Supreme Court struck down. The numbers presented in this chapter are based on data in Congressional Research Service, *The Constitution of the United States of America: Analysis and Interpretation, 2002 Edition* and *2008 Supplement* (Washington, D.C.: Government Printing Office, 2004, 2008), with one addition to the list of federal laws for 2008. There are some errors and inconsistencies in the Congressional Research Service data, but the broad patterns shown in Table 5-2 are clearly accurate.
5. Linda Camp Keith, *The U.S. Supreme Court and the Judicial Review of Congress* (New York: Peter Lang, 2008), 26.
6. The distinctions made in the paragraphs that follow are drawn chiefly from Robert A. Dahl, "Decision-Making in a Democracy: The Supreme Court as a National Policy-Maker," *Journal of Public Law* 6 (fall 1957): 279–295.
7. *Scott v. Sandford* (1857); *Hammer v. Dagenhart* (1918); *Bailey v. Drexel Furniture Co.* (1922). Decisions overturning New Deal economic legislation include *United States v. Butler* (1936) and *Schechter Poultry Corp. v. United States* (1935).
8. See Keith E. Whittington, *Political Foundations of Judicial Supremacy: The Supreme Court and Constitutional Leadership in U.S. History* (Princeton: Princeton University Press, 2007).

9. The decisions were *McConnell v. Federal Election Commission* (2003); *Federal Election Commission v. Wisconsin Right to Life, Inc.* (2007); and *Davis v. Federal Election Commission* (2008).

10. The cases were, respectively, *Rothgery v. Gillespie County* (2008); *Snyder v. Louisiana* (2008); and *Giles v. California* (2008).

11. Robert Scigliano, "The Presidency and the Judiciary," in *The Presidency and the Political System*, 3d ed., ed. Michael Nelson (Washington, D.C.: CQ Press, 1990), 471–499. See David A. Yalof, "The Presidency and the Judiciary," in *The Presidency and the Political System*, 8th ed., ed. Michael Nelson (Washington, D.C.: CQ Press, 2006), 501–504.

12. The decisions were *Rasul v. Bush* (2004); *Hamdi v. Rumsfeld* (2004); *Hamdan v. Rumsfeld* (2006); and *Boumediene v. Bush* (2008).

13. See, for example, *Desert Palace, Inc. v. Costa* (2003).

14. *Griggs v. Duke Power Co.* (1971).

15. *Meritor Savings Bank v. Vinson* (1986); *Burlington Industries v. Ellerth* (1998).

16. Sandra L. Wood, Linda Camp Keith, Drew Noble Lanier, and Ayo Ogundele, "The Supreme Court, 1888–1940: An Empirical Overview," *Social Science History* 22 (summer 1998): 215–216; William G. Ross, *A Muted Fury: Populists, Progressives, and Labor Unions Confront the Courts, 1890–1937* (Princeton: Princeton University Press, 1994).

17. To obtain these figures and others to be presented later in the chapter, I categorized decisions that struck down laws according to whether they pertained to economics, civil liberties, or other subjects. The criteria that I used were necessarily arbitrary; other criteria would have resulted in somewhat different totals.

18. *Santa Clara County v. Southern Pacific Railroad Co.* (1886).

19. James W. Ely Jr., *Railroads and American Law* (Lawrence: University Press of Kansas, 2001); Richard C. Cortner, *The Iron Horse and the Constitution: The Railroads and the Transformation of the Fourteenth Amendment* (Westport, Conn.: Greenwood Press, 1993).

20. Benjamin Twiss, *Lawyers and the Constitution* (Princeton: Princeton University Press, 1942).

21. This discussion draws from John Braeman, *Before the Civil Rights Revolution: The Old Court and Individual Rights* (Westport, Conn.: Greenwood Press, 1988).

22. *Twining v. New Jersey* (1908).

23. See, for example, *Schenck v. United States* (1917). See also David Rabban, *Free Speech in Its Forgotten Years* (New York: Cambridge University Press, 1997).

24. Henry Steele Commager, "Judicial Review and Democracy," *Virginia Quarterly Review* 19 (summer 1943): 428. The possible exception was *Wing v. United States* (1896).

25. Robert H. Jackson, *The Struggle for Judicial Supremacy* (New York: Knopf, 1941), 187.

26. William E. Leuchtenburg, *The Supreme Court Reborn: The Constitutional Revolution in the Age of Roosevelt* (New York: Oxford University Press, 1995), 235.

27. *United States v. Cardiff* (1952).

28. Ken Alexander, *San Francisco Examiner*, December 14, 1967, 42.

29. The decisions were, respectively, *Roper v. Simmons* (2005) and *Atkins v. Virginia* (2002).

30. *Miller v. California* (1973).

31. The punitive damages decision was *Exxon Shipping Company v. Baker* (2008); the preemption decision was *Riegel v. Medtronic, Inc.* (2008).

32. Joan Biskupic, "High Court Rulings Come Down on Side of Business," *USA Today*, June 20, 2007, 3B.

33. See Jeffrey Rosen, "Supreme Court Inc.," *New York Times Magazine*, March 16, 2008, 38–45, 66–71.

34. Lucas A. Powe Jr., *The Warren Court and American Politics* (Cambridge: Harvard University Press, 2000).

35. See Keith E. Whittington, "Taking What They Give Us: Explaining the Court's Federalism Offensive," *Duke Law Journal* 51 (2001): 477–520.

36. See Powe, *Warren Court and American Politics*, 485–501.

37. Charles R. Epp, *The Rights Revolution: Lawyers, Activists, and Supreme Courts in Comparative Perspective* (Chicago: University of Chicago Press, 1998), chaps. 3 and 4.

38. See John R. Howard, *The Shifting Wind: The Supreme Court and Civil Rights from Reconstruction to Brown* (Albany: State University of New York Press, 1999).

39. Jeffrey Rosen, "The Dissenter," *New York Times Magazine*, September 23, 2007, 52–53.

40. Dahl, "Decision-Making in a Democracy," 285.

41. Fred Rodell, *Nine Men* (New York: Random House, 1955), 9. The original aphorism was coined by Finley Peter Dunne and put in the mouth of his character Mr. Dooley in 1901. See Finley Peter Dunne, *Mr. Dooley on Ivrything and Ivrybody*, selected by Robert Hutchinson (New York: Dover Publications, 1963), 160.

Chapter 6

The Court's Impact

In June 2008, the Supreme Court decided *District of Columbia v. Heller*. By a 5–4 vote, the Court struck down the Washington, D.C., law that generally prohibited people from possessing handguns. The Court based that ruling on the principle that the Second Amendment protects the right of individuals to possess guns and use them for lawful purposes.

The Supreme Court's decision was a landmark, garnering headlines throughout the country and attracting a flurry of positive and negative reactions. But the decision was hardly the last word on the subject of gun rights and gun control. The District of Columbia government quickly enacted new gun laws in response to the *Heller* decision. The U.S. House of Representatives passed a bill in September to further limit gun regulation in the District of Columbia, but the Senate did not act on the bill. The decision spurred legislators elsewhere to reconsider their own gun laws, and a few local governments repealed laws.

Inevitably, new legal cases arose, cases that would require courts to determine what kinds of gun regulations were acceptable under the Supreme Court's decision. Indeed, thirty-two days after the *Heller* decision, its winning litigant, Dick Heller, was a plaintiff in a lawsuit challenging one of the new District of Columbia gun laws.[1] The first wave of decisions by lower courts upheld nearly all the gun laws that were challenged, based on judges' interpretations of language in the Court's opinion in *Heller*.[2] Inevitably, the Supreme Court will decide new cases to resolve issues that its 2008 decision left open. But even so, the Court will be only one of many decision makers that shape gun policy in the United States.

The aftermath of *Heller* underlines an important reality. The Supreme Court is the highest interpreter of federal law, and people often think that its decisions bring an end to the issues they address. But most of the time a Supreme Court decision is only one part of the processes that shape law and policy on an issue.

This is true for several reasons. Often the Court decides only one aspect of an issue or offers general guidelines that other policymakers have to fill in. Even when the Court fully decides an issue, other institutions may reinforce that ruling, limit its impact, or negate it altogether. Congress and the president can write a new statute to override the Court's interpretation of an old one. Congress and the states can amend the Constitution to overcome a constitutional decision. Judges and administrators exercise discretion as to how they carry out a Supreme Court policy. And the Court's ultimate impact on society depends on the actions of people in and out of government. The Court affects the structure of industries and the status of women, but so do many other forces—including some that have far greater impact than the Court's decisions.

This chapter explores the impact of Supreme Court decisions. I begin by looking at what happens to the litigants themselves. In the remainder of the chapter I examine the broader effects of the Court's policies: their implementation, responses of legislatures and chief executives to them, and their effects on society as a whole.

Outcomes for the Parties

Whatever else it does, a Supreme Court decision affects the parties in the case. But the Court's ruling does not always determine the final outcome for the two sides. Indeed, a great deal can happen to the parties after the Court rules in their case.

If the Court affirms a lower-court decision, that decision usually becomes final. If the Court reverses, modifies, or vacates a decision, it almost always remands (sends back) the case to the lower court for "further proceedings consistent with this opinion," or the like. When it remands a case, the Court sometimes gives the lower court little leeway about what to do, and that court usually follows the Supreme Court's lead. But often the lower court has wide discretion about how to apply the Court's ruling, and the party that wins in the Court may end up the ultimate loser.

Cases in which the Court overturns a criminal conviction on procedural grounds are good examples. The defendant is often retried, and the retrial sometimes produces a second conviction. A similar result can occur on the civil side of the law.

Most such outcomes are quite consistent with the Supreme Court rulings that preceded them, although lower-court judges occasionally respond to remands in ways that conflict with the Court's intent. In either situation, a litigant who won in the Court but then lost in a lower court can ask the Court to hear the case once again. In *Smith v. Texas* (2004), the Court held that a Texas death sentence was inappropriate because of the judge's instruction to the jury. On remand, the Texas Court of Criminal

Appeals reinstated the death sentence, with a dissenting justice protesting that "the majority misapprehends the plain directive of the United States Supreme Court in its reversal of this court." Smith brought the case back to the Supreme Court, which once again reversed the Texas court and gently reprimanded it for its decision on remand.[3]

The ultimate outcome for the parties is often determined outside of court. Sometimes the parties settle the case, with the Court's decision providing leverage for the party that it favored. After decisions by the Court in 1989 and 2001 that overturned his death sentences, a Texas inmate in 2008 agreed to a plea bargain that would keep him in prison for life.[4] In 2005 an Alabama teacher won a Supreme Court decision that allowed him to sue his school district for retaliation after he complained about discrimination against the girls' basketball team that he coached. The next year, the school board agreed to pay the teacher monetary damages to settle the case.[5]

Implementation of Supreme Court Policies

More important than the outcome of a case for the litigants are the broader effects of the legal rules that the Court lays down in its opinions. Like statutes or presidential orders, these rules have to be implemented by administrators and judges. Judges are obliged to apply the Court's interpretations of law whenever they are relevant to a case. Similarly, administrators such as cabinet officers and police officers are expected to follow Court-created rules that are relevant to their work.

The responses of judges and administrators to the Court's rules of law can be examined in terms of their compliance or noncompliance with these rules. But the Court's decisions may evoke responses ranging from complete rejection to enthusiastic acceptance and extension, and the concept of compliance does not capture all the possible variations.

The Effectiveness of Implementation

In March 2007 federal district judge William Schwarzer ruled that a defendant in a patent infringement suit was not entitled to summary judgment in its favor. The defendant, a company in the computer industry, had argued that the plaintiff's patent was invalid because it failed to meet the statutory requirement that an invention be "nonobvious" to obtain a patent. Judge Schwarzer said that under the law, there was insufficient basis for a summary judgment. A month later, the Supreme Court reached a decision in which it tightened the requirement of nonobviousness. In response, Judge Schwarzer reconsidered the defendant's motion for summary judgment. Citing the Supreme Court's decision, he reversed himself and dismissed the case.[6]

What Judge Schwarzer did fits the image that most people have about the implementation of Supreme Court decisions. Having ruled one way on a legal issue, he changed his stance in order to follow a subsequent Court ruling. Because judges and administrators are subordinate to the Supreme Court as interpreters of the law, it is expected that they will follow the Court's lead and carry out its decisions fully.

Indeed, this is what happens a great deal of the time. Yet implementation of the Court's policies is often quite imperfect. In this respect the Court is in the same position as Congress. For the Court, as for Congress, the record of implementation is mixed. Some Court rulings are carried out more effectively than others, and specific decisions often are implemented better in some places or situations than in others.

Implementation of the Court's decisions is most successful in lower courts, especially appellate courts. When the Court announces a new rule of law, judges generally do their best to follow its lead. And when a series of decisions indicates that the Court has changed its position in a field of policy, lower courts tend to follow the new trend.

But even appellate judges sometimes diverge from the Court's rulings. Seldom do they explicitly refuse to follow the Court's decisions. More common is what might be called implicit noncompliance, in which a court purports to follow the Supreme Court's lead but actually evades the implications of the Court's ruling. To take one example, the federal Court of Appeals for the Eleventh Circuit in Atlanta has given a narrow interpretation to a Supreme Court decision limiting the immunity of law enforcement officers from lawsuits, and one legal scholar charged that "the circuit essentially has thumbed its nose" at the Court.[7]

The Court enjoys considerable success in gaining compliance from administrative bodies, especially at the federal level.[8] Like Judge Schwarzer, the Patent and Trademark Office acted to adopt new standards for the granting of patents in response to the Court's 2007 decision.[9] Yet implementation problems seem more common among administrators than among judges. For example, there is a long history of incidents in which public school students are punished for refusing to salute the flag, despite a 1943 decision to the contrary.[10]

State trial courts resemble administrative agencies in some respects, and similar implementation problems arise. In particular, some of the Court's decisions about criminal procedure have suffered from evasion by prosecutors and judges. One observer in a Chicago court found substantial deviations from the Court's decisions on judicial oversight of jailing after arrest, the prosecutor's obligation to turn evidence over to the defense, and discrimination in jury selection.[11] Indeed, the Court's efforts to prevent discriminatory challenges to prospective jurors have suffered from widespread noncompliance by prosecutors and defense attorneys, as

Justice Breyer noted in a 2005 opinion, and trial judges are often less than vigilant about reining in that noncompliance. A 2008 decision was one of several in which the Court has reversed convictions because of a failure to follow its rulings on challenges to jurors.[12]

Two Case Studies of Implementation

The implementation process can be illuminated with two case studies. School desegregation and police investigations highlight the difficulties of implementation and variation in its success.

School Desegregation. Before the Supreme Court's 1954 decision in *Brown v. Board of Education*, separate schools for black and white students existed throughout the Deep South and in most districts of border states such as Oklahoma and Maryland. The Court's decision required that these dual school systems be eliminated. There was considerable compliance with the Court's ruling in the border states within a few years. In contrast, policies in the Deep South changed very slowly. As late as 1964–1965, there was no Deep South state in which even 10 percent of the black students went to school with any white students—a minimal definition of desegregation.[13]

Judges and school officials in the Deep South responded to the *Brown* decision in an atmosphere that was hostile to desegregation. Most white citizens were strongly opposed to desegregation; the opinions of black citizens had only limited impact, in part because a large proportion of them were prevented from voting. Throughout the South, public officials encouraged resistance to the Supreme Court.

Because of this political atmosphere and their own opposition to *Brown,* most school administrators did everything possible to preserve segregation. Those administrators who wanted to comply with the Court's ruling were deterred from doing so by pressure from state officials and local citizens.

In places where the schools did not comply on their own, parents could file suits in the federal district courts to challenge the continuation of segregated systems. In many districts no suits were ever brought, in part because of potential retaliation.

Even where suits were brought, their success was hardly guaranteed. In its second decision in *Brown* in 1955, the Supreme Court gave federal district judges great freedom to determine the appropriate schedule for desegregation in a school district. Many judges themselves disagreed with the *Brown* decision, and all felt local pressure against *Brown.* As a result, few judges demanded speedy desegregation of the schools, and some actively resisted desegregation. Some judges did support the Court wholeheartedly, but they found it difficult to overcome delaying tactics by school administrators and elected officials.

TABLE 6-1
Percentage of Black Elementary and Secondary Students Going to School with Any Whites, in Eleven Southern States, 1954–1973

School year	Percentage	School year	Percentage
1954–1955	0.001	1964–1965	2.25
1956–1957	0.14	1966–1967	15.9
1958–1959	0.13	1968–1969	32.0
1960–1961	0.16	1970–1971	85.6
1962–1963	0.45	1972–1973	91.3

Sources: For 1954–1967, Southern Education Reporting Service, *A Statistical Summary, State by State, of School Segregation-Desegregation in the Southern and Border Area from 1954 to the Present* (Nashville: Southern Education Reporting Service, 1967); for 1968–1973, U.S. Bureau of the Census, *Statistical Abstract of the United States* (Washington, D.C.: Government Printing Office, 1971 and 1975).

Note: The states are Alabama, Arkansas, Florida, Georgia, Louisiana, Mississippi, North Carolina, South Carolina, Tennessee, Texas, and Virginia.

After a long period of resistance, officials in the southern states began to comply. In the second decade after *Brown,* most dual school systems in the South were finally dismantled. Although school segregation was not eliminated altogether, the proportion of black students attending school with whites increased tremendously, as shown in Table 6-1.

The major impetus for this change came from Congress. The Civil Rights Act of 1964 allowed federal funds to be withheld from institutions that practiced racial discrimination. In carrying out that provision, President Johnson's administration required that schools make a "good-faith start" toward desegregation to receive federal aid. Faced with a threat to important financial interests, school officials felt some compulsion to go along. The 1964 act also allowed the Justice Department to bring desegregation suits where local residents were unable to do so, and this provision greatly increased the potential for litigation against school districts that refused to change their policies. The Court reinforced the congressional action with decisions in 1968 and 1969 that demanded effective desegregation without further delay.[14]

In the 1970s the Court turned its attention to the North. In many northern cities, housing patterns and school board policies had combined to create a situation in which white and nonwhite students generally went to different schools. In a Denver case, *Keyes v. School District No. 1* (1973), the Court held that segregation caused by government in such cities violated the Fourteenth Amendment and required a remedy. In a line of decisions over the next decade, the Court spelled out rules with which to identify segregation that violated the Constitution and to devise remedies for that segregation.

Federal district judges in the North supported the Court more than had their southern counterparts. Many ordered sweeping remedies for segregation in the face of strong local opposition to those remedies, especially busing of students. One judge ordered the imposition of higher property taxes to pay for school improvements that might facilitate desegregation in Kansas City, Missouri. Another held a city in New York State and some of its council members in contempt for failing to approve new public housing for a similar purpose.[15] Ironically, the Court found some of these remedies *too* sweeping.

Few northern school districts took significant steps to eliminate segregation until they were faced with a court order or pressure from federal administrators. But most northern districts complied with desegregation orders. One reason was the willingness of some district judges to supervise school desegregation closely. Congress and some presidents took steps to limit northern desegregation, but their actions were mostly symbolic and had little impact.

Once desegregation plans were put in place, it was uncertain whether and when such plans could be terminated. In a pair of decisions in 1991 and 1992, the Court indicated that these plans need not remain permanent even if ending them would produce high levels of racial segregation within a school district.[16] With support for desegregation declining, many administrators have accepted this invitation and returned to systems in which students are assigned to schools based on where they reside.

In contrast, administrators in Seattle and Louisville designed school assignment plans to reduce segregation, and lower federal courts upheld those plans. But the Supreme Court struck down these plans in *Parents Involved v. Seattle School District No. 1* (2007) on the ground that they impermissibly took race into account. The ultimate impact of that ruling on school district policies remains to be seen.

Police Investigation. The Warren Court imposed substantial procedural requirements on the police in two areas of criminal investigation, issuing a landmark decision in each. In search and seizure, *Mapp v. Ohio* (1961) extended to the states the "exclusionary rule," under which evidence illegally seized by the police cannot be used against a defendant in court. The *Mapp* decision provided an incentive for police to follow rules for legal searches that the Court established in other decisions. In the area of interrogation, *Miranda v. Arizona* (1966) required that suspects be given a series of warnings before police questioned them if their statements were to be used as evidence.

Lower-court responses to *Mapp* and *Miranda* have been mixed. Some state supreme courts criticized the decisions and interpreted them narrowly. At the trial level, many judges who sympathize with the police are reluctant to exclude evidence from trials on the basis of Supreme Court rules. But some lower-court judges have applied the Court's rulings vigorously.

Although the basic rules of *Mapp* and *Miranda* remain standing, since the 1970s the Court has narrowed their protections of suspects in some respects. This is especially true of the exclusionary rule for illegal searches. *Herring v. United States* (2009) is the most recent in a series of decisions that has limited the reach of the exclusionary rule. Many lower courts have followed this new direction enthusiastically. In contrast, some state supreme courts that support the rulings of the 1960s have found a legitimate means to establish broader protections of procedural rights by declaring that rights denied by the Supreme Court under the U.S. Constitution are protected independently by state constitutions.

Inevitably, *Mapp* and *Miranda* were unpopular in the law enforcement community. Most police officers want maximum freedom for their investigative activities and resent court decisions that impose constraints on them, but they also want their evidence to stand up in court. The result has been a complex pattern of police behavior.

In regard to police questioning, it appears that reading the *Miranda* warnings to suspects gradually has become standard practice in most places.[17] Perhaps the primary reason is that reading the warnings generally has little effect. As one legal scholar concluded in 2008, "the *Miranda* ritual makes almost no practical difference in American police interrogation."[18] The great majority of suspects waive their *Miranda* rights and answer questions, in part because officers structure the situation to encourage waivers. Even if suspects invoke their right to remain silent or to wait for a lawyer, officers sometimes can get them to change their minds.

Some of the means that officers use to encourage suspects to talk are of questionable legality. In some California police departments, for example, officers have told suspects who invoke their *Miranda* rights that they want to ask questions off the record and that nothing the suspect says can be used in court. What most suspects do not know is that under *Harris v. New York* (1971), statements obtained by officers who do not comply with *Miranda* can be used to discredit a defendant's testimony in court. The California Supreme Court acknowledged and condemned this practice in a 2003 decision, and a year later Justice Souter noted the existence of this and other mechanisms to evade the dictates of *Miranda*.[19]

To a considerable degree, then, police officers have learned to live with *Miranda*, complying partially with its requirements and continuing to get the information they seek from most suspects. Indeed, *Miranda* serves them well in one important respect. As one scholar put it, "if warnings

WARNING AS TO YOUR RIGHTS

You are under arrest. Before we ask you any questions, you must understand what your rights are.

You have the right to remain silent. You are not required to say anything to us at any time or to answer any questions. Anything you say can be used against you in court.

You have the right to talk to a lawyer for advice before we question you and to have him with you during questioning.

If you cannot afford a lawyer and want one, a lawyer will be provided for you.

If you want to answer questions now without a lawyer present you will still have the right to stop answering at any time. You also have the right to stop answering at any time until you talk to a lawyer.   P-4475

A "Miranda card" with warnings that police officers read to suspects before questioning them. The Supreme Court's decision in *Miranda v. Arizona* (1966) has changed police practices, but the effects of *Miranda* are limited by several realities of the law enforcement process.

were delivered by the police and a waiver was given or signed, it is almost impossible to persuade a judge that the resultant confession or admission is 'involuntary.' "[20] For this reason, although many officers still resent *Miranda*, police condemnation of the decision is far from universal.[21]

Before the *Mapp* decision, as one scholar put it, state and local law enforcement officers "*systematically* ignored the requirements of the Fourth Amendment because there was no reason to pay attention to it."[22] *Mapp* was intended to achieve greater compliance with search rules by providing a reason for compliance—potential exclusion of evidence from cases in court. To a degree, it has achieved this goal.[23] Faced with potential loss of evidence, many police departments changed their practices substantially. Most important, some made much greater use of search warrants.[24]

However, the available evidence indicates that compliance is far from perfect. One example is a study based on a sample of searches by a metropolitan police department in the early 1990s. The authors of the study concluded that at least 30 percent of the searches violated constitutional rules.[25]

Some noncompliance is inadvertent, reflecting the complexity and ambiguity of the rules that police are asked to follow in searches and seizures. Other noncompliance is intentional, resulting most fundamentally from the conflict that police officers often perceive: if they follow the applicable legal rules, they cannot obtain evidence they see as critical.

Because violations of the rules for searches often do not result in the exclusion of evidence, officers may resolve this conflict by violating those rules. Indeed, one scholar concluded that "for many police officers," the exclusionary rule "is not a significant influence when contemplating a search or seizure."[26]

Explaining the Implementation Process

It should be clear by now that the effectiveness with which Supreme Court policies are implemented varies a great deal. That effectiveness depends on several conditions: communication of policies to relevant officials, the motivations of those officials to follow or resist the Court's policies, the Court's authority, and the sanctions it can use to deter noncompliance.

Communication. Judges and administrators can carry out Supreme Court decisions well only if they know what the Court wants them to do. The communication process begins with the Court's opinions. Ideally, an opinion would state the Court's legal rules with sufficient precision and specificity that an official who reads the opinion would know how to apply those rules to any other case or situation. Frequently, however, opinions fall far short of that ideal: the Court's messages contain considerable ambiguity.

Much of this ambiguity is unavoidable. The Court's opinions proclaim general legal principles in the context of specific cases. As the example of police searches indicates, the application of those principles to other cases or situations often is uncertain. Thus, it was not surprising when two courts disagreed in 2007 about whether a Supreme Court decision on public access to criminal proceedings required the disclosure of jurors' names.[27] The problem of interpretation is greater when the Court's decisions are murky. A 2006 decision on protection of wetlands under the Clean Water Act lacked a majority opinion and a clear position on the appropriate standards to apply, and judges understandably have disagreed on how to interpret the decision.[28]

Officials who are uncertain about what the Court wants may not carry out the Court's intent properly even if they would like to do so. When officials do *not* want to carry out the Court's intent, ambiguity gives them leeway to interpret decisions as they see fit. For example, the Court's vague timetable for school desegregation gave southern judges and school administrators an excuse to delay desegregation.

Whether the Court's position on an issue is clear or ambiguous, its decisions must be transmitted to relevant judges and administrators. The communication of decisions is not usually automatic. Even judges seldom monitor the Supreme Court's output systematically to identify relevant decisions. Instead, decisions come to the attention of officials through other channels.

One channel is the mass media. A few Supreme Court decisions are sufficiently interesting that they receive heavy publicity in newspapers and on television. But most decisions garner little or no coverage in the mass media, and what the media report is sometimes misleading.[29] And even the best-publicized decisions may not get through to everyone. Few of the Court's rulings have received as much media coverage as the 1989 decision that struck down state laws against flag desecration. Yet in recent years prosecutors in Illinois and Utah have charged individuals under those laws. After the Illinois prosecution, an ACLU official asked in some surprise, "Have they not heard of *Texas v. Johnson* down there?"[30]

Attorneys communicate decisions to some officials. Through their arguments in court proceedings and administrative hearings, lawyers bring favorable precedents to the attention of judges and administrators. Staff lawyers in administrative agencies often inform agency personnel of relevant decisions. But such administrators as teachers and public welfare workers lack that source of information.

Another channel of information is professional hierarchies. State trial judges often become aware of the Court's decisions when they are cited by state appellate courts. Police officers learn of decisions from department superiors. Here, too, there is considerable potential for misinformation, especially when the communicator disagrees with a decision. Many state supreme courts and most police officials conveyed negative views of liberal criminal justice decisions by the Warren Court when they informed their subordinates of those decisions.

Effective communication of decisions depends on the receivers as well as the channels of transmission. Legally trained officials are the most capable of understanding decisions and their implications. Police officers and other nonlawyers who work regularly with the law also have some advantage in interpreting decisions. On the whole, administrators who work outside the legal system have the greatest difficulty in interpreting what they learn about Supreme Court rulings.

Transmission problems have an obvious impact. Policymakers who do not know of a decision cannot implement it, and those who misunderstand the Court's requirements will not follow them as intended. Police officers who do not fully understand the complex body of rules for searches cannot fully comply with those rules. In sum, effective transmission of the Court's policies, like clarity in the policies themselves, is needed for their effective implementation.

Motivations for Resistance. If policymakers know of a Supreme Court policy that is relevant to a choice they face, they must decide what to do with that policy. Not surprisingly, officials are likely to carry out a policy faithfully if they think it is a good policy and that they will benefit from doing so. But if that policy conflicts with their policy preferences or their self-interest, they may resist the Court's lead.

When judges fail to implement Supreme Court decisions fully, the most common reason is a conflict between those decisions and their policy preferences. After the Court adopts a new policy, lower-court judges may conclude that it has made a serious mistake. Those judges sometimes rebel against the Court's policy, although their rebellion is usually quiet.

Disagreement about judicial policy tends to follow ideological lines. For many years the federal Court of Appeals for the Ninth Circuit on the West Coast has been the most liberal court of appeals, distinctly more liberal than the Supreme Court. As a result, it is relatively common for three-judge panels of the Ninth Circuit to take positions that diverge from those of the Supreme Court. Similarly, the conservative Fifth Circuit in the Deep South has given narrow interpretations to Court decisions that favor criminal defendants, especially on the death penalty. The stances of both courts have been reflected in reversals by the Supreme Court, sometimes accompanied by rebukes for deviating from the Court's positions. In a 2006 decision, the Court held that a Ninth Circuit ruling was "legally erroneous" and that the error was "obvious" in light of a prior Court decision.[31]

Like judges, administrators may disagree with Supreme Court decisions. Beginning with a pair of decisions in 1962 and 1963, the Court prohibited organized religious observances, such as classroom prayer and Bible reading exercises, in public schools.[32] A great many teachers and school administrators disapprove of those decisions, and some disapprove strongly. As a result, many schools have maintained the prohibited practices or modified them only marginally.[33]

Supreme Court policies conflict with officials' self-interest if they threaten existing practices that serve important purposes. Many trial judges who handle criminal cases feel considerable time pressure because of their heavy caseloads. As a result, they often fail to comply with decisions that would slow down their disposition of cases. There is widespread noncompliance with the Court's 1990 decision that prohibited the hiring of low-level public employees on the basis of their partisan affiliation and political ties. That noncompliance is understandable, because elected officials have strong incentives to use government jobs to reward supporters.[34]

Elected officials sometimes have good reason not to carry out highly unpopular decisions. Rulings in favor of criminal defendants may provide an issue to opponents of elected judges, and some judges have lost their positions as a result. The Texas Court of Criminal Appeals, the state's highest court for criminal cases, has deviated from some Supreme Court decisions expanding defendants' rights. One reason appears to be the electoral advantage of taking pro-prosecution positions.[35]

Because their positions are secure, federal judges might seem to be immune from these political concerns. But they too may wish to avoid incurring public wrath. Full adherence to *Brown v. Board of Education* would have made the lives of district judges less pleasant because of the reactions of their friends and neighbors.[36] A federal judge in Florida said that he had "lost more friends in the last four years following the Constitution of the United States than I made in the first forty."[37] Only a few federal judges in the Deep South were willing to accept the costs of following *Brown* wholeheartedly.

Differences in the implementation of Supreme Court policies result chiefly from differences in the policy preferences and self-interest of implementers. Police departments tend to resist decisions that limit their powers but follow with alacrity those that expand them. The Deep South and the border states responded differently to the *Brown* decision because attitudes toward race and segregation were not the same in the two regions.

The Court's Authority. In a 2007 opinion, federal court of appeals Judge Timothy Tymkovich argued that a Supreme Court decision was entirely wrong as an interpretation of federal bankruptcy law. Having reached that conclusion, he asked, "What happens when the Supreme Court ignores the plain meaning of a statute?" His answer was clear: "As tempting as it would be to ignore the Supreme Court's interpretation of the text in favor of the actual text, that is not our role at the circuit court level."[38] Judge Tymkovich was accepting both the Supreme Court's authority to make conclusive judgments about the law and his own obligation to comply with the Court's decisions. This acceptance, broadly shared among judges and administrators, helps to foster faithful implementation of Supreme Court decisions.

The Court's authority is strongest for judges, who have been socialized to accept the leadership of higher courts and who benefit from acceptance of judicial authority, but on rare occasions a judge denies the Supreme Court's authority. An Alabama Supreme Court justice rebuked his colleagues "because they chose to passively accommodate—rather than actively resist—the unconstitutional opinion of five liberal justices on the U.S. Supreme Court."[39] More often, judges give narrow interpretations to Court decisions with which they disagree, thereby limiting the impact of those decisions while acknowledging the Court's authority. In some instances, these narrow interpretations seem inconsistent with the Court's decisions.

The Court's authority extends to administrators. To take one important example, some school officials eliminate religious observances that they would prefer to maintain because they accept their duty to follow Supreme Court rulings.[40] On the whole, however, the Court's authority is weaker for administrators than it is for judges. Administrative agencies are somewhat removed from the judicial system and its norm of obedience to higher courts, and most administrators have not had the law school training that supports this norm. As a result, administrative officials find it somewhat easier to justify deviation from Supreme Court policies than judges do.

The Court's authority tends to decline as organizational distance from the Court increases. State trial judges typically orient themselves more closely to appellate courts in their state than to the Supreme Court, several steps away from them in the judicial hierarchy. For administrators at the grassroots level, both state courts and administrative superiors may seem far more relevant than the Court. The effect of distance is suggested by an episode in which a Pennsylvania justice of the peace was told that his practice of taking part of each fine as a personal fee was unconstitutional. "Who said that?" he asked. When he was told that it was the Supreme Court, the JP "shrugged and said, 'Oh well, I didn't think it was any Pennsylvania court.' "[41]

Sanctions for Disobedience. Alongside its intangible authority, the Court also has more concrete sanctions with which to secure effective implementation of its rulings. For judges, the most common sanction is reversal. If a judge does not follow an applicable Supreme Court policy, the losing litigant may appeal the case and secure a reversal of the judge's decision. This sanction is significant, chiefly because it suggests that a judge erred. Indeed, lawyers and judges sometimes gauge judges' performance by the frequency of reversals.

In practice, however, the threat of reversal may have only a limited effect. The primary reason is that reversal has its limits as a sanction. Judges who feel strongly about an issue may be willing to accept reversals on that issue as the price of following their personal convictions. For that matter, failure to follow the Supreme Court's lead does not always lead to reversal. The losing litigant may not appeal. Moreover, the great majority of judges are reviewed by a court other than the Supreme Court, and the reviewing court may share their opposition to the Court's policies. Even for judges on the federal courts of appeals—who *are* reviewed directly by the Court—other motivations, such as acceptance of the Court's authority, seem to be more important than the desire to avoid reversal in inducing them to follow the Court's lead.[42]

For administrators, the most common sanction is a court order that directs compliance with a decision. If a public welfare agency fails to follow an applicable Supreme Court policy, someone who is injured by its failure may bring a lawsuit to compel compliance with the Court's decision. An agency finds any suit unwelcome because of the trouble and expense it entails. A successful suit is even worse, because an order to comply with a Supreme Court rule puts an agency under judicial scrutiny and may embarrass agency officials. The agency may also be required to pay monetary damages to the person who brought the lawsuit. For instance, an Arkansas school district and its officials were ordered to pay damages and later were held in contempt by a federal court for maintaining religious observances that the Supreme Court had prohibited.[43]

But this sanction has weaknesses. Most important, it can occur only if people bring lawsuits against agencies, and agency noncompliance often goes unchallenged. If a lawsuit is threatened or actually brought, agencies can usually change their practices in time to avoid serious costs. And in situations in which compliance is difficult to ascertain, sanctions lose some of their efficacy.

Still, to follow a policy that conflicts with a Supreme Court ruling carries risks that officials usually prefer to avoid. This attitude helps to account for the frequency with which administrative organizations on their own initiative eliminate practices that the Court prohibits. Administrators whose actions require court enforcement, such as some regulatory officials, have even more reason to avoid noncompliance that may cost them judicial support.

Police practices in searches and seizures illustrate both the strength and limitations of sanctions. Under *Mapp*, noncompliance with constitutional rules for searches prevents the use of evidence in court. Largely for this reason, officers frequently comply with rules they would prefer to ignore. Officers, however, seldom receive any personal sanctions for noncompliant practices that cause evidence to be thrown out. Moreover, illegal searches may not prevent convictions. Most defendants plead guilty, and by doing so they generally waive their right to challenge the legality of searches. Trial judges usually give the benefit of the doubt to police officers on borderline evidentiary questions. And evidence that is ruled illegal may not be needed for a conviction. Thus, police officers have an incentive to avoid illegal searches, but not so strong an incentive that they always try to follow the applicable rules.

This discussion points to two conditions that affect the implementation process. First, interest groups can play an important part in enforcement of Supreme Court decisions. The ACLU frequently challenges religious observances in public schools, and by doing so it has enhanced compliance with the Court's rules. Second, the Court's decisions are easiest to enforce when the affected policymakers are few in number and highly visible. It is relatively simple for the Court to oversee the fifty state governments that must carry out its decisions on the drawing of legislative districts. It is far more difficult for the Court to oversee the day-to-day activities of all the police officers who investigate crimes.

In general, the sanctions available to the Court are fairly weak, so help from Congress and the president can make a great deal of difference when the Court faces widespread noncompliance. In enforcing school desegregation, that help was a necessity.

Summary. The Supreme Court's policies are implemented more effectively in some settings than in others. Judges generally carry out the Court's policies more fully than administrators for several reasons: communication of decisions to judges is relatively good; most judges accord the Court considerable authority; and their self-interest is less likely to conflict with the implementation of decisions. For similar reasons, federal judges and administrators probably implement decisions more faithfully than their state counterparts. The Court's decisions are communicated to them more effectively, and its authority and sanctions affect them more directly.

On the whole, the Court's policies are implemented fairly well. But there is often a substantial gap between the rules of law that the Court establishes and the actions taken by judges and administrators. To a degree, this gap reflects the Court's limited power, in that it can exert little control over the implementation process. Most important, the sanctions that the Court can apply to disobedient officials are relatively weak compared with those available to Congress and the president. But more striking than this difference is the similarity in the basic positions of Court, Congress, and president. Each proclaims policies that have uncertain and often unhappy fates in the implementation process.

Responses by Legislatures and Chief Executives

Congress, the president, and their state counterparts also respond regularly to Supreme Court decisions. Their responses shape the impact of the Court's decisions and affect the Court itself.

Congress

Congressional responses to the Court's rulings take several forms. Within some limits, Congress can modify or override the Court's decisions. It also shapes the implementation of decisions, and it can act against individual justices or the Court as a whole.

Statutory Interpretation. In *Ledbetter v. Goodyear Tire and Rubber Co.* (2007), the Supreme Court ruled on the time limit for lawsuits for discrimination in pay under Title VII of the Civil Rights Act of 1964. The Court held by a 5–4 vote that a lawsuit must be brought within 180 days of the discriminatory act, even though the effects of pay discrimination continue in future paychecks.

There was an immediate effort in Congress to override the Court's decision with a new statute. An override bill failed in 2008 because of opposition from Senate Republicans and President George W. Bush. But the Democrats gained a larger Senate majority in 2009 and President Obama made an

Lily Ledbetter, speaking at the 2008 Democratic National Convention. After Ledbetter lost her pay discrimination case in the Supreme Court in 2007, many Democrats disagreed with the Court's interpretation of a federal statute in the case. Shortly after taking office in January 2009, President Barack Obama signed a new statute that Congress had adopted to override the Court's interpretation of the law.

override of *Ledbetter* a high priority, guaranteeing success for a new bill. Indeed, both houses passed an override within a week of Obama's inauguration, and he signed the bill two days after Congress completed its action.

The override of *Ledbetter* was legitimate, because Congress is superior to the Supreme Court in statutory law: it can nullify the Court's interpretation of a statute simply by adopting a new statute with different language. Congress can also ratify or extend the Court's interpretation of a statute, and it frequently does so. But overrides of statutory decisions are especially significant.

A high proportion of statutory decisions receive some congressional scrutiny, and proposals to override decisions are common. Most of these proposals fail, for the same reasons that most bills of any type fail: bills go through several decision points and can be killed at any of them, and there is usually a presumption in favor of the status quo. Still, overrides are far from rare. Over a recent period of three decades, an average of more than ten statutory decisions were overturned in part or altogether in each two-year Congress. A study of Supreme Court tax decisions from 1954 to 2004 found that Congress overrode at least 8 percent of them.[44]

Most of these overrides come within a few years of the decisions that triggered them.

Members of Congress themselves sometimes initiate efforts to override decisions, but more often they respond to interest groups. Just as groups that are unsuccessful in Congress frequently turn to the courts for relief, groups whose interests suffer in the Supreme Court frequently turn to Congress. Sometimes the initiative comes from the Court itself. Dissenting in *Ledbetter* on behalf of three colleagues, Justice Ginsburg pointedly referred to a 1991 statute that had overturned some narrow interpretations of Title VII by the Court. "Once again," she wrote, "the ball is in Congress' court. As in 1991, the Legislature may act to correct this Court's parsimonious reading of Title VII."[45] Sometimes the Court's majority opinion invites members of Congress to override the Court's decision if they believe that the Court misinterpreted their intent or they think the Court's decision created an undesirable result.

The success of efforts to overturn statutory decisions depends on the same broad array of factors that influence the fates of other bills. The political strength of the groups that favor or oppose overrides is important. So is the political coloration of Congress and the executive branch, as the *Ledbetter* override indicates.

Like other legislation, many successful overrides are enacted not as separate bills but as provisions of broader bills, such as appropriations. *Zadvydas v. Davis* (2001), which limited the detention of noncitizens, was overridden by a provision of the long and complex Patriot Act of 2001. Members of Congress who vote for these broader bills sometimes do not know that they are overriding a Supreme Court decision.

Statutes that override the Court's decisions, like any other statutes, are subject to the Court's interpretation in later cases. Sometimes those interpretations limit the impact of an override—in effect, restoring part of the policy that Congress sought to reverse. Thus neither institution necessarily has the last word on the issues that both address.

Constitutional Interpretation. When the Supreme Court strikes down a statute as unconstitutional, Congress can simply let the decision stand or choose from a wide range of responses. A study of decisions in which the Court struck down federal statutes between 1954 and 1997 found that about half the time Congress acted to restore at least a portion of the policy that the Court had invalidated.[46] All but one of those actions involved adoption of a new statute aimed at avoiding the constitutional problems the Court had found in its predecessor.

When Congress enacts such a statute, the Court often hears a case to determine whether the new statute avoids the constitutional problem it was designed to overcome. In recent years the Court has done so on two sets of laws regulating sexually oriented material, and this area illustrates the interplay that can occur between Congress and the Court after the Court strikes down a statute.

The first set concerns child pornography. In *Ashcroft v. Free Speech Coalition* (2002) the Court struck down the Child Pornography Protection Act of 1996 on the ground that it was too broad, in that it prohibited material that was protected by the First Amendment. The next year Congress passed a new statute that was designed to avoid the problem of overbreadth. In *United States v. Williams* (2008), the Court upheld the 2003 statute. Thus Congress was able to achieve its original aim.

The second set concerns children's exposure to sexually oriented material on the Internet. In *Reno v. American Civil Liberties Union* (1997), the Court held that a 1996 statute aimed at limiting this exposure violated the First Amendment. In 1998 Congress enacted a new statute, written to achieve the same goal without running into the First Amendment problems that the Court had cited in *Reno*. There has been a complicated series of federal court decisions about whether the 1998 statute is constitutionally acceptable. The Supreme Court addressed that question in 2002 and 2004 without reaching a final judgment. In 2008 a court of appeals struck down the statute. The Supreme Court denied certiorari in that case in 2009, leaving the court of appeals decision standing. The result was to make the law unenforceable.[47]

When the Court holds that a right is not protected by the Constitution, Congress can protect that right by statute, so long as it acts within its constitutional powers and does not violate other constitutional rights. In 1993 Congress enacted the Religious Freedom Restoration Act (RFRA) to overcome a 1990 decision that had made it easier for the government to justify neutral rules that put a burden on particular religious practices. The Court held in 1997 that RFRA was unconstitutional as applied to state and local governments because it went beyond congressional power to enforce the Fourteenth Amendment. Congress tried a second time in 2000 with a narrower version of RFRA based on two other constitutional provisions. In 2005 the Court rejected one constitutional argument against a section of this second law but did not address a second argument that it might consider later.[48]

In situations in which constitutional decisions cannot be negated by statute, members of Congress often introduce resolutions to overturn them with constitutional amendments. These efforts seldom win the two-thirds majorities needed for Congress to propose an amendment. Only five times has Congress proposed an amendment that was aimed directly at Supreme Court decisions. One of these, proposed in 1924 to give Congress the power to regulate child labor, was not ratified by the states. (A few amendments have indirectly negated Supreme Court decisions.)

Since the child labor proposal, the only amendment that Congress has proposed in order to overturn a decision was the Twenty-sixth Amendment, adopted in 1971. In *Oregon v. Mitchell* (1970), the Court had ruled that Congress could not regulate the voting age in elections to state office; Congress quickly proposed an amendment overturning the decision, and the states quickly ratified it.

The difficulty of the constitutional amendment route is illustrated by the repeated failures of efforts to overturn Supreme Court rulings by restoring organized prayer in public schools and criminal penalties for flag burning. Both efforts have had considerable support in Congress and the general public, but neither has yet succeeded. The failure of flag-burning amendments is striking. In 1989 and 1990, the Supreme Court struck down state and federal statutes prohibiting flag burning on the ground that they punished people for political expression. Shortly after the 1989 decision, some members of Congress began working for a constitutional amendment to allow prohibition of flag desecration. Its passage might seem inevitable, because most members of Congress share an abhorrence of flag burning and because a member's vote against the amendment could provide an election opponent with a powerful issue. Indeed, the House approved flag-desecration amendments in every Congress from 1995 to 2006, and in 2006 the Senate came within one vote of sending an amendment to the states. But the general reluctance to amend the Constitution was compounded by a special reluctance to limit the protections of the Bill of Rights. Those concerns were just enough to keep any anti-flag-burning amendment from getting through Congress.

Affecting the Implementation of Decisions. By passing legislation, Congress can influence the implementation of Supreme Court decisions by other institutions. Its most important tool is money. Congress can provide or fail to provide funds to carry out a decision. It can also affect responses to decisions by state and local governments through its control over federal grants to them. Congressional use of this latter power was critical to school desegregation in the Deep South.

In a 2001 education statute, Congress employed the same power in two different ways. The first was related to *Boy Scouts of America v. Dale* (2000), in which the Court held that the First Amendment allows the Boy Scouts to prohibit membership to gay men and boys. In response, some schools ended their ties with the Scouts. One provision of the 2001 law required that no federal funds be provided to schools that "deny equal access" to the Scouts or "discriminate against" them. Another provision required that schools receiving federal money allow "constitutionally protected prayer." By enacting this provision, Congress gave school districts an incentive to adopt narrow interpretations of the Court's limitations on school religious observances.[49]

In 2006 the House passed a bill that would prohibit courts from awarding attorneys' fees to people who bring legal cases to enforce the First Amendment's prohibition of an establishment of religion. The bill was designed to discourage challenges to government links with religion, including challenges based on Supreme Court rulings. The Senate took no action on the bill.[50]

When a Supreme Court decision requires Congress itself to comply with the decision, Congress generally does so. The legislative veto is an exception. In *Immigration and Naturalization Service v. Chadha* (1983), the Court indicated that any statutes allowing Congress as a whole, one house, or a committee to veto proposed executive branch actions are invalid. After the decision, Congress eliminated legislative veto provisions from several statutes. But it has maintained others and adopted more than five hundred new legislative veto provisions—most requiring that specific congressional committees approve action by administrative agencies. To maintain good relations with congressional committees and to avoid even more stringent controls by Congress, agency officials are willing to accept these provisions rather than challenge their legality. Thus, political realities have allowed noncompliance with *Chadha* to continue.[51]

Attacks on Justices and the Court. When members of Congress are unhappy with the Supreme Court's policies, they can attack the Court or the justices directly. The easiest way to do so is verbally, and members of Congress sometimes denounce the Court publicly. More concretely, Congress can take several types of formal action against the Court or its members.

One type is reduction of the Court's jurisdiction.[52] The Constitution allows Congress to alter the Court's appellate jurisdiction and the jurisdiction of other federal courts through legislation, although some scholars argue that there are limits to congressional power over the Court's jurisdiction. Such limits aside, if members of Congress are unhappy with the Court's decisions in a field of policy, they can eliminate the Court's appellate jurisdiction in that field.

Congress frequently changes the jurisdiction of the Supreme Court alone or the federal courts in general. In a few instances, it has done so because of a concern with the Court's decisions. The best-known example is unusual because Congress acted to limit the Court's jurisdiction even before the Court had ruled on the issue in question. In 1869 it withdrew the Court's right to hear appeals in habeas corpus actions in order to prevent the Court from deciding a pending challenge to the post–Civil War Reconstruction legislation. In *Ex parte McCardle* (1869), the Court ruled that Congress had acted properly. In 1932 Congress withdrew the federal courts' power to hear certain kinds of cases in labor law, partly in reaction to Supreme Court decisions that were perceived as antagonistic to labor unions.[53]

Beyond habeas corpus, since the 1960s Congress has considered many bills that would have limited the Court's jurisdiction on issues such as abortion and school busing, and occasionally one house passes such a bill. In 2004 and 2006 the House passed bills to eliminate the jurisdiction of all federal courts over issues involving the Pledge of Allegiance. In 2004 the House passed a bill barring federal court jurisdiction over the Defense of Marriage Act, the 1996 federal statute intended to limit legal recognition of same-sex marriages. None of these bills passed the Senate.

Congress controls the Court budget, limited only by the constitutional prohibition against reducing the justices' salaries. In 1964 Congress singled out the justices by increasing their salaries by $3,000 less than those of other federal judges. A year later the House defeated a proposal to restore the $3,000, after a debate in which several members attacked the Court and Robert Dole, a Kansas Republican, suggested that this pay increase be contingent on the Court's reversing a legislative districting decision that he disliked.[54] Dissatisfaction with the Court's decisions can affect congressional responses to its budget requests, and in 2005 a Republican member of the House introduced an amendment to reduce the Court's budget by $1.5 million to express his unhappiness with *Kelo v. City of New London* (2005), in which the Court gave a broad interpretation to government power to take property through eminent domain.[55]

The most extreme action that Congress can take against individual justices is to remove them through impeachment. Members of Congress sometimes talk of impeachment when they dislike a justice's policy position. In 2005 the chief of staff for Senator Tom Coburn, an Oklahoma Republican, suggested "mass impeachment" of many federal judges, including Justices Breyer, Ginsburg, Kennedy, and Souter.[56]

In light of the range of congressional powers over the Court and the frequency with which their use is threatened, it is striking how little Congress has actually employed its powers during the past century. Of the many actions that members of Congress contemplated using against the conservative Court in the early part of the twentieth century, culminating in Franklin Roosevelt's Court-packing plan, almost none were carried out.[57] All the attacks on the liberal Court in the second half of the century resulted in nothing more serious than the salary "punishment" of 1964 and 1965. Why has Congress been so hesitant to use its powers, even at times when most members are unhappy about the Court's direction?

Several factors help to explain this hesitancy.[58] First, there are always some members of Congress who agree with the Court's policies and lead its defense. Second, serious forms of attack against the Court, such as impeachment and reducing its jurisdiction, seem illegitimate to many people. Finally, when threatened with serious attack, the Court occasionally retreats to reduce the impetus for congressional action. For these reasons, the congressional bark at the Supreme Court has been a good deal worse than its bite.

In the past half century most congressional attacks on the Court and its members have come from conservative members, and that has remained true even as the Court itself has become more conservative. For that reason the prospects for congressional action against the Court declined when both houses gained Democratic majorities in 2007 and those majorities grew in 2009. Several bills were introduced by conservatives in 2007 and 2008 to restrict the Court's jurisdiction, but none got very far. However, the shift in control of Congress made conservative decisions such as *Ledbetter* more vulnerable to overrides.

The President

Presidents affect the use of congressional power over the Court, and they may also act on their own to shape the outcomes of decisions.

Influencing Congressional Response. The president can influence congressional responses to the Supreme Court by taking a position on proposals for action. Sometimes it is the president who first proposes anti-Court action. The most noteworthy example in the last century was Franklin Roosevelt's Court-packing plan.

Since the 1960s, conservative presidents have encouraged efforts in Congress to limit or overturn some of the Court's liberal rulings on civil liberties. For example, George H. W. Bush led the effort to overturn the Court's flag-burning decisions in 1989 and 1990, and George W. Bush supported a constitutional amendment to prohibit flag desecration. For his part, Bill Clinton supported legislation in response to conservative decisions on regulation of tobacco and prohibition of guns in and around schools. In 2006 President George W. Bush proposed that Congress give the president the power to veto portions of budget laws. In *Clinton v. City of New York* (1998), the Court had struck down a statute establishing a line-item veto. The president's proposal took a somewhat different form, one that might meet the Court's objections to the earlier statute. Congress, however, did not act on the president's proposal.

Using Executive Power. As chief executive, the president has means to shape the implementation of Supreme Court decisions. Most directly, presidents help to determine how the executive branch carries out decisions that require agencies to change their policies. One example was *Massachusetts v. Environmental Protection Agency* (2007), in which the Supreme Court ruled that the Clean Air Act required the EPA to regulate emissions of pollutants from automobiles unless the agency determined that those emissions did not contribute to climate change. The EPA responded a few months later by producing a report that supported regulation of emissions. White House officials refused to open the e-mail message containing the report, and they persuaded the EPA to issue a second report that was less favorable to regulation.[59]

Presidents also decide whether to support the Court with the power of the federal government when decisions encounter open resistance from state and local officials. The most coercive form of federal power is deployment of the military. In 1957, when a combination of state interference and mob action prevented court-ordered desegregation of the schools in Little Rock, Arkansas, President Dwight Eisenhower abandoned his earlier position against the use of federal troops to enforce *Brown v. Board of Education*. In 1962 President John Kennedy used federal troops to enforce desegregation at the University of Mississippi.

Presidents can also employ litigation and their control over federal funds, and the Johnson administration used both mechanisms vigorously to break down segregated school systems in the Deep South. President George W. Bush reinforced a Supreme Court decision allowing drug tests of public school students who participated in extracurricular activities by using federal monetary grants to encourage drug testing in schools.[60]

Compliance with Decisions. Occasionally, a Supreme Court decision requires compliance by the president, either as a party in the case or—more often—as head of the executive branch. Some presidents and commentators have argued that the president need not obey an order of the Supreme Court, on the ground that the Court is a coequal body rather than a legal superior. In any case, presidents would seem sufficiently powerful to disobey the Court with impunity.

In reality, their position is not that strong. The president's political power is based largely on the ability to obtain support from other policymakers. This ability, in turn, depends in part on perceptions of the president's legitimacy. Because disobedience of the Court would threaten this legitimacy, presidents feel some pressure to comply with the Court's decisions.

That conclusion is supported by presidential responses to two highly visible Court orders. In *Youngstown Sheet and Tube Co. v. Sawyer* (1952), the Court ruled that President Harry Truman had acted illegally during the Korean War when he seized steel mills to keep them operating if a threatened strike took place. The Court ordered an end to the seizure, and Truman immediately complied.

Even more striking is *United States v. Nixon* (1974). During the investigation of the Watergate scandal, President Richard Nixon withheld recordings of certain conversations in his offices that were sought by special prosecutor Leon Jaworski. In July 1974 the Supreme Court ruled unanimously that Nixon must yield the tapes.

In oral argument before the Court, the president's lawyer had indicated that Nixon might not comply with an adverse decision. But he did comply. At the least, this compliance speeded Nixon's departure from office. The content of the tapes provided strong evidence of presidential misdeeds, and opposition to impeachment evaporated. Fifteen days after the Court's ruling, Nixon announced his resignation.

In light of that result, why did Nixon comply with the Court order? He apparently did not realize how damaging the evidence in the tapes actually was. Perhaps more important, noncompliance would have fatally damaged his remaining legitimacy. For many members of Congress, noncompliance in itself would have constituted an impeachable offense, one for which there would be no dispute about the evidence. Under the circumstances, compliance may have been the better of two unattractive choices.

State Legislatures and Governors

State governments have no direct power over the Supreme Court as an institution. But like Congress and the president, state legislatures and governors can influence the impact of the Court's decisions. They do so most often through their responses to decisions that strike down a state statute directly or to a ruling that a similar law from another state is unconstitutional.

Like Congress, state legislatures sometimes respond to such a decision by doing nothing, leaving an unconstitutional statute on the books. That inaction creates a problem only if the statute is actually enforced. When legislatures do respond to a Supreme Court decision, they sometimes enact new statutes that clearly fail to comply with the decision. This has been true of some statutes that states enacted to restore religious observances in public schools that the Court had invalidated. When challenged, these noncomplying statutes are usually overturned by the federal courts. Adopting such laws might seem futile, but they allow legislators to gain personal satisfaction and political credit by expressing opposition to the Court's rulings.

In contrast, legislatures frequently rewrite a statute to try to meet the Court's constitutional objections to it. After the Court struck down existing death penalty laws in *Furman v. Georgia* (1972), by 1975 thirty-one states wrote new laws that were designed to avoid arbitrary use of capital punishment and thus meet the objections raised by the pivotal justices in *Furman*.[61] In a series of decisions that followed, the Court upheld some of the new statutes and overturned others. States whose laws were rejected by the Court then adopted the forms that the Court had found acceptable.

In *Granholm v. Heald* (2005), the Supreme Court struck down state laws that allowed in-state wineries to sell wine directly to consumers but that required out-of-state wineries to sell through wholesalers.[62] The Court held that these provisions violated the Commerce Clause of Article I because they discriminated against out-of-state companies. Responding to lobbying by in-state wineries and wholesalers, several states enacted new laws intended to limit the impact of the Court's decision. Some states allowed only small wineries to ship directly to consumers, thereby protecting their own small wine producers against competition from large wineries in states such as California. Other states required consumers to travel to the wineries with which they wanted to place orders. Federal courts have reached conflicting decisions on such provisions,[63] and the Supreme Court ultimately may have to decide whether the new laws comply with its 2005 decision.

Like presidents, governors can influence both legislative responses to the Court's decisions and their implementation. Southern governors helped to block school desegregation in the 1950s and 1960s through their efforts to stir up resistance. Some governors have played a similar role in opposition to the Court's limitations on religious observances in public schools. In 2002 Texas governor Rick Perry appeared at a mandatory public school assembly in which a minister led students in a prayer, contrary to the Court's long-standing rules.[64]

Legislatures, governors, and their local counterparts sometimes must do more than eliminate unconstitutional statutes in order to put Supreme Court decisions into effect. *Gideon v. Wainwright* (1963) and later decisions required that indigent criminal defendants be provided with legal counsel. The Court's decisions spurred state and local governments to increase their commitment to provide attorneys for indigent defendants. That commitment has been reflected in much higher levels of funding, and low-income defendants are now in a far better position than they were prior to 1963. But funding of counsel has often been inadequate, and studies of the quality of indigent defense in states and local areas regularly report serious deficiencies.[65]

A quite different situation arises when the Supreme Court has held that a right is unprotected by the Constitution. State governments do not need to take any action in response to such a decision, but occasionally legislatures act to protect such a right under state law. In *Kelo v. City of New London* (2005), the Court upheld broad government power to take private property with compensation through eminent domain. *Kelo* evoked a strong negative reaction, and within eighteen months two-thirds of the states had enacted legislation to limit the use of eminent domain by local governments.[66] Their action was fully consistent with *Kelo,* since such a decision leaves the states free to protect rights that the U.S. Constitution does not.

Two Policy Areas

Patterns of response to the Court's decisions by the other two branches of government can be examined more closely by looking at two areas in which the Court and other policymakers interact. One involves a long-standing issue in which the Court's decisions evoke responses by the federal and state governments; the other involves a set of issues triggered by the federal government's efforts to attack terrorism.

Abortion. The Supreme Court's decision in *Roe v. Wade* (1973) marked the beginning of an interplay between the courts and the other branches of government that continues today. Legislatures and chief executives frequently adopt measures to limit abortion, opponents of these measures usually challenge them in court, and the other branches respond to favorable or unfavorable court decisions with new measures.

State legislatures have been the most active in responding to *Roe.* Across the country, legislators have enacted a variety of laws intended to reduce the number of abortions. These laws deal with such matters as the facilities in which abortions can be performed, waiting periods for women seeking abortions, and requirements for the consent of parents or husbands for abortions.

In the first fifteen years after *Roe,* the Supreme Court and lower federal courts generally struck down laws that created substantial limits to access to abortion, although the Court upheld prohibitions of state funding for abortion. The Court's decisions in 1989 and 1992 seemed to give states more room to restrict abortion, and they helped to spur additional state legislation.[67] However, federal courts have continued to strike down much of this legislation. The Supreme Court has reviewed only a few laws since 1992. During the 1990s a majority of states enacted a new type of regulation, one prohibiting an abortion method that opponents label "partial-birth abortion." The Court struck down these laws in *Stenberg v. Carhart* (2000). Following a well-established pattern in this field, legislators immediately began to draft new laws that might meet the Court's objections to the existing ones. Lower courts struck down some of these new laws on the basis of *Stenberg,* but the Court upheld a similar federal law in *Gonzales v. Carhart* (2007).

The Court's 1989 decision encouraged Louisiana and Utah to enact general prohibitions of abortion in the belief that the Court might uphold them. Its 1992 decision in *Planned Parenthood v. Casey* retained most of *Roe v. Wade* and thus ruled out such laws. In 2006, after the appointment of Justice Alito seemed to make the Court more sympathetic to limits on abortion, South Dakota enacted a bill to prohibit all abortions except those necessary to save the pregnant woman's life. But this statute was never tested in court because it was repealed by the state's voters.

At the federal level, many bills to overturn *Roe* with a constitutional amendment and to limit the Supreme Court's jurisdiction over abortion cases have been introduced but not adopted. Congress has enacted some restrictions on abortion, including annual provisions limiting the use of federal Medicaid funds for abortion (upheld by the Supreme Court) and the 2003 law on partial-birth abortion that the Court upheld in 2007.

Chief executives have played an active role in this field. Governors in some states have encouraged restrictions on abortion, but other governors have prevented their enactment. Federal legislation that significantly restricts abortion has better prospects during Republican administrations, although in fact little legislation of that type has been enacted. When the Court ruled in 1993 that abortion clinics could not use a civil rights law to sue people who engaged in protests obstructing access to the clinics, the Clinton administration encouraged enactment of a 1994 statute that allowed criminal prosecutions and civil lawsuits against those engaged in activities such as blockading abortion clinics.[68]

Presidents have also used their unilateral powers to shape federal policy on abortion. For example, President Reagan prohibited U.S. foreign aid to groups that use their own money to promote abortion, President Clinton repealed that prohibition, President George W. Bush reinstated it, and President Obama repealed it once again. Presidents have acted on other issues, such as the availability of abortion to members of the military. Because any legislation overturning such actions is subject to veto, presidents can effectively determine the rules on abortion in areas where they have power to act.

Detainees at Guantánamo. After the terrorist attacks of 2001, the George W. Bush administration created a detention facility for suspected terrorists at the Guantánamo Bay Naval Station. Two sets of issues about the legal rights of detainees arose.

The first set of issues concerned the right of detainees to challenge their imprisonment. In *Rasul v. Bush* (2004) the Supreme Court ruled that federal courts had jurisdiction to hear challenges by detainees through habeas corpus suits. A week after the decision, the Defense Department created Combat Status Review Tribunals (CSRTs) to determine whether detainees were properly being held at Guantánamo. The CSRTs, staffed by military officers, were intended to provide an alternative to habeas corpus actions. The Bush administration's hope was that the federal courts would find the CSRTs an adequate substitute for habeas corpus.

Congress then enacted the Detainee Treatment Act of 2005, which prohibited federal courts from hearing habeas corpus suits brought by detainees. The only judicial review available to detainees would be limited scrutiny of CSRT decisions by the federal court of appeals in the District of Columbia. But in *Hamdan v. Rumsfeld* (2006) the Court ruled that the prohibition of habeas corpus actions did not apply to lawsuits that had been brought before the law was enacted.

Congress soon overrode that part of the *Hamdan* decision with the Military Commissions Act of 2006, which made the bar on habeas corpus actions retroactive. In *Boumediene v. Bush* (2008) the Court ruled that this provision of the Military Commissions Act was unconstitutional because detainees had the right to habeas corpus and the procedures in the Detainee Treatment Act were not an adequate substitute for it.

The second set of issues concerned the form of trials for Guantánamo detainees. In 2001 President Bush established military commissions to prosecute some detainees for criminal offenses. In *Hamdan v. Rumsfeld* the Supreme Court ruled that there was no legal authority for the president's action. The Military Commissions Act included a provision that authorized the commissions, and the commissions went into operation.

Congressional action in response to the Court's decisions on these two sets of issues reflected President Bush's strong advocacy of action and a degree of unhappiness with the Court's interventions on matters relating to national security. (A month after the *Boumediene* decision, a Republican member of the House from Texas introduced legislation mandating that Guantánamo detainees be moved to the grounds around the Supreme Court building.) On the availability of habeas corpus, the Court's decisions eventually blunted action by the other branches. On the use of military commissions, Congress and the president overrode the Court's ruling against the use of commissions, and the override stands. However, the *Hamdan* decision left open the possibility of new challenges to the commissions in the future. The course of events on both habeas corpus and the commissions illustrates the interplay between the Court and the other branches that occurs in many areas of policy.

Impact on Society

The impact of the Supreme Court on government policy is important in itself, but its impact on American society as a whole is even more important. Some scholars have argued that the Court's effect on society is quite limited, but that is a minority view. Indeed, there is a widely held belief that the Court is one of the most powerful institutions in the country.

That belief is reflected in the praise that the Court receives from people who think that it has made the country better. Among other things, they point to the Court's role in advancing racial equality. People who disapprove of the Court's policies tend to be even more emphatic in portraying the Court as a source of great harm to the country. A 2008 book focused on twelve Supreme Court decisions that "radically expanded government and eroded freedom."

According to a 2007 commentary, the result of a 1969 decision on the rights of public school students was that "much of the cultural disarray of the past 35 years flowed out of schools and into society." Members of the Court themselves sometimes join in the criticism. Dissenting in *Boumediene v. Bush* (2008), Justice Scalia said that the Court's decision upholding the right of Guantánamo detainees to seek writs of habeas corpus "will make the war" with radical Islamists "harder on us. It will almost certainly cause more Americans to be killed."[69]

The belief that the Court shapes society is reflected in the attention that it gets from interest groups, the mass media, and political leaders. But just how strong is the Court's impact?

A General View

The question of the Supreme Court's impact on society is difficult to answer. Any effects the Supreme Court has on "cultural disarray" or national security operate alongside those of other policymakers and social forces, and the extent of the Court's own impact is uncertain. Even with this uncertainty, however, there is reason to be skeptical about assertions that the Court has a sweeping impact on American society. In reality, any impact is limited considerably by the context in which the Court's policies operate.

Much of that context is governmental. The Supreme Court seldom issues directives to people or institutions outside government. Rather, its decisions establish legal rules to govern decisions within government. This means that the Court's impact on society is mediated by other public policymakers.

This mediation reduces the impact of many Court policies. Some opponents of the Court's limits on religious exercises in public schools have argued that eliminating such exercises does considerable harm to schools and their students. But we know that compliance with the Court's decisions on school religion is far from complete, and that reality limits any good or bad effects of those decisions.

More broadly, the Court is seldom the only government body that deals with a particular set of issues. Rather, in most areas the Court is one policymaker among many that make decisions and undertake initiatives. In environmental policy, for instance, Congress sets the basic legal rules, administrative agencies elaborate on these rules and apply them to specific cases, and lower courts resolve most challenges to agency decisions. The Court's participation is limited to resolving a few of the legal questions that arise in the lower courts. Under these conditions, the Court can hardly determine environmental policy by itself.

The Court's policies also operate within a context of nongovernmental action. The direct impact of most decisions depends heavily on the responses of people outside government. Especially important are the actions of individuals and institutions to which the Court's decisions give greater freedom to act. These beneficiaries of the Court's policies may not take full advantage of the freedom that the Court provides them. One reason is that they may not be aware of favorable decisions. But even those who know about such decisions do not always act on them. For example, welfare recipients may not insist on their procedural rights because they do not want to alienate officials who hold power over them.

Forces outside of government also limit the broad impact of Supreme Court decisions on societal conditions. The crime rate and the quality of education are affected by family socialization, the mass media, and the economy. Those forces are likely to exert a much stronger impact on the propensity to commit crimes or the performance of students than does any Supreme Court policy. This limitation is common to all public policies, no matter which branch issues them. But the Supreme Court is in an especially weak position, because it has little control over the behavior of the private sector and because it seldom makes comprehensive policy in a particular area.

Despite all these limitations, Supreme Court decisions can and do affect society in significant ways. By helping to allocate legal rights, the Court shapes the balance between competing values and segments of society. A 1938 decision that allowed companies to hire new employees as permanent replacements for striking workers was increasingly used by employers in the 1980s, and it has helped to weaken the power of organized labor since then.[70] The Court's decisions on interest rates and other charges to credit card customers in 1978 and 1996 loosened regulation of these charges and thereby affected the financial situations of millions of people.[71] One commentator has argued that the Court's 1978 decision helped precipitate the economic downturn of 2008.[72] The Court's decisions on regulation of political campaign finance have shaped campaigns and elections since the 1970s, and its 2008 decision upholding laws that require voters to provide certain forms of identification will affect election results in the future.[73] But even in these areas of major impact, the Court is hardly the only institution that shapes outcomes.

Some Areas of Court Activity

We can gain a better sense of the Court's impact on society and the forces that determine that impact by looking at a few areas of the Court's activity. These examples demonstrate that the Court's impact is complex, highly variable, and sometimes quite difficult to measure.

Abortion. Prior to the Court's 1973 decisions in *Roe v. Wade* and *Doe v. Bolton*, two-thirds of the states prohibited abortion altogether or allowed abortions only under quite limited circumstances, and abortion was generally legal in only four states. With its decisions the Court disallowed nearly all significant legal restrictions on abortion. In every year since 1975, more than one million legal abortions have been performed. In light of the sequence of events, it seems reasonable to conclude that the Court is responsible for the large number of legal abortions. Indeed, people who care about the abortion issue typically treat the Court as the source of the current state of abortion in the United States. But the reality is more complicated, and it is impossible to determine the Court's impact with any precision.[74]

As shown in Figure 6-1, the number of legal abortions increased by about 150 percent between 1972 and 1979. This massive change suggests that the Court made a great deal of difference. But the rate of increase was actually greater between 1969 and 1972, before *Roe v. Wade.* That increase reflected changes in state laws before and during that period, as some states relaxed their general prohibitions of abortion and a few eliminated most restrictions. If the Court had never handed down *Roe,* the number of legal abortions probably would have continued to rise because of more changes in state laws and an increasing abortion rate in the states that allowed abortion. But it is impossible to know with any certainty how state laws would have evolved and how the abortion rate would have changed if the Court had not intervened.

After the Court decided *Roe v. Wade,* its impact was shaped by the policies of the other branches of government. For instance, decisions by the federal government and most states to fund abortions through Medicaid only under limited circumstances affect the rate of abortion among low-income women. Decisions not to perform abortions in government-run medical facilities also affect the abortion rate. The Court influences these policies through its rulings on what kinds of restrictions on abortion are allowable, but that influence falls far short of full control.

Conditions other than government policy also affect the abortion rate.[75] First, the number of abortions largely depends on the number of unintended pregnancies and on women's choices to seek abortions. A second condition is the ability of women who want abortions to obtain them. Only a small minority of privately owned hospitals perform abortions. Urban areas generally have clinics that perform abortions, but many rural areas lack such clinics. The number of facilities that perform abortions has declined substantially in the past two decades. These patterns reflect the personal beliefs of medical personnel as well as restrictive laws and pressures against providing abortions, ranging from disapproval in the local community to threatened and actual violence. The decline in facilities that perform abortions helps to explain the lower numbers of abortions in recent years.

All this does not mean that the Supreme Court has had little effect on abortion in the United States. In all likelihood, the Court has made

FIGURE 6-1

Estimated Number of Legal Abortions and Related Government Policy Actions, 1966–2005

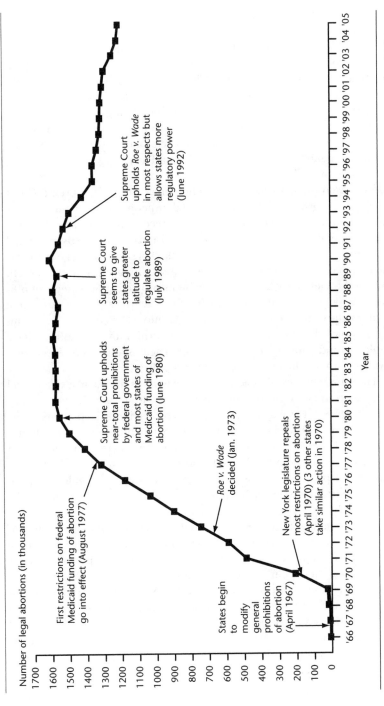

Sources: Estimated number of abortions for 1968–1985 taken from Gerald N. Rosenberg, *The Hollow Hope: Can Courts Bring about Social Change?* (Chicago: University of Chicago Press, 1991), 180; for 1986–2005, Rachel K. Jones, Mia R. S. Zolna, Stanley K. Henshaw, and Lawrence B. Finer, "Abortion in the United States: Incidence and Access to Services, 2005," *Perspectives on Sexual and Reproductive Health* 40 (March 2008): 6–16.

considerable difference. But its impact is more limited and less certain than most people think.

Roe v. Wade certainly has shaped American politics. The Court helped to make abortion a major issue in national politics, one that affects both political activity and government policy on a variety of issues. *Roe* strengthened and energized the groups that opposed the legalization of abortion by creating a perceived need for action and a target to attack. More broadly, reaction against *Roe v. Wade* played a part in the development of the religious right as a major political force, one that strengthened the conservative movement and the Republican Party.

Political Expression. In its First Amendment cases, the Supreme Court often reviews government policies aimed at people who take unpopular political positions. The Court has a mixed record in these cases, but over the past half century it has made many decisions limiting censorship and punishment of political dissenters. In the 1960s it struck down government policies that penalized people for association with groups on the far left. During the Vietnam War it issued decisions protecting opponents of official U.S. policy from punishment for their activities. In the past three decades, the Court has established some additional protections. For example, it struck down criminal penalties for burning the flag as a political statement and limited economic retaliation against public employees and business owners who criticize government policy.

The impact of these decisions is difficult to measure, but in all likelihood they have restrained government action against dissent and thereby encouraged dissenters. For example, the Court's protection of opponents of the war in Vietnam probably encouraged the open expression of opposition.

Yet the Court has not brought about a massive increase in the level of political expression in the United States. One reason is that the Court's support for political expression has not gone as far as it could have. But more important are forces that limit the impact of the Court's support for free speech.

For one thing, government officials do not always comply with the letter of the Court's decisions, and noncompliance with their spirit is quite common. Thus public school administrators sometimes punish students who express their political beliefs in ways that the Court has protected. Local governments occasionally establish limits on political demonstrations despite Court decisions that protect such demonstrations.

But perhaps most important are conditions in the private sector. First Amendment rights protect people only against actions by government. As a result, people may suffer serious consequences for political expression. Millions of Americans live in places that are governed by homeowners' associations, and many of these associations limit or prohibit political

Some homeowners' associations restrict the display of political signs. This is one of the limitations on freedom of expression that Supreme Court decisions cannot affect directly.

signs. Private employers sometimes fire people for taking political positions that differ from those of the employer. Threats and violence have been directed at environmentalists who oppose economic activities that are important in their area and at opponents of government-sponsored religious activities.[76] At a more prosaic level, people who express unpopular opinions may be ostracized by others in their community. As Mark Twain put it, people often "suppress an unpopular opinion because we cannot afford the bitter cost of putting it forth. None of us likes to be hated, none of us likes to be shunned."[77]

Incentives to avoid unpopular speech become especially strong in times of perceived danger to national security. Beginning in 2001 concern about terrorism and later the U.S. war in Iraq produced pressures against dissent from national policy. In the best-publicized case, members of the Dixie Chicks music group were subjected to boycotts, vandalism, and death threats after one member said that the group's members were "ashamed" to share the home state of President George W. Bush.[78]

It is not surprising, then, that people often choose to remain silent rather than express controversial views. Even if the Supreme Court made an even stronger commitment to protection of free speech than it does, its decisions would not reach the formal and informal actions in the private sector that discourage people from expressing themselves freely.

This result underlines the limits on the Supreme Court's ability to change social realities.

Racial Equality. In debates over the Supreme Court's impact, no issue receives as much attention as racial equality. The Warren Court of the 1950s and 1960s did a great deal to combat racial discrimination. It ruled against discrimination in education and voting, it upheld federal laws prohibiting discrimination, and it sought to protect the civil rights movement from legal attacks. To a degree, that line of policy extended back to the Court of the 1940s and forward to the Court of the 1970s. Implicitly, the Court was making a commitment to improve the status of black Americans. To what extent have the Court's policies achieved that goal?

That question has no clear answer, because this is a complicated matter. To start with, the extent of change in the status of black Americans over the past half century is ambiguous. The most dramatic progress has been political. Racial barriers to black voting in the South were overcome. Growth in the number of black elected officials is symbolized by the election of President Obama.[79] The social segregation of American life has broken down unevenly. Official segregation of public schools, the target of *Brown v. Board of Education*, was eliminated. But the level of actual school segregation remains high, largely reflecting segregation in housing.[80] In the economic arena, reduced employment discrimination and growth in average levels of education have helped to improve the economic status of black Americans. But there remain substantial differences in economic well-being by race.[81]

To the extent that we have come closer to racial equality, there is no reason to think that the Supreme Court was the primary source of that progress. Other relevant forces include the other branches of government, the mass media, and the civil rights movement. In some respects these sources are considerably more powerful than the Court.

The Court's relative weakness is clear in education and voting, the areas in which it was most active from the 1940s to the 1970s. The Court's rulings against dual school systems and devices to limit black voting in the South had only limited effects in themselves. In the Deep South it was the enactment of the Civil Rights Act of 1964 and the Voting Rights Act of 1965 and their vigorous enforcement by the Lyndon Johnson administration that broke down official school segregation and made the right to vote effective.

Because constitutional protections against discrimination apply to the private sector only to a limited degree, policies to attack housing and employment discrimination had to come from the other branches. Congress enacted statutes in the 1960s that mandated equal treatment in housing and employment, and the executive branch is responsible for enforcing them. In the 1970s and early 1980s, the Court generally gave broad interpretations to the laws against employment discrimination, interpretations that strengthened those laws. Some evidence indicates that these laws have affected the economic status of black citizens significantly. The Court's decisions may have played a part in bringing about that effect, but that part could only be minor.

Perhaps the Court played a crucial indirect role in bringing about racial equality. As some observers see it, its early civil rights decisions—especially *Brown v. Board of Education*—helped to spur passage of federal legislation and served as a catalyst for the civil rights movement. The development of a mass civil rights movement in the South was probably inevitable, and the Supreme Court was hardly the major force contributing to its development. But the Court may have speeded the movement's growth. Its decisions in education and other areas created hope for change and established rights to be vindicated by political action.

The series of civil rights laws adopted from 1957 on also may owe something to the Court. In education and voting, the Court initiated government action against discrimination and helped to create expectations that Congress and the executive branch were pressed to fulfill. It is true that congressional action was most directly responsible for bringing about school desegregation in the Deep South. But if the Court had not issued the *Brown* decision, Congress might have had less impetus to act against segregation at all.

Overall, the Supreme Court has had little direct impact on discrimination in the private sector. Even in the public sector, it has been weak in the enforcement of rights. In part for these reasons, some assessments of the Court's impact half a century after *Brown* were gloomy.[82]

But the Court helped to initiate and support processes of change, and its members probably can take some credit for progress toward racial equality. If the Court's impact has been more limited than many people had hoped, the Court *has* contributed to significant social change.[83]

Conclusion: The Court, Public Policy, and Society

It is now possible to reach some tentative conclusions about the role of the Supreme Court as a public policymaker. As suggested in Chapter 5 and this chapter, that role is fundamentally limited in some respects but still quite important.

The most obvious limitation on the Court's role is that it decides relatively few issues. One effect is that the Court can be only a minor participant in fields such as foreign policy, in which it does not address most major issues. Even in its areas of specialization, the Court intervenes only in limited ways. It makes decisions on a small sample of the issues that affect the rights of criminal defendants or freedom of expression.

The justices are not always shy about intervening on major issues of public policy, and the Court often reaches decisions that mandate significant changes in government policy. The impact of these decisions, however, is mediated and frequently reduced by the actions of other institutions and individuals. A ruling that public schools must eliminate organized prayers does not guarantee that those observances will disappear. Efforts to broaden freedom of expression may be stymied by conditions in society that the Court cannot influence.

These limitations must be balanced against the Court's strengths. Certainly, a great many Supreme Court decisions have significant direct effects. Interpretations of the Voting Rights Act and the Constitution shape politics at all levels of government. The Court's decisions influence business practices and the outcome of conflicts between different economic groups. Decisions on capital punishment are literally matters of life and death for some people.

The Court also helps to shape political and social change. Its partial opposition to government regulation of private business in an earlier era was ultimately overcome, but the Court slowed a fundamental change in the role of government. If *Roe v. Wade* was not as consequential as most people think, it *has* been the focus of a major national debate and struggle for more than three decades. The Court's decisions have not brought about racial equality, even in conjunction with other forces, but they have helped to spur changes in race relations.

As the examples of abortion and civil rights suggest, the Court is perhaps most important in creating conditions for action by others. Its decisions help to put issues on the national agenda so that other policymakers and the general public consider them. The Court is not highly effective in enforcing rights, but it often legitimates efforts to achieve rights. By doing so, it provides an impetus for people to take legal and political action. Its decisions affect the positions of interest groups and social movements, strengthening some and weakening others.

The Supreme Court, then, is neither all-powerful nor inconsequential. Rather, it is one of many institutions that shape American society in significant ways. That is a more limited role than some have claimed for the Court. But the role that the Court does play is an extraordinary one for a single small body that possesses little tangible power. In this sense, perhaps more than any other, the Supreme Court is a remarkable institution.

NOTES

1. Del Quentin Wilber and Paul Duggan, "D.C. Is Sued Again over Handgun Rules," *Washington Post,* July 29, 2008, B1.
2. Adam Winkler, "*Heller*'s Catch-22," *UCLA Law Review* 56 (June 2009): 1565–1567; Adam Liptak, "Gun Ruling Was Called a Landmark, But That Remains to Be Seen," *New York Times,* March 17, 2009, A14.

3. *Smith v. Texas* (2007). The quotation is from *Ex parte Smith*, 185 S.W.3d 455, 474 (Texas Ct. Crim. App. 2006).

4. Mike Tolson, "Deal Keeps Penry Imprisoned for Life," *Houston Chronicle*, February 16, 2008, B1. The decisions were *Penry v. Lynaugh* (1989) and *Penry v. Johnson* (2001).

5. Patrick Hickerson and Val Walton, "Board Settles Gender Bias Suit," *Birmingham News*, November 29, 2006, 1A. The decision was *Jackson v. Birmingham Board of Education* (2005).

6. The Supreme Court's decision was *KSR International Co. v. Teleflex Inc.* (2007). The second district court decision was *Friskit, Inc. v. Realnetworks, Inc.* (N.D. Calif. 2007).

7. Karen M. Blum, "11th Circuit Is Out of Step," *National Law Journal*, April 21, 2003, A13; see Jonathan Ringel, "Divided 11th Circuit Panel Backs Immunity for Cops," *National Law Journal*, December 8, 2003, 7. The Supreme Court decision was *Hope v. Pelzer* (2002).

8. James F. Spriggs II, "Explaining Federal Bureaucratic Compliance with Supreme Court Opinions," *Political Research Quarterly* 50 (September 1997): 577–578.

9. Patent and Trademark Office, "Examination Guidelines for Determining Obviousness under 35 U.S.C. 103 ...," *Federal Register* 72 (October 10, 2007), 57526–57535. See Ryan H. Flax, "Patent Counsel Adjust to the Post-'KSR' Landscape," *National Law Journal*, December 3, 2007, S2.

10. Richard Ellis, *To the Flag: The Unlikely History of the Pledge of Allegiance* (Lawrence: University Press of Kansas, 2004). The decision was *West Virginia Board of Education v. Barnette* (1943).

11. Steve Bogira, *Courtroom 302: A Year behind the Scenes in an American Criminal Courthouse* (New York: Knopf, 2005), 16–17, 67, 157–158, 261. The decisions were, respectively, *Gerstein v. Pugh* (1975), *Brady v. Maryland* (1963), and *Batson v. Kentucky* (1986).

12. *Miller-El v. Dretke*, 545 U.S. 231, 267–269 (2005); *Snyder v. Louisiana* (2008). See Adam Liptak, "Oddity in Picking Jurors Opens Door to Racial Bias," *New York Times*, June 4, 2007, A12.

13. Harrell R. Rodgers Jr. and Charles S. Bullock III, *Law and Social Change: Civil Rights Laws and Their Consequences* (New York: McGraw-Hill, 1972), 75.

14. *Green v. School Board* (1968); *Alexander v. Holmes County Board of Education* (1969).

15. *Missouri v. Jenkins* (1990); *Spallone v. United States* (1989). On *Spallone*, see Lisa Belkin, *Show Me a Hero: A Tale of Murder, Suicide, Race, and Redemption* (Boston: Little, Brown, 1999).

16. *Board of Education v. Dowell* (1991); *Freeman v. Pitts* (1992).

17. Richard A. Leo, "The Impact of *Miranda* Revisited," *Journal of Criminal Law and Criminology* 86 (spring 1996): 652–653; Paul G. Cassell and Bret S. Hayman, "Police Interrogation in the 1990s: An Empirical Study of the Effects of *Miranda*," *UCLA Law Review* 43 (February 1996): 887–892.

18. Richard A. Leo, *Police Interrogation and American Justice* (Cambridge: Harvard University Press, 2008), 124.

19. *People v. Neal* (Calif. 2003); *Missouri v. Seibert*, 542 U.S. 600, 609–611 (2004).

20. Steven B. Duke, "Does Miranda Protect the Innocent or the Guilty?" *Chapman Law Review* 10 (spring 2007): 562.

21. Marvin Zalman and Brad W. Smith, "The Attitudes of Police Executives toward *Miranda* and Interrogation Policies," *Journal of Criminal Law and Criminology* 97 (2007): 873–942.

22. Jerome H. Skolnick, *Justice without Trial: Law Enforcement in Democratic Society*, 3d ed. (New York: Macmillan, 1994), 277, emphasis in original.

23. Evidence on the impact of *Mapp* is discussed in L. Timothy Perrin, H. Mitchell Caldwell, Carol A. Chase, and Ronald W. Fagan, "If It's Broken, Fix It: Moving beyond the Exclusionary Rule," *Iowa Law Review* 83 (May 1998): 678–711.

24. Bradley C. Canon, "Is the Exclusionary Rule in Failing Health? Some New Data and a Plea against a Precipitous Conclusion," *Kentucky Law Journal* 62 (1974): 702–725; Myron W. Orfield Jr., "The Exclusionary Rule and Deterrence: An Empirical Study of Chicago Narcotics Officers," *University of Chicago Law Review* 54 (summer 1987): 1024–1049; and Craig D. Uchida and Timothy S. Bynum, "Search Warrants, Motions to Suppress and 'Lost Cases': The Effects of the Exclusionary Rule in Seven Jurisdictions," *Journal of Criminal Law and Criminology* 81 (winter 1991): 1034–1066.

25. Jon B. Gould and Stephen D. Mastrofski, "Suspect Searches: Assessing Police Behavior under the U.S. Constitution," *Criminology and Public Policy* 3 (2004): 901–948.

26. Christopher Slobogin, "Why Liberals Should Chuck the Exclusionary Rule," *University of Illinois Law Review*, 1999, 369.

27. *Commonwealth v. Long* (Pa. Sup. Ct. 2007); *United States v. Black* (N.D. Ill. 2007). The Supreme Court decision was *Press-Enterprise Co. v. Superior Court* (1986).

28. *United States v. Johnson* (1st Cir. 2006); *United States v. Robison* (11th Cir. 2008). See Amanda Bronstad, "Wetlands Protection Muddied by Court Rulings," *National Law Journal*, June 25, 2007, 1, 21.

29. Elliot E. Slotnick and Jennifer A. Segal, *Television News and the Supreme Court: All the News That's Fit to Air?* (New York: Cambridge University Press, 1998).

30. Caleb Hale, "Man Pleads Guilty to Desecrating U.S. Flag," *Southern Illinoisian*, December 3, 2003. The Utah case is described in *Winsness v. Yocom* (10th Cir. 2006).

31. *Gonzales v. Thomas*, 547 U.S. 183, 185 (2006).

32. *Engel v. Vitale* (1962); *Abington School District v. Schempp* (1963).

33. See Kevin T. McGuire, "Public Schools, Religious Establishments, and the U.S. Supreme Court: An Examination of Policy Compliance," *American Politics Research* 37 (January 2009): 50–74.

34. The decision was *Rutan v. Republican Party of Illinois* (1976). See Ray Long, John Chase, and David Kidwell, "Hiring Law? What Hiring Law?" *Chicago Tribune*, September 17, 2006, sec. 1, 1, 16; David Kocieniewski, "New Jersey's State Medical School Provides a Blatant Lesson in the Spoils System," *New York Times*, April 5, 2006, A20.

35. Cragg Hines, "Supremes to Texas Appeals Court: You Still Don't Get It," *Houston Chronicle*, November 21, 2004, 3; Michael Hall, "And Justice for Some," *Texas Monthly*, November 2004, 154–157, 259–263.

36. J.W. Peltason, *Fifty-Eight Lonely Men: Southern Federal Judges and School Desegregation* (Urbana: University of Illinois Press, 1971), 9.

37. Robert Carp and Russell Wheeler, "Sink or Swim: The Socialization of a Federal District Judge," *Journal of Public Law* 21 (1972): 373.

38. *Troff v. State of Utah*, 488 F.3d 1237, 1243 (10th Cir. 2007).

39. Tom Parker, "Alabama Justices Surrender to Judicial Activism," *Birmingham News*, January 1, 2006, 4B. The case was *Adams v. State* (Ala. 2005).

40. William K. Muir Jr., *Prayer in the Public Schools: Law and Attitude Change* (Chicago: University of Chicago Press, 1967); Richard Johnson, *The Dynamics of Compliance* (Evanston, Ill.: Northwestern University Press, 1967).

41. George D. Braden, "Legal Research: A Variation on an Old Lament," *Journal of Legal Education* 5 (1952): 41n1.

42. David E. Klein and Robert J. Hume, "Fear of Reversal as an Explanation of Lower Court Compliance," *Law & Society Review* 37 (2003): 579–606; Jennifer K. Luse, Geoffrey McGovern, Wendy L. Martinek, and Sara C. Benesh, "'Such Inferior Courts …': Compliance by Circuits with Jurisprudential Regimes," *American Politics Research* 37 (January 2009): 75–106.

43. *Warnock v. Archer* (8th Cir. 2004, 2006).

44. William N. Eskridge Jr., "Overriding Supreme Court Statutory Interpretation Decisions," *Yale Law Journal* 101 (November 1991): 338; Lori Hausegger and Lawrence Baum, "Behind the Scenes: The Supreme Court and Congress in Statutory Interpretation," in *Great Theatre: The American Congress in Action*, ed. Herbert F. Weisberg and Samuel C. Patterson (New York: Cambridge University Press, 1998), 228; Nancy Staudt, René Lindstädt, and Jason O'Connor, "Judicial Decisions as Legislation: Congressional Oversight of Supreme Court Tax Cases, 1954–2005," *New York University Law Review* 82 (November 2007): 1354.

45. *Ledbetter v. Goodyear Tire & Rubber Company*, 550 U.S. 618, 660 (2007).

46. J. Mitchell Pickerill, *Constitutional Deliberation in Congress: The Impact of Judicial Review in a Separated System* (Durham, N.C.: Duke University Press, 2004), 42. This discussion draws from the Pickerill book.

47. This history is summarized in *American Civil Liberties Union v. Mukasey*, 534 F.3d 181, 184–186 (3d Cir. 2008). The Supreme Court decisions were *Ashcroft v. American Civil Liberties Union* (2002, 2004) and *Mukasey v. American Civil Liberties Union* (2009).

48. The Court's decisions were *Employment Division v. Smith* (1990), *City of Boerne v. Flores* (1997), and *Cutter v. Wilkinson* (2005).

49. The provision on school religion is at *U.S. Code*, Title 20, sec. 7904; the provision on the Boy Scouts is at *U.S. Code*, Title 20, sec. 7905.

50. See Erwin Chemerinsky, "Legislating Violations of the Constitution," *Washington Post*, September 30, 2006.

51. Louis Fisher, *Constitutional Conflicts between Congress and the President*, 5th ed., revised (Lawrence: University Press of Kansas, 2007), 152–154.

52. This discussion draws from Brett W. Curry, "The Courts, Congress, and the Politics of Federal Jurisdiction" (Ph.D. diss., Ohio State University, 2005), chaps. 6–7; and Lauren C. Bell and Kevin M. Scott, "Policy Statements or Symbolic Politics? Explaining Congressional Court-Limiting Attempts," *Judicature* 89 (January–February 2006): 196–201.

53. George I. Lovell, *Legislative Deferrals: Statutory Ambiguity, Judicial Power, and American Democracy* (New York: Cambridge University Press, 2003), 162.

54. *Congressional Record*, 89th Cong., 1st sess., 1965, 111, pt. 4: 5275. See John R. Schmidhauser and Larry L. Berg, *The Supreme Court and Congress: Conflict and Interaction, 1945–1968* (New York: Free Press, 1972), 8–12.

55. Sheryl Gay Stolberg, "Republican Lawmakers Fire Back at Judiciary," *New York Times*, July 1, 2005, A10.

56. Ruth Marcus, "Booting the Bench," *Washington Post,* April 11, 2005, A19.
57. William G. Ross, *A Muted Fury: Populists, Progressives, and Labor Unions Confront the Courts, 1890–1937* (Princeton: Princeton University Press, 1994).
58. See Charles Gardner Geyh, *When Courts and Congress Collide: The Struggle for Control of America's Judicial System* (Ann Arbor: University of Michigan Press, 2006).
59. Felicity Barringer, "White House Refused to Open E-Mail on Pollutants," *New York Times,* June 25, 2008, A15.
60. Donna Leinwand, "More Schools Test for Drugs," *USA Today,* July 12, 2006, 1A; "Conference Call Briefing ... on the 2008 National Drug Control Strategy," Business Wire, March 1, 2008, at www.businesswire.com. The decision was *Board of Education v. Earls* (2002).
61. Lee Epstein and Joseph F. Kobylka, *The Supreme Court and Legal Change: Abortion and the Death Penalty* (Chapel Hill: University of North Carolina Press, 1992), 87.
62. The aftermath of the Court's decision is discussed in Alan E. Wiseman and Jerry Ellig, "The Politics of Wine: Trade Barriers, Interest Groups, and the Commerce Clause," *Journal of Politics* 69 (August 2007): 859–875; and Maureen K. Ohlhausen and Gregory P. Luib, "Moving Sideways: Post-*Granholm* Developments in Wine Direct Shipping and Their Implications for Competition," *Antitrust Law Review* 75:505–547.
63. *Baude v. Heath* (7th Cir. 2008); *Cherry Hill Vineyards v. Lilly* (6th Cir. 2008).
64. Jay Root, "Falwell Backs Perry Prayer Push," *Fort Worth Star-Telegram,* November 1, 2001, 5B.
65. One example is Commission on the Future of Indigent Defense Services, *Final Report to the Chief Judge of the State of New York* (Albany: New York State Unified Court System, 2006).
66. David G. Savage, "Even a Supreme Court Loss Can Propel a Cause," *Los Angeles Times,* January 3, 2007, A10.
67. The decisions were *Webster v. Reproductive Health Services* (1989) and *Planned Parenthood v. Casey* (1992).
68. The decision was *Bray v. Alexandria Women's Health Clinic* (1993).
69. The quotations are from, respectively, Robert A. Levy and William Mellor, *The Dirty Dozen: How Twelve Supreme Court Cases Radically Expanded Government and Eroded Freedom* (New York: Sentinel, 2008); Daniel Henninger, "Bong Hits 4 Jesus—Final Episode," *Wall Street Journal,* June 28, 2007, A12; and *Boumediene v. Bush,* 171 L. Ed. 2d 41, 178 (2008).
70. The decision was *National Labor Relations Board v. Mackay Radio & Telegraph Company* (1938).
71. The decisions were *Marquette National Bank v. First of Omaha Service Corp.* (1978) and *Smiley v. Citibank* (1996).
72. Thomas Geoghegan, "Infinite Debt: How Unlimited Interest Rates Destroyed the Economy," *Harper's Magazine,* April 2009, 31–39.
73. The major decisions on campaign finance were *Buckley v. Valeo* (1976) and *McConnell v. Federal Election Commission* (2003). The decision on voter identification laws was *Crawford v. Marion County Election Board* (2008).
74. This discussion of abortion is based in part on Gerald N. Rosenberg, *The Hollow Hope: Can Courts Bring about Social Change?* 2d ed. (Chicago: University of Chicago Press, 2008), 175–201; and Matthew E. Wetstein,

"The Abortion Rate Paradox: The Impact of National Policy Change on Abortion Rates," *Social Science Quarterly* 76 (September 1995): 607–618.

75. See Rachel K. Jones, Mia R. S. Zolna, Stanley K. Henshaw, and Lawrence B. Finer, "Abortion in the United States: Incidence and Access to Services, 2005," *Perspectives on Sexual and Reproductive Health* 40 (March 2008): 6–16.

76. See Neela Banerjee, "School Board to Pay in Jesus Prayer Suit," *New York Times,* February 28, 2008, A15.

77. Mark Twain, "The Privilege of the Grave," *The New Yorker,* December 22–29, 2008, 50. (The essay was written in 1905 but first published in 2008.)

78. See Dick Polman, "A Clash Over Who Is a Patriot," *Philadelphia Inquirer,* March 23, 2003, C1.

79. Figures on the number of black elected officials over time are in U.S. Census Bureau, *Statistical Abstract of the United States: 2008* (Washington, D.C.: Census Bureau, 2007), 255.

80. Gary Orfield and Chungmei Lee, *Racial Transformation and the Changing Nature of Segregation* (Cambridge, Mass.: Civil Rights Project, Harvard University, 2006).

81. Alemayehu Bishaw and Jessica Semega (U.S. Census Bureau), *Income, Earnings, and Poverty Data from the 2007 American Community Survey* (Washington, D.C.: Government Printing Office, 2008), 3, 20.

82. Charles J. Ogletree Jr., *All Deliberate Speed: Reflections on the First Half Century of* Brown v. Board of Education (New York: Norton, 2003); Derrick Bell, *Silent Covenants:* Brown v. Board of Education *and the Unfulfilled Hopes for Racial Reform* (New York: Oxford University Press, 2004).

83. See Michael J. Klarman, *From Jim Crow to Civil Rights: The Supreme Court and the Struggle for Racial Equality* (New York: Oxford University Press, 2004), 443–468.

Glossary of Legal Terms

Affirm. In an appellate court, to reach a decision that agrees with the result reached in the case by the lower court.

Amicus curiae. "Friend of the court." A person, private group or institution, or government agency, not a party to a case, that participates in the case (usually through submission of a brief) at the invitation of the court or on its own initiative.

Appeal. In general, a case brought to a higher court for review. In the Supreme Court, a small number of cases are designated as appeals under federal law; formally, these must be heard by the Court.

Appellant. The party that appeals a lower-court decision to a higher court.

Appellee. A party to an appeal who wishes to have the lower-court decision upheld and who responds when the case is appealed.

Brief. A document submitted by counsel to a court, setting out the facts of the case and the legal arguments in support of the party represented by the counsel.

Certiorari, Writ of. A writ issued by the Supreme Court, at its discretion, to order a lower court to send a case to the Supreme Court for review. Most cases come to the Court as petitions for writs of certiorari.

Civil cases. All legal cases other than criminal cases.

Class action. A lawsuit brought by one person or group on behalf of all persons in similar situations.

Concurring opinion. An opinion by a member of a court that agrees with the result reached by the court in the case but offers its own rationale for the decision.

Dicta. *See* Obiter dictum.

Discretionary jurisdiction. Jurisdiction that a court may accept or reject in particular cases. The Supreme Court has discretionary jurisdiction over most cases that come to it.

Dissenting opinion. An opinion by a member of a court that disagrees with the result reached by the court in the case.

Habeas corpus. "You have the body." A writ issued by a court to inquire whether a person is lawfully imprisoned or detained. The writ demands that the persons holding the prisoner justify the detention or release the prisoner.

Holding. In a majority opinion, the rule of law necessary to decide the case. That rule is binding in future cases.

In forma pauperis. "In the manner of a pauper." In the Supreme Court, cases brought in forma pauperis by indigent persons are exempt from the Court's usual fees and from some formal requirements.

Judicial review. Review of legislation or other government action to determine its consistency with the federal or state constitution; includes the power to strike down policies that are inconsistent with a constitutional provision. The Supreme Court reviews government action only under the federal Constitution, not state constitutions.

Jurisdiction. The power of a court to hear a case in question.

Litigants. The parties to a court case.

Majority opinion. An opinion in a case that is subscribed to by a majority of the judges who participated in the decision. Also known as the opinion of the court.

Mandamus. "We command." An order issued by a court that directs a lower court or other authority to perform a particular act.

Mandatory jurisdiction. Jurisdiction that a court must accept. Cases falling under a court's mandatory jurisdiction must be decided officially on their merits, although a court may avoid giving them full consideration.

Modify. In an appellate court, to reach a decision that disagrees in part with the result reached in the case by the lower court.

Moot. A moot case is one that has become hypothetical, so that a court need not decide it.

Obiter dictum. (Also called *dictum* [sing.] or *dicta* [pl.].) A statement in a court opinion that is not necessary to resolve the case before the court. Dicta are not binding in future cases.

Original jurisdiction. Jurisdiction as a trial court.

Per curiam. "By the court." An unsigned opinion of the court, often quite brief.

Petitioner. One who files a petition with a court seeking action or relief, such as a writ of certiorari.

Remand. To send back. When a case is remanded, it is sent back by a higher court to the court from which it came, for further action.

Respondent. The party in opposition to a petitioner or appellant, who answers the claims of that party.

Reverse. In an appellate court, to reach a decision that disagrees with the result reached in the case by the lower court.

Standing. A requirement that the party who files a lawsuit have a legal stake in the outcome.

Stare decisis. "Let the decision stand." The doctrine that principles of law established in earlier judicial decisions should be accepted as authoritative in similar subsequent cases.

Statute. A written law enacted by a legislature.

Stay. To halt or suspend further judicial proceedings. The Supreme Court sometimes issues a stay to suspend action in a lower court while the Supreme Court considers the case.

Vacate. To make void or annul. The Supreme Court sometimes vacates a lower-court decision, requiring the lower court to reconsider the case.

Writ. A written court order commanding the designated recipient to perform or not perform acts specified in the order.

Selected Bibliography

General References

Epstein, Lee, Jeffrey A. Segal, Harold J. Spaeth, and Thomas G. Walker. *The Supreme Court Compendium: Data, Decisions, and Developments*. 4th ed. Washington, D.C.: CQ Press, 2007.

Hall, Kermit L., James W. Ely Jr., and Joel B. Grossman, eds. *The Oxford Companion to the Supreme Court of the United States*. 2d ed. New York: Oxford University Press, 2005.

Savage, David G. *Guide to the U.S. Supreme Court*. 4th ed. Washington, D.C.: CQ Press, 2004.

Chapter 1

Hoekstra, Valerie J. *Public Reaction to Supreme Court Decisions*. New York: Cambridge University Press, 2003.

Peppers, Todd C. *Courtiers of the Marble Palace: The Rise and Influence of the Supreme Court Law Clerk*. Stanford: Stanford University Press, 2006.

Perry, Barbara A. *The Priestly Tribe: The Supreme Court's Image in the American Mind*. Westport, Conn.: Praeger, 1999.

Rehnquist, William H. *The Supreme Court*. New ed. New York: Knopf, 2001.

Slotnick, Elliot E., and Jennifer A. Segal. *Television News and the Supreme Court: All the News That's Fit to Air?* New York: Cambridge University Press, 1998.

Ward, Artemus, and David L. Weiden. *Sorcerers' Apprentices: 100 Years of Law Clerks at the United States Supreme Court*. New York: New York University Press, 2006.

Zimmerman, Joseph F. *Interstate Disputes: The Supreme Court's Original Jurisdiction*. Albany: State University of New York Press, 2006.

Chapter 2

Abraham, Henry J. *Justices, Presidents, and Senators: A History of the U.S. Supreme Court Appointments from Washington to Bush II*. Rev. ed. Lanham, Md.: Rowman and Littlefield, 2008.

Comiskey, Michael. *Seeking Justices: The Judging of Supreme Court Nominees.* Lawrence: University Press of Kansas, 2004.

Dean, John W. *The Rehnquist Choice.* New York: Free Press, 2001.

Greenberg, Jan Crawford. *Supreme Conflict: The Inside Story of the Struggle for Control of the United States Supreme Court.* New York: Penguin Press, 2007.

Nemacheck, Christine L. *Strategic Selection: Presidential Nomination of Supreme Court Justices from Herbert Hoover through George W. Bush.* Charlottesville: University of Virginia Press, 2007.

Ward, Artemus. *Deciding to Leave: The Politics of Retirement from the United States Supreme Court.* Albany: State University of New York Press, 2003.

Yalof, David Alistair. *Pursuit of Justices: Presidential Politics and the Selection of Supreme Court Nominees.* Chicago: University of Chicago Press, 1999.

Chapter 3

Baird, Vanessa A. *Answering the Call of the Court: How Justices and Litigants Set the Supreme Court Agenda.* Charlottesville: University of Virginia Press, 2007.

Collins, Paul M., Jr. *Friends of the Supreme Court: Interest Groups and Judicial Decision Making.* New York: Oxford University Press, 2008.

Lawrence, Susan E. *The Poor in Court: The Legal Services Program and Supreme Court Decision Making.* Princeton: Princeton University Press, 1990.

McGuire, Kevin T. *The Supreme Court Bar: Legal Elites in the Washington Community.* Charlottesville: University Press of Virginia, 1993.

Pacelle, Richard L., Jr. *Between Law and Politics: The Solicitor General and the Structuring of Civil Rights, Gender, and Reproductive Rights Litigation.* College Station: Texas A&M Press, 2003.

Sorauf, Frank J. *The Wall of Separation: The Constitutional Politics of Church and State.* Princeton: Princeton University Press, 1976.

Walker, Samuel. *In Defense of American Liberties: A History of the ACLU.* 2d ed. Carbondale: Southern Illinois University Press, 1999.

Chapter 4

Biskupic, Joan. *Sandra Day O'Connor: How the First Woman on the Supreme Court Became Its Most Influential Justice.* New York: HarperCollins, 2005.

Brenner, Saul, and Joseph M. Whitmeyer. *Strategy on the United States Supreme Court.* New York: Cambridge University Press, 2009.

Devins, Neal, and Davison M. Douglas, eds. *A Year at the Supreme Court.* Durham, N.C.: Duke University Press, 2004.

Epstein, Lee, and Jack Knight. *The Choices Justices Make.* Washington, D.C.: CQ Press, 1998.

Greenhouse, Linda. *Becoming Justice Blackmun: Harry Blackmun's Supreme Court Journey.* New York: Times Books, 2005.

Hansford, Thomas G., and James F. Spriggs II. *The Politics of Precedent on the U.S. Supreme Court.* Princeton: Princeton University Press, 2006.

Johnson, Timothy R. *Oral Arguments and Decision Making on the United States Supreme Court.* Albany: State University of New York Press, 2004.

Maltzman, Forrest, James F. Spriggs II, and Paul J. Wahlbeck. *Crafting Law on the Supreme Court: The Collegial Game.* New York: Cambridge University Press, 2000.

Maveety, Nancy. *Queen's Court: Judicial Power in the Rehnquist Era.* Lawrence: University Press of Kansas, 2008.

Segal, Jeffrey A., and Harold J. Spaeth. *The Supreme Court and the Attitudinal Model Revisited.* New York: Cambridge University Press, 2002.

Spaeth, Harold J., and Jeffrey A. Segal. *Majority Rule or Minority Will: Adherence to Precedent on the U.S. Supreme Court.* New York: Cambridge University Press, 1999.

Chapter 5

Epp, Charles R. *The Rights Revolution: Lawyers, Activists, and Supreme Courts in Comparative Perspective.* Chicago: University of Chicago Press, 1998.

Kahn, Ronald, and Ken I. Kersch, eds. *The Supreme Court and American Political Development.* Lawrence: University Press of Kansas, 2006.

Keith, Linda Camp. *The U.S. Supreme Court and the Judicial Review of Congress.* New York: Peter Lang, 2008.

McCloskey, Robert G. *The American Supreme Court.* 4th ed., rev. Sanford Levinson. Chicago: University of Chicago Press, 2005.

Pacelle, Richard L., Jr. *The Transformation of the Supreme Court's Agenda: From the New Deal to the Reagan Administration.* Boulder, Colo.: Westview Press, 1991.

Whittington, Keith E. *Political Foundations of Judicial Supremacy: The Supreme Court and Constitutional Leadership in U.S. History.* Princeton: Princeton University Press, 2007.

Chapter 6

Bell, Derrick. *Silent Covenants: Brown v. Board of Education and the Unfulfilled Hopes for Racial Reform.* New York: Oxford University Press, 2004.

Canon, Bradley C., and Charles A. Johnson. *Judicial Policies: Implementation and Impact.* 2d ed. Washington, D.C.: CQ Press, 1999.

Geyh, Charles Gardner. *When Courts and Congress Collide: The Struggle for Control of America's Judicial System.* Ann Arbor: University of Michigan Press, 2006.

Klarman, Michael J. *From Jim Crow to Civil Rights: The Supreme Court and the Struggle for Racial Equality.* New York: Oxford University Press, 2004.

Leo, Richard A. *Police Interrogation and American Justice.* Cambridge: Harvard University Press, 2008.

Miller, Mark C. *The View of the Courts from the Hill: Interactions between Congress and the Federal Judiciary.* Charlottesville: University of Virginia Press, 2009.

Pickerill, J. Mitchell. *Constitutional Deliberation in Congress: The Impact of Judicial Review in a Separated System.* Durham, N.C.: Duke University Press, 2004.

Rosenberg, Gerald N. *The Hollow Hope: Can Courts Bring about Social Change?* 2d ed. Chicago: University of Chicago Press, 2008.

Stone, Geoffrey R. *Perilous Times: Free Speech in Wartime from the Sedition Act of 1798 to the War on Terrorism.* New York: Norton, 2004.

Sources on the Web

There are many sources on the Supreme Court on the World Wide Web. Some of the most useful ones are listed here; several of these Web sites have links to other useful sites. Access to each of these Web sites is available without charge.

Many colleges and universities subscribe to the LexisNexis Academic database, which provides access to all published court decisions as well as articles in newspapers, law reviews, and other sources. The database includes the text of briefs submitted to the Supreme Court in cases with oral arguments.

As is true of Web sites in general, the content of these sites can change over time, and Web sites sometimes disappear altogether. However, most of the sites listed below have been maintained for many years.

Supreme Court of the United States (www.supremecourtus.gov/). This is the Court's official Web site. The site includes the Court's rules and the calendar for oral arguments in the current term. The Web site also includes the docket sheets in each case that comes to the Court, sheets that list all the briefs filed and the actions taken by the Court. The site provides transcripts of oral arguments and briefs submitted by the parties in cases accepted for argument.

SCOTUSBlog (www.scotusblog.com/wp/). This site, founded by Supreme Court litigator Tom Goldstein, is the most extensive source of news about the Court. Postings report and provide analysis on cases filed in the Court, oral arguments, the Court's decisions, and related subjects. The postings are arranged chronologically, but a search function can be used to call up all postings on a particular case.

SCOTUSWiki (www.scotuswiki.com/index.php?title=Main_Page). This site is a companion to the SCOTUSBlog. Its most important feature is a collection of sources on cases that the Court has accepted for oral argument. The site posts briefs (including amicus briefs) and adds the oral argument transcript and the Court's opinions when they are issued. Analyses and commentaries on cases are also included. Materials on cases extend back to the 2007 term. The site also provides a collection of statistics on the Court's work that Tom Goldstein has compiled since the 1995 term.

FindLaw (www.findlaw.com/casecode/supreme.html/). This Web site includes a database of Supreme Court decisions since 1893 and separate files of decisions by year since 1999. Under "Supreme Court Link Index" and "Findlaw Supreme Court Center" the site has links to a wide range of other sites, including those of several media organizations.

Legal Information Institute (www.law.cornell.edu/supct/). The law school at Cornell University provides this Web site, which includes collections of Supreme Court decisions and other kinds of information about the Court as well as links to other sites. Connected with the Web site is a free e-mail subscription service that sends previews of cases prior to oral argument and syllabi that summarize the Court's decisions on the same day they are handed down. Those syllabi are linked to the text of the opinions in the case.

The Oyez Project (www.oyez.org). Jerry Goldman of Northwestern University has created this site, which has several types of information about the Supreme Court. The most important feature is an extensive collection of audiotapes and transcripts of oral arguments and announcements of decisions in the Court.

Office of the Solicitor General (www.usdoj.gov/osg/). This Web site provides information on the solicitor general's office and on the Court. The site includes a file of briefs filed by the solicitor general's office in the Supreme Court. The "help/glossary" file (under "briefs") provides detailed information about technical matters related to the Court such as jurisdiction and the assignment of docket numbers to cases.

The Constitution of the United States of America: Analysis and Interpretation (www.gpoaccess.gov/constitution/browse.html). For many years the Congressional Research Service of the Library of Congress has compiled a highly detailed summary of the Supreme Court's interpretations of each provision of the Constitution, along with citations of the relevant cases. Also included are lists of all federal, state, and local statutes that the Court has declared unconstitutional and all Supreme Court decisions overruled by subsequent decisions. Editions of this compilation and supplements to those editions since 1992 are available at this site.

Case Index

Case titles normally are followed by case citations. These begin with the volume of the reporter in which the case appears, for example, 374 in the first case listed below. This is followed by the abbreviated name of the reporter; "U.S." is the United States Reports, the official reporter of Supreme Court decisions. The last part of the citation is the page on which the case begins (203 in the first case below). There is some delay before cases are published in the United States Reports; recent Supreme Court decisions therefore are cited to unofficial reporters. In this text, the Lawyers' Edition (L. Ed. 2d) is the unofficial reporter used for that purpose. Lower court decisions have their own reporters, including the Federal Reports (F.3d) for the federal courts of appeals and various regional reporters for decisions of state supreme courts. For lower courts, the year of the decision is preceded by a designation of the specific court— the circuit for the federal courts of appeals, the district for the federal district courts, and the state for state supreme courts.

Index